P9-DGS-263

The EXTREME SEARCHER'S
Internet Handbook
2nd Edition

The EXTREME SEARCHER'S
Internet Handbook
2nd Edition

A Guide for the Serious Searcher

Randolph Hock

Foreword by Greg R. Notess

Andrew Carnegie Library
Livingstone College
701 W. Monroe St.
Salisbury, NC 28144

CyberAge Books
Medford, New Jersey

Second printing, January 2008

**The Extreme Searcher's Internet Handbook:
A Guide for the Serious Searcher, 2nd Edition**

Copyright © 2007 by Randolph E. Hock.

All rights reserved. No part of this book may be reproduced in any form or by any electronic or mechanical means including information storage and retrieval systems without permission in writing from the publisher, except by a reviewer, who may quote brief passages in a review. Published by CyberAge Books, an imprint of Information Today, Inc., 143 Old Marlton Pike, Medford, New Jersey 08055.

Publisher's Note: The author and publisher have taken care in preparation of this book but make no expressed or implied warranty of any kind and assume no responsibility for errors or omissions. No liability is assumed for incidental or consequential damages in connection with or arising out of the use of the information or programs contained herein.

Many of the designations used by manufacturers and sellers to distinguish their products are claimed as trademarks. Where those designations appear in this book and Information Today, Inc. was aware of a trademark claim, the designations have been printed with initial capital letters.

Library of Congress Cataloging-in-Publication Data
Hock, Randolph, 1944-
  The Extreme searcher's Internet handbook : a guide for the serious
searcher / Randolph Hock. -- 2nd ed.
      p. cm.
  Includes index.
  ISBN 978-0-910965-76-7
  1. Internet searching--Handbooks, manuals, etc. 2. Web search
engines--Handbooks, manuals, etc. 3. Computer network resources--Handbooks,
manuals, etc. 4. Web sites--Directories. 5. Internet
addresses--Directories. I. Title.

  ZA4230.H63 2007
  025.04--dc22

                                                          2006036791
Printed and bound in the United States of America.

President and CEO: Thomas H. Hogan, Sr.
Editor-in-Chief and Publisher: John B. Bryans
Managing Editor: Amy M. Reeve
VP Graphics and Production: M. Heide Dengler
Book Designer: Kara Mia Jalkowski
Cover Design: Laura Hegyi
Copyeditor: Barbara Brynko
Proofreader: Pat Hadley-Miller
Indexer: Sharon Hughes

DEDICATION

To my wife, Pamela,
without whom I would be a boat without a port and a sail without wind

CONTENTS

Chapter 8   Sights and Sounds: Finding Images, Audio, and Video 189

Chapter 9   News Resources 219

FIGURES AND TABLES

FOREWORD

The Internet has become a tremendous information resource, with Web searching supplying quick access to facts, opinion, news, commentary, and so much more. Enter a word or two into a search box and—voilà!—links to all kinds of answers appear. While basic Internet searching is often easy, with simple answers to popular topics and basic descriptions readily available, everyone comes across searches that fail. The results are overly commercial, refer to a different meaning of the search word, or just do not have helpful information.

When the first search fails, all kinds of alternative approaches are available, from rewording the search to switching to a different search engine to going straight to a known, reliable site. Which direction should you take, and what sources should you use? Ran Hock draws from his extensive background in training thousands of searchers, from the novice to the skilled professional, and distills the best and most important elements of searching. With this new edition of his classic work, Ran has expanded coverage to include many new sources and topics related to the ever-changing realm of the Internet.

For those who aspire to become more proficient searchers, this is a treasure trove of tips, techniques, and great resources. Expert searchers use a combination of skill in search techniques along with knowledge of top sources in multiple subject areas. This handbook covers both. The early chapters present a solid foundation about Internet basics, search strategies, and search engines. Chapter 7, An Internet Reference Shelf, lists key resources in many fields, all of which are well worth knowing.

For the frequent Internet user, the author expands his coverage to crucial Internet topics beyond searching. Internet technologies both new and old are approached with an eye to the important aspects for searchers. Look closely at each of the chapters, since many significant points are covered ranging from citing Web pages and mailing lists to mashups and podcasts to auction sites and Weblogs.

Read *The Extreme Searcher's Internet Handbook* straight through to become a proficient searcher. Then keep it handy near your Internet computer as a reference for the future. On the go? Just bookmark Ran's companion Extreme Searcher site for quick access to the hundreds of URLs from the book.

While most extreme sports enthusiasts find themselves in the great outdoors, the extreme searchers ply their craft on their desktop, laptop, or mobile device. So sit back, grab a drink, and learn from Ran's expertise how to become an extreme searcher!

—Greg R. Notess
Author of *Teaching Web Search Skills:*
Techniques and Strategies of Top Trainers
Founder and author of SearchEngineShowdown.com
Reference Librarian and Professor at Montana State University

ACKNOWLEDGMENTS

First, I am particularly appreciative of the many enthusiastic and kind comments I have received from readers of the first edition. Those comments were a major factor in my deciding to do a second edition of this book.

Second, as with my previous books, I owe immense gratitude to the wonderful people at Information Today, Inc. They continue to be great people to work with and great people to know. I particularly want to acknowledge Amy Reeve, Managing Editor. She has indeed gone above and beyond her ordinary duties in getting this book out. I truly appreciate her flexibility, understanding, enthusiasm, and knowledge. John Bryans, Editor-in-Chief and Publisher, Books Division, continues to be a friend and advocate who provides welcome and excellent perspectives for all steps of the process. I am also grateful to Heide Dengler (VP of Graphics and Production), Kara Mia Jalkowski (Book Designer), Sharon Hughes (Indexer), Laura Hegyi (Cover Designer), and Rob Colding (Marketing Coordinator) for all the hard work and creativity they have applied in getting this book from manuscript to the hands of the reader. I continue to appreciate and admire Information Today, Inc. President and CEO, Tom Hogan, Sr., not just for the many things he has done for me, but for what he has done for the information community.

Finally, I thank my wife, Pamela, for her continued love, support, understanding, tolerance, and much more. Like "Web 2.0" products, I, myself, am still "in Beta," perpetual Beta, and appreciate my wife's willingness to put up with the bugs in my program.

INTRODUCTION

Several years ago, Thomas's English Muffins had an ad that proclaimed that the tastiness of its muffins was due to the presence of myriad "nooks and crannies." The same may be said of the Internet. It is in the Internet's nooks and crannies that the true "tastiness" often lies. Almost every Internet user has used Google and probably Yahoo!, and any group of experienced searchers could probably come up with a dozen or so sites that every one of them had used. But even for experienced searchers, time and task constraints have meant that some nooks and crannies have not been explored and exploited. These unexplored areas may be broad Internet resources (newsgroups), specific types of resources (multimedia), or the nooks and crannies of a specific site (even Google). This book is intended to be an aid in that exploration.

Back on the culinary scene, I am told that some people don't take the few extra seconds to split their English muffins with a fork, but, driven by their busy schedules, just grab a knife and slice them. This book is written for those seeking to savor the extra tastiness from the Internet. It will hopefully tempt you to discover what the nooks and crannies have to offer, and how to split the Internet muffin with a fork almost as quickly as you can slice it with a knife.

Less metaphorically, this book is written as a guide for researchers, writers, librarians, teachers, and others, covering what serious users need to know to take full advantage of Internet tools and resources. It focuses on what the serious searcher "has to know" but, for flavor, a dash of the "nice-to-know" is occasionally thrown in. It assumes that you already know the basics, you are signed up for and frequently use the Internet, and you know how to use your browser. For those who are not experienced online searchers, my aim is to provide a lot that is new and useful. For those of you with more experience, I hope to reinforce what you know while introducing some new perspectives and new content.

If you are among those who find themselves not just using the Internet but *teaching* it, the book should help you address an extensive range of questions. Much of what is included is based on my experience training thousands of Internet users from a wide range of professions, across a broad age range, and from more than 40 countries.

BRIEF OVERVIEW OF THE CHAPTERS

The chapter topics reflect congruence between the types of things that experienced Internet users most frequently inquire about and a categorization of the kinds of resources available on the Internet. An argument could certainly be made that the content should have been divided differently. While there is a chapter on Finding Products Online, for example, you may wonder why there is not one specifically on "company information." This is because company information pervades almost every chapter. Not every chapter will be of utmost interest to every reader, but it's worth giving each chapter at least a quick glimpse. You may be surprised what some nooks (and crannies, of course) contain.

Although the nature of each chapter means that each has its own organization, they all share some common elements. Typically, each chapter includes these aspects:

- Useful background information, along with suggestions, tips, and strategies for finding and making the most effective use of sites in that area.
- Resource guides that will lead you to collections of links to major sites on the topic.
- Selected sites, which were chosen because (1) they are sites that many if not most readers should be aware of, and (2) they are *representative* of types of sites that are useful for the topic. Deciding which sites to include was often difficult. Many of the sites included in this book are considered to be "the best" in their area, but space limitation meant that hundreds of great sites had to be excluded. These difficult decisions were made more palatable, however, because the resource guides included in the chapters will lead you quickly to those great sites—you're only one or two clicks away.

Following is a quick rundown of what each chapter covers.

Chapter 1: Basics for the Serious Searcher

This chapter covers background information that serious searchers need to know in order to be conversant with Internet content and issues. The background it includes helps users understand more fully the characteristics, content, and searchability of the Internet. For those who teach others how to use the Internet, it provides answers to some of the more frequently asked questions. Among the things included in Chapter 1 are a brief history of the Internet, a look at the kinds of available "finding tools," issues such as retrospective coverage and copyright, resources regarding citing Internet sources, and others for keeping up-to-date.

Chapter 2: General Web Directories and Portals

Although they have quite a bit in common with Web search engines, general Web directories such as the Yahoo! Directory and Open Directory also differ tremendously. This chapter addresses where these tools fit and when they may be best used. Even though their databases may include less than 1 percent of what search engine databases cover, general Web directories still serve unique research purposes and in many cases may be the best starting point. This chapter looks at their strengths, weaknesses, and special characteristics. Since these general directories are positioned to varying degrees as "portals," this chapter also addresses the "portal" concept.

Chapter 3: Specialized Directories

For accessing immediate expertise in Web resources on a specific topic, there is no better starting point than the right "specialized directory" (resource guide). These sites bring together well-organized collections of Internet resources on specific topics and provide not just a good starting place, but also—importantly—confidence in knowing that no important tools in that area are being missed. Add some content such as news headlines, and you don't just have a resource guide but a portal, making these tools even more important as starting points.

Chapter 4: Search Engines: The Basics

This chapter provides background and details about search engines that the serious searcher needs to know in order to get the best results. It also presents a case for not getting too excited about metasearch engines.

Chapter 5: Search Engines: The Specifics

This chapter examines the largest engines in detail, identifying their strengths, weaknesses, and special features, and also includes an overview of other engines. It also describes "visualization" engines (for a very different and fruitful "look" at search engine results).

Chapter 6: Groups, Newsgroups, Forums, and Their Relatives

Newsgroups, discussion groups, mailing lists, and other interactive forums form a class of Internet resources that too few researchers take advantage of. These tools, which can be useful for a broad range of applications from solving a software problem to competitive intelligence, can be gold mines. This chapter outlines what they are, why they are useful, and how to locate the ones you need.

Chapter 7: An Internet Reference Shelf

All serious searchers have a collection of tools they use for quick answers—the Web equivalent of a personal reference shelf. This chapter emphasizes the variety of resources that are available for finding quick facts, offers some direction on finding the right site for a specific need, and suggests several dozen sites of which most serious searchers should be aware.

Chapter 8: Sights and Sounds: Finding Images, Audio, and Video

Not only are there billions of images, audio files, and video files available on the Web, but they are searchable (and, even better, they are findable). Whether you are looking for photos of world leaders or rare birds, a famous speech, the sound of an elephant seal, or your favorite song, this chapter provides a look at what resources and tools are available for finding the needed file and discusses techniques for doing so effectively.

Chapter 9: News Resources

This chapter covers the range of news resources available on the Internet—news services and newswires, newspapers, news aggregation services, and more—and explains how to find what you are looking for effectively and efficiently. The chapter not only emphasizes the searchability of these resources, but also the limitations the researcher faces, particularly in regard to archival and exhaustivity issues.

Chapter 10: Finding Products Online

Whether for one's own purchase, an organization's purchase, or competitive analysis purposes, some searchers find themselves tracking and comparing products online. This chapter shows where to look and how to do it efficiently and effectively.

Chapter 11: Becoming Part of the Internet: Publishing

Beyond using the Internet to gather information, many serious searchers need to have a way of "publishing" on the Internet, by means of a Weblog, a podcast, or a Web site of their own. Reasons may range from communicating information about the services or products one may provide, to sharing knowledge and resources, to providing a syllabus and links for classes you may be teaching. Although this chapter does not provide extensive details about how to become a blogger, a podcaster, or a Webmaster, it does offer an overview of what is needed and the options that are available to those who want to move in that direction.

SOME INTRODUCTORY ODDS AND ENDS

Most of the sites I discuss in the book do not charge for access. Occasionally, reference is made to sites that require a paid subscription or offer information for a fee; these are included here in part as a reminder that (as the serious searcher is already aware) not all of the good stuff is available for free on the Internet. Commercial services such as LexisNexis, Factiva, and Dialog contain proprietary information that is critical for many kinds of research and is not available on the free Web.

Sites are included here because they have useful content. Except for association, government, and academic sites, most of the sites mentioned are supported by ads. On the Internet, just as with television and radio, if the ratio of advertisements to useful content is too high, we can switch to another channel or another Web site. Some of us have come to appreciate the ads to some extent, aware as we are that advertising makes many valuable sites possible.

A Word on "Usage"

Although Internet and Web are not synonymous, most users do not distinguish between them. When it makes a difference, I use the appropriate term. Where I refer to resources that are generally on the Web part of the Internet, Web is used. Where the terms are interchangeable, either term may be used.

About the Second Edition

I have been very gratified by the warm reception the first edition of this book received, which is the major impetus for a second edition. Much has changed since the first edition was published, but much has also stayed the same. Almost all of the "old standby" Web sites are still there, still providing similar services and content, though they are often enhanced and have had occasional name changes. Among the major changes are those in the search engine "leaders" and in the new, different, and exciting services they are providing. Other major changes include the vastly increased prevalence of Weblogs, new multimedia content, and several other Web phenomena. You will find quite a few additions to the list of Web sites included here and some fairly lengthy discussion of topics that were only briefly mentioned in the first edition. Overall, the size of the book has increased by about one-third.

Some Final Basic Advice
Before You Proceed

As we have encountered the Internet over the last decade or so, most of us have learned much of what we know about it in a rather piecemeal fashion, for instance, having been told about a great site, having bumped into it, or having read about it. Although this is, in many ways, an effective approach to exploring the Internet, it can leave gaps in our knowledge. Because each user has individual needs, no single book can fill all of the gaps, but this one attempts to help by providing a better understanding of what is out there as well as some starting points and suggestions for getting what you need—to help you find your way to the most useful nooks and crannies.

As you explore, keep in mind the following three guidelines to help you get the most value from the Internet:

One: "Click everywhere."

Two: "Click where you have never clicked before."

Three: "Split your muffins with a fork."

ABOUT THE EXTREME SEARCHER'S WEB PAGE

As a supplement to this book (and his other books), the author maintains a Web site, The Extreme Searcher's Web Page at www.extremesearcher.com. There you will find information about and links to sites included in this and his other books. The collection of links for all of the Web sites included in this book can be found at that site. URLs for sites covered in this book occasionally change, and once in a while (hopefully not very often), a Web site covered may just disappear. This Web site is updated on a continuing basis just to account for those changes, and you will sometimes also find some new sites added there. (If you should find a "dead link" on the site before the author does, you are encouraged to report it to him at the e-mail address below.)

Since links to all Web sites in the book are on the Extreme Searcher's site, if you make use of that site (and bookmark it), you will not have to type in any of the URLs included in the book. You should find the site particularly helpful for browsing through the sites covered here.

Enjoy your visit and please send any feedback to ran@extremesearcher.com.

Disclaimer

Neither the publisher nor the author makes any claim as to the results that may be obtained through the use of The Extreme Searcher's Web Page or of any of the Internet resources it references or links to. Neither publisher nor author will be held liable for any results, or lack thereof, obtained by the use of this page or any of its links; for any third-party changes; or for any hardware, software, or other problems that may occur as the result of using it. The Extreme Searcher's Web Page is subject to change or discontinuation without notice at the discretion of the publisher and author.

CHAPTER 1

BASICS FOR THE SERIOUS SEARCHER

In writing this book, I have made the assumption that the reader knows the Internet basics—what it is, how to get connected, and so forth. The "basics" covered in this chapter involve background information that serious searchers need to know to be fully conversant with Internet content and issues as well as general ways of approaching Internet resources to find just what you need. I go into some details already familiar to many readers, but I include this background material for two purposes: (1) so readers might understand more fully the characteristics, content, utility, and nuances of the Internet in order to use it more effectively, and (2) to help those who find themselves teaching others how to use the Internet by providing answers to some of the more frequently asked questions.

As for the general approaches to finding the right resources, this chapter provides an overview and comparison of the kinds of "finding tools" available and a set of strategies that can be applied. The strategies coverage goes into some detail on topics (such as Boolean logic) that will also be encountered elsewhere in the book. Integral to all of this are some aspects and issues regarding the *content* that is found on the Internet. These aspects include the questions of retrospective coverage, quality of content, and general accessibility of content, particularly the issue of the Invisible Web. Woven into this content fabric are issues, such as copyright, that affect how information found on the Internet can be used. Although only lightly touched upon, it is important that every serious user have an awareness of these issues. Lastly, the chapter provides some useful resources for keeping up with the latest Internet tools, content, and issues.

THE PIECES OF THE INTERNET

First, the "Internet" and the "Web" are not synonymous, although they are frequently used interchangeably. As late as the mid-1990s, the Internet had some clearly distinguishable parts, as defined by their functions. Much

Internet usage could be thought of as Internet *sans* content. It was simply a communications channel that allowed easy transfer of information. Typically, a user at one university could use the Internet to send or request a file from someone at another university using FTP (File Transfer Protocol). Sending e-mail via the Internet was becoming tremendously popular at that time. A user of a commercial search service such as Dialog or LexisNexis could harness it as an alternative to proprietary telecommunications networks, basically sending and receiving proprietary information. "Content" parts of the Internet could indeed be found, such as Usenet newsgroups, where anyone with a connection could access a body of publicly available information. Gophers (menu-based directories allowing access to files, mainly at universities) were also beginning to provide access to content.

The world changed and content was destined to become king, when Tim Berners-Lee at CERN (Conseil European pour la Recherché Nucleaire) in Geneva created the World Wide Web in 1991. The Web provided an easy-to-use interface for both potential content providers and users, with a GUI (Graphical User Interface) incorporating hypertext point-and-click navigation of text, graphics, and sounds, and created what was for most of us at that time an unimaginable potential for access to information.

Within less than five years, the Web had overtaken e-mail and FTP in terms of Internet traffic. By 2000, usage of the other parts of the Internet was becoming fused into the Web. Usenet newsgroups were being accessed through a Web interface, and Web-based e-mail was becoming the main—or only—form of e-mail for millions. FTP was typically being done through a Web interface. Gophers were replaced by Web directories and search engines, and any gophers you now find are likely to be in your backyard.

A VERY BRIEF HISTORY

The following selection of historical highlights provides a perspective for better understanding the nature of the Internet. It should be emphasized that the Internet is the result of many technologies (computing, time-sharing of computers, packet-switching, etc.) and many visionaries and great technical thinkers coming together over a period of a few decades. In addition, what they were able to accomplish was dependent upon minds and technologies of preceding decades. This selection of highlights is merely a sampling and leaves out many essential technical achievements and notable contributors.

The points here are drawn primarily from the resources listed at the end of this timeline.

1957	The USSR launches *Sputnik*.
1958	Largely as a result of the *Sputnik* launch, ARPA (Advanced Research Projects Agency) is established to push the U.S. ahead in science and technology. High among its interests is computer technology.
1962	J. C. R. Licklider writes about his vision of a globally interconnected group of computers providing widespread access to data and programs; the RAND Corporation begins research on distributed communications networks for military purposes.
Early 1960s	Packet-switching moves from theory to practice.
Mid- to Late-1960s	ARPA develops ARPANET to promote the "cooperative networking of time-sharing computers" with four host computers connected by the end of 1969 (Stanford Research Institute, UCLA, UC Santa Barbara, and the University of Utah).
1965	The term "hypertext" is coined by Ted Nelson.
1968	The Tymnet nationwide time-sharing network is built.
1971	ARPANET grows to 23 hosts, including universities and government research centers.
1972	The International Network Working Group (INWG) is established to advance and set standards for networking technologies; the first chairman is Vinton (Vint) Cerf, who is later often referred to as the "Father of the Internet."
1972–1974	Commercial database services—Dialog, SDC Orbit, Lexis, The New York Times DataBank, and others—begin making their subscription services available through dial-up networks.
1973	ARPANET makes its first international connections at the University College of London (England) and the Royal Radar Establishment (Norway).
1974	"A Protocol for Packet Network Interconnection," which specifies the details of TCP (Transmission Control Protocol), is published by Vint Cerf and Bob Kahn.

1974   Bolt, Beranek & Newman, contractor for ARPANET, opens a commercial version of the ARPANET called Telenet, the first public packet-data service.

1977   There are 111 hosts on the Internet.

1978   TCP is split into TCP and IP (Internet Protocol).

1979   The first Usenet discussion groups are created by Tom Truscott, Jim Ellis, and Steve Bellovin, graduate students at Duke University and the University of North Carolina, and it quickly spreads worldwide.

The first emoticons (smileys) are suggested by Kevin McKenzie.

1980s   The personal computer becomes a part of millions of people's lives.

There are 213 hosts on ARPANET.

BITNET (Because It's Time Network) is started, providing e-mail, electronic mailing lists, and FTP service.

CSNET (Computer Science Network) is created by computer scientists at Purdue University, University of Washington, RAND Corporation, and BBN, with National Science Foundation (NSF) support. It provides e-mail and other networking services to researchers without access to ARPANET.

1982   The term "Internet" is first used.

TCP/IP is adopted as the universal protocol for the Internet.

Name servers are developed, allowing a user to get to a computer without specifying the exact path.

There are 562 hosts on the Internet.

France Telecom begins distributing Minitel terminals to subscribers free of charge, providing videotext access to the Teletel system. Initially providing telephone directory lookups, then chat and other services, Teletel is the first widespread home implementation of these types of network services.

Orwell's vision, fortunately, is not fulfilled, but computers are soon to be in almost every home.

There are more than 1,000 hosts on the Internet.

1985   The WELL (Whole Earth 'Lectronic Link) is started. Individual users, outside universities, can now easily participate on the Internet.

There are more than 5,000 hosts on the Internet.

1986	NSFNET (National Science Foundation Network) is created. The backbone speed is 56K. (Yes, as in the total transmission capability of a 56K dial-up modem.)
1987	There are more than 10,000 hosts on the Internet.
1988	The NSFNET backbone is upgraded to a T1 at 1.544 Mbps (megabits per second).
1989	There are more than 100,000 hosts on the Internet.
	ARPANET fades away.
	There are more than 300,000 hosts on the Internet.
1991	Tim Berners-Lee at CERN (Conseil European pour la Recherché Nucleaire) in Geneva introduces the World Wide Web.
	NSF removes the restriction on commercial use of the Internet.
	The University of Minnesota releases the first gopher, which allows point-and-click access to files on remote computers.
	The NSFNET backbone is upgraded to a T3 (44.736 Mbps).
1992	There are more than 1,000,000 hosts on the Internet.
	Jean Armour Polly coins the phrase "surfing the Internet."
1994	The first graphics-based browser, Mosaic, is released.
	Internet talk radio begins.
	WebCrawler, the first successful Web search engine, is introduced.
	A law firm introduces Internet "spam."
	Netscape Navigator, the commercial version of Mosaic, is shipped.
1995	NSFNET reverts to being a research network; Internet infrastructure is now primarily provided by commercial firms.
	RealAudio is introduced, meaning that you no longer have to wait for sound files to download completely before you begin hearing them, and allowing for continued ("streaming") downloads.
	Consumer services such as CompuServe, America Online, and Prodigy begin to provide access through the Internet instead of only through their private dial-up networks.
1996	There are more than 10,000,000 hosts on the Internet.
1999	Microsoft's Internet Explorer overtakes Netscape as the most popular browser.

1999	Testing of the registration of domain names in Chinese, Japanese, and Korean languages begins, reflecting the internationalization of Internet usage.
2001	Mysterious monolith does not emerge from the Earth and no evil computers take over any spaceships (as far as we know).
2002	Google is indexing more than 3 billion Web pages.
2003	There are more than 200,000,000 IP hosts on the Internet.
2004	Weblogs, which started in the mid-1990s, gain widespread popularity and attention.
2005	More than 50 percent of Americans who access the Internet at home have a high-speed connection.
2006	Developmental focus is on a more interactive, personalized Web, with collaboration, sharing, desktop-type programs, and use of APIs (Application Program Interfaces) to integrate data from multiple sources over the Web.

Internet History Resources

Anyone interested in information on the history of the Internet beyond this selective list is encouraged to consult the following resources.

A Brief History of the Internet, version 3.1

www.isoc.org/internet-history/brief.shtml

By Barry M. Leiner, Vinton G. Cerf, David D. Clark, Robert E. Kahn, Leonard Kleinrock, Daniel C. Lynch, Jon Postel, Larry G. Roberts, and Stephen Wolff, this site provides historical commentary from many of the people who were actually involved in the Internet's creation.

Internet History and Growth

www.isoc.org/internet/history/2002_0918_Internet_History_and_Growth.ppt

This PowerPoint presentation by William F. Slater provides a good look at the Internet's pioneers and provides an excellent collection of statistics on Internet growth.

Hobbes' Internet Timeline

www.zakon.org/robert/internet/timeline

This detailed timeline emphasizes technical developments and who was behind them.

THE "NEW" WEB

By 2006, most heavy-duty Internet users had begun to hear the term "Web 2.0" fairly frequently—a term coined (and trademarked) in conjunction with a series of Web development conferences that began in 2004. Web 2.0 refers to a "second generation" of the Web that provides a much greater focus on—and use of—desktop applications made available on the Web, and collaboration and sharing by users. Forerunners of this include wikis, Weblogs, RSS, folksonomies (tagging), and podcasts. Though Web 2.0 has no precise definition, some people also define this new generation of the Web in terms of the kinds of programs and techniques used, including APIs (Application Programming Interfaces), social software, and Ajax (Asynchronous JavaScript and XML). The glossary of this book has brief definitions of those terms. From one perspective, what the new Web is really about is " the user," with a focus on areas of user interaction such as participation, publication, social software, sharing, and "the Web as platform."

Though Web sites are not usually "labeled" as part of this trend, if you look closely, you will see these elements in more and more Web sites. You are seeing manifestations of it when you encounter sites that allow for user-applied "tags" (such as Flickr), in the way a search engine might "suggest" search phrases as you type in your terms, in the ability to zoom and drag maps, and in using instant windows that open on pages in response to moving your cursor or clicking (such as some of the tabs on Yahoo!'s main page). This flexible interactivity with Web pages and with the Web carries over into increased interactivity with others on the Web and can also make Web-based programs (such as Google spreadsheets) flow as smoothly as similar programs on your desktop.

SEARCHING THE INTERNET: WEB "FINDING TOOLS"

Whether your hobby or profession is cooking, carpentry, chemistry, or anything in-between, the right tool can make all the difference. The same is true for searching the Web. A variety of tools are available to help you find what you need, and each tool does things a little differently, sometimes with a different purpose and different emphasis, as well as different coverage and different search features.

To understand the variety of tools, it can be helpful to think of most finding tools as falling into one of three categories (although many tools will be hybrids): (1) general directories, (2) search engines, and (3) specialized directories. The third category could indeed be lumped in with the first because both are directories, but for a couple of reasons discussed later, it is worthwhile to treat them separately.

All three categories may incorporate another function, that of a portal, which is a Web site that provides a gateway not only to links, but also to a number of other information resources going beyond just the searching or browsing function. These resources may include news headlines, weather, stock market information, alerts, yellow pages, and other kinds of handy information. A portal can be general, as in the case of My Yahoo!, or it can be specific for a particular discipline, region, or country.

Other finding tools serve other kinds of Internet content, such as newsgroups, mailing lists, images, and audio. These tools may exist either on their own sites or they may be incorporated into the three main categories of tools. These specialized tools will be covered in later chapters.

General Web Directories

The general Web directories are Web sites that provide a large collection of links arranged in categories to enable browsing by subject area, such as the Yahoo! Directory and Open Directory. Their content is (usually) handpicked by people who ask: "Is this site of enough interest to enough people that it should be included in the directory?"

If the answer is yes (and in some cases, if the owner of the site has paid a fee), the site is added and placed in the directory's database (catalog), and is listed in one or more of the subject categories. As a result of this process, these tools have two major characteristics: They are *selective* (sites have had to meet the selection criteria), and they are *categorized* (all sites are arranged in categories; see Figure 1.1). Because of the selectivity, the directory user is working, theoretically, with higher quality sites—the wheat and not the chaff. Because the sites included are arranged in categories, the user has the option of starting at the top of the category hierarchy and browsing down until the appropriate level of specificity is reached. Also, only one entry is usually made for each site, instead of including, as in search engines, many pages from the same site. The size of the database of general Web directories is much smaller than that created and used by Web search engines, the former containing perhaps a few million sites and the latter billions of pages. Web directories are designed primarily for browsing and for general questions. Sites on very specific topics, such as "UV-enhanced dry stripping of silicon nitride films" or "social security retirement program reform in Croatia," are generally not included. As a result, directories are most successfully used for *general* rather than *specific* questions, for example, "types of chemical reactions" or "social security." Although browsing through the categories is the major design idea behind general Web directories, they do provide a search box to allow you to bypass the browsing and go directly to the sites in the database.

The Role of General Directories

General Web directories are a good starting place when you have a very general question (museums in Paris, dyslexia), or when you don't quite know where to go with a broad topic and would like to browse down through a category to get some guidance.

General Web directories are discussed in detail in Chapter 2.

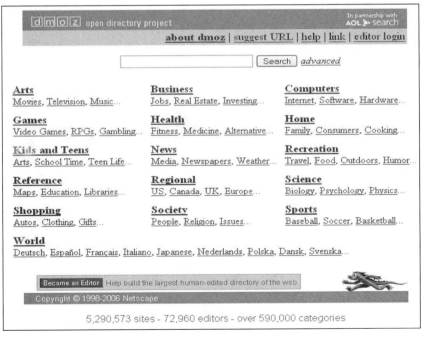

Figure 1.1

Open Directory's main page

Web Search Engines

Whereas a directory is a good start when you want to be directed to just a few selected items on a fairly general topic, search engines are the place to go when you want something on a fairly specific topic (ethics of human cloning, Italian paintings of William Stanley Haseltine). Instead of searching brief descriptions of a few million Web sites, these services allow you to search virtually every word from several billion Web pages. In addition, Web search engines allow you to use much more sophisticated techniques, so you can focus on your topic more effectively (Figure 1.2). The pages included in Web search engines are not placed in categories (hence, you cannot browse a hierarchy), and no prior human selectivity was involved in determining what is in the search engine's database. As the searcher, you provide the selectivity by the search terms you choose and by the further narrowing techniques you may apply.

The Role of Search Engines

If your topic is very specific or you expect that very little is written on it, a search engine will be a much better starting place than a directory. If your

TIP:

If your question contains one or two concepts, consider a directory. If it contains three or more, definitely start with a search engine.

Figure 1.2

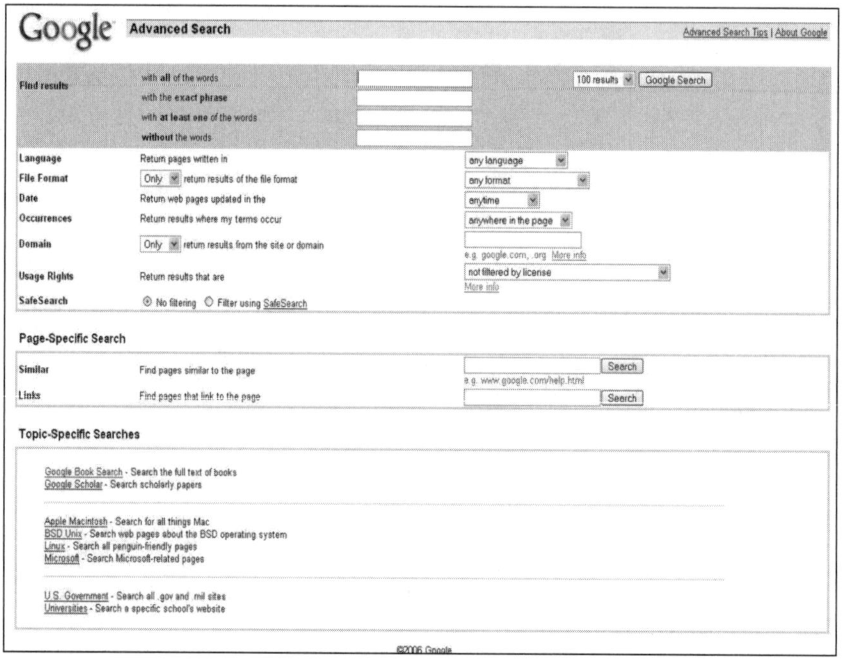

Google's advanced search page

search needs to be exhaustive, use a search engine. If your topic is a combination of three or more concepts (e.g., "Italian" "paintings" "Haseltine"), use a search engine. Find out more about search engines in Chapter 4 and Chapter 5.

Specialized Directories (Resource Guides, Research Guides, and Metasites)

Specialized Web directories are collections of selected Internet resources (collections of links) on a particular topic. The topic could range from something as broad as medicine to something as specific as biomechanics. These sites go by a variety of names such as resource guides, research guides, metasites, cyberguides, and Webliographies. Although their main function is to provide links to resources, they may also incorporate some additional portal features such as news headlines.

Indeed, this category could have been lumped in with the general Web directories, but it is kept separate for two main reasons. First, the large general directories, such as the Yahoo! Directory and Open Directory, have several things in common besides being general: They provide categories you can browse, they have a search feature, and when you get to know them, they tend to have the same "look and feel" in other ways as well. The second main reason for keeping the specialized directories as a separate category is that they deserve greater attention than they often get. More searchers need to tap into their extensive utility.

The Role of Specialized Directories

Use specialized directories when you need to get to know the Web literature on a topic, in other words, when you need a general familiarity with the major resources for a particular discipline or area of study. These sites can be thought of as providing *some* immediate expertise in using Web resources in the area of interest. When you are not sure of how to narrow your topic and would like to browse, these sites can also often be better starting places than a general directory because they may reflect a greater expertise in the choice of resources for a particular area than would a general directory, and they often include more sites on the specific topic than are found in the corresponding section of a general directory.

Specialized directories are discussed in detail in Chapter 3.

GENERAL STRATEGIES

For starters, there is no right or wrong way to search the Internet. If you find what you need and find it quickly, your strategy is good. Keep in mind, though, that finding what you need involves other issues: Was it really the correct answer? Was it the best answer? Was it the complete answer?

At the broadest level, assuming that your question is one for which the Internet is the best starting place, one approach to a finding what you need on the Internet is to first answer the following three questions:

1. Exactly what is my question? (Identify what you need and how exhaustive or precise you need to be.)

2. What is the most appropriate tool to start with? (See the previous sections on the categories of finding tools.)

3. What search strategy should I start with?

These three steps often take place without much conscious effort and may take a matter of seconds. For instance, if you wanted to find out who General Carl Schurz was, you could go to your favorite search engine and type in those three words. The quick-and-easy, keep-it-simple approach is often the best.

Even for a more complicated question, it is often worthwhile to start with a very simple approach to get a sense of what is out there, then develop a more sophisticated strategy based on an analysis of your topic into concepts.

Organizing Your Search by Concepts

Thinking in terms of concepts is both a natural way of organizing the world around us and a way of organizing your thoughts about a search. Thinking in concepts is a central part of most searches. The concepts are the ideas that must be present in order for a resultant answer to be relevant, each concept corresponding to a required criterion. Sometimes a search is so specific that only a single concept may be involved, but most searches involve a combination of two, three, or four concepts. For instance, if our search is for *hotels in Albuquerque*, our two concepts are "hotels" and "Albuquerque." If we are trying to identify Web pages on this topic, any Web page that includes both concepts possibly contains what we are looking for, and any page that is missing either of those concepts is not going to be relevant.

The experienced searcher knows that for any concept, more than one term present in a record (on a Web page) may indicate the presence of the concept, and these alternate terms also need to be considered. Alternate terms may include, among other things, (1) grammatical variations (e.g., electricity, electrical), (2) synonyms, near-synonyms, or closely related terms (e.g., culture, traditions), and (3) a term and its narrower terms. For an exhaustive search on the concept of "Baltic states," you may also want to search for Latvia, Lithuania, and Estonia. In an exhaustive search for information on the production of electricity in the Baltic states, you would not want to miss the Web page that dealt specifically with "Production of Electricity in Latvia."

When the idea of thinking in concepts is expanded further, it naturally leads to a discussion of Boolean logic, which will be covered in Chapter 4. In the meantime, the major point here is that, in preparing your search strategy, think about what concepts are involved, and remember that, for most concepts, looking for alternate terms is important.

A Basic Collection of Strategies

Just as there is no one right or wrong way to search the Internet, there can be no list of definitive steps or one specific strategy to follow in preparing and performing every search. Rather, it is useful to think in terms of a toolbox of strategies and select whichever tool or combination of tools seems most appropriate for the search at hand. Among the more common strategies, strategic tools, or approaches for searching the Internet are the following:

1. Identify your basic ideas (concepts) and *rely on the built-in relevance ranking* provided by search engines. When you enter terms in the major search engines and many other search sites, only those records (Web pages) that contain all those terms will be retrieved, and the engine will automatically rank the order of output based on various criteria (Figure 1.3).

2. Use simple *narrowing techniques* if your results need narrowing:

   • Add another concept to narrow your search (instead of *hotels Albuquerque*, try *inexpensive hotels Albuquerque*).

   • Use quotation marks to indicate phrases when a phrase defines your concept(s) more exactly than if the words occur in different places on the page, for example, "*foreign policy.*" Most Web sites that have a search function allow you to specify a phrase (a combination of two or more adjacent words in the order written) by the use of quotation marks.

- Use a more specific term for one or more of your concepts (i.e., instead of *intelligence*, try *military intelligence*).
- Narrow your results to only those items that contain your most important terms in the title of the page. (These kinds of techniques will be discussed in Chapter 4.)

3. *Examine your first results* and look for, and then use, terms you might not have thought of at first.

4. *If you do not seem to be getting enough relevant items, use the Boolean OR operation to allow for alternate terms; for example, electrical OR electricity* would find all items that have either the term *electrical* or the term *electricity*. How you express the OR operation varies a bit with the finding tool (but in most cases it is the word OR, capitalized).

5. *Use a combination of Boolean operations* (AND, OR, NOT, or their equivalents) to identify those pages that contain a specific combination of concepts and alternate terms for those concepts (for example,

Figure 1.3

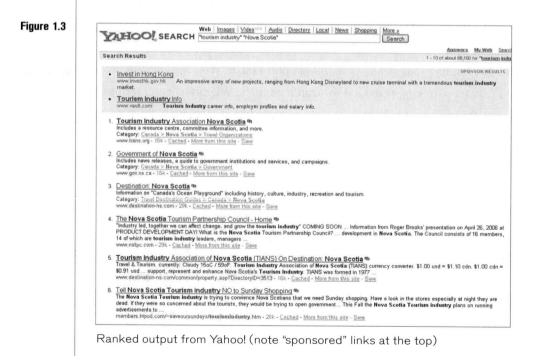

Ranked output from Yahoo! (note "sponsored" links at the top)

to get all pages that contain either the term *cloth* or the term *fabric* and also contain the words *flax* and *shrinkage*). As will be discussed later, Boolean is not necessarily complicated and is often implied without you doing anything; it can be as simple as choosing between "all of these words" or "any of these words" options.

6. *Look at what else the finding tools (particularly search engines) can do* to allow you to get as much as you need—and only what you need. Advanced search pages are probably the first place you should look.

Ask five different experienced searchers and you will get five different lists of strategies. The most important thing is to have an awareness of the kinds of techniques that are available to you for getting everything you need and, at the same time, only what you need.

CONTENT ON THE INTERNET

Not only the amount of information but the kinds of information available and searchable on the Internet continue to increase rapidly. In understanding what you are getting—and not getting—as a result of a search of the Internet requires consideration of a number of factors, such as the time frames covered, quality of content, and a recognition that various kinds of material exist on the Internet that are not readily accessible by search engines. In *using* the content found on the Internet, other issues must also be considered, such as copyright.

Assessing Quality of Content

A favorite complaint by those who are still a bit shy of the Internet is that the quality of information they find is often low. The same could be said about information available from a lot of other resources. A newsstand may have both the *Economist* and the *National Enquirer* on its shelves. On television, you will find both The History Channel and infomercials. Experience has taught us how, in most cases, to make a quick determination of the relative quality of the information we encounter in our daily lives. In using the Internet, many of the same criteria can be successfully applied, particularly those criteria we are accustomed to applying to traditional literature resources, both popular and academic.

TIP:

If you don't immediately see a link to get back to the home page of a site, try clicking on the site's logo. It usually works.

These traditional literature evaluation techniques/criteria that can be applied in the Internet context include:

1. Consider the source.

From what organization does the content originate? Look for the organization identified both on the Web page itself and in the URL. Is the content identified as coming from known sources such as a news organization, a government, an academic journal, a professional association, or a major investment firm? Just because it does not come from such a source is certainly not cause enough to reject it outright. On the other hand, even if it does come from such a source, don't bet the farm on this criterion alone.

Look at the URL. Often you will immediately be able to identify the owner. Peel back the URL to the domain name. If that does not adequately identify it, you can check details of the domain ownership for U.S. sites (and some non-U.S.) on sites that provide access to a Whois database, such as Network Solution's Whois Search (www.networksolutions.com/cgi-bin/whois/whois) or Whois Source (www.whois.sc). For other countries, similar sites are available. The Internet Assigned Numbers Authority provides a list of Whois sites by country (www.iana.org/cctld/cctld-whois.htm).

Be aware that some look-alike domain names are intended to fool the reader as to the origin of the site. The top-level domain (.edu, .com, etc.) may provide some clues about the source of the information, but do not make too many assumptions here. An .edu or .ac domain does not necessarily assure academic content, given that students as well as faculty can often easily get a space on the university server.

A tilde "~" in a directory name is often an indication of a personal page. Again, don't reject something on such a criterion alone. There are some very valuable personal pages out there.

Is the actual author identified? Is there an indication of the author's credentials, the author's organization? Search for other things by the same author. Does she or he publish a lot on spontaneous human combustion and extraterrestrial origins of life on Earth? If you recognize an author's name and the work does not seem consistent with other works from the same author, question it. It is easy to impersonate someone else on the Internet.

2. Consider the motivation.

What seems to be the purpose of the site—academic, consumer protection, sales, entertainment (don't be taken in by a spoof), political? There is nothing inherently bad (or for that matter necessarily inherently good) in any of those purposes, of course, but identifying the motivation can be helpful in assessing the degree of objectivity. Is any advertising on the page clearly identified, or is advertising disguised as something else?

3. Look at the quality of the writing.

If there are spelling and grammatical errors, assume that the same level of attention to detail probably went into the gathering and reporting of the "facts" given on the site.

4. Look at the quality of the documentation of sources cited.

First, remember that even in academic circles, the number of footnotes is not a true measure of a work's quality. On the other hand, and more importantly, if facts are cited, does the page identify the origin of the facts? If a lot rests on the information you are gathering, check out a few of the cited sources to be sure they really do give the facts that were quoted.

5. Is the site and its contents as current as it should be?

If a site is reporting on current events, the need for currency and the answer to the question of currency will be apparent. If the content is something that should be up to date, look for indications of timeliness, such as a "last updated" date on the page or telling examples of outdated material. For example, if it is a site that recommends which search engines to use, and WebCrawler is still listed, don't trust the currency (or for that matter, accuracy) of other things on the page. What is the most recent material that is referred to? If you find a number of "dead links," assume the author of the page is not giving it much attention.

6. For facts you are going to use, verify using multiple sources, or choose the most authoritative source.

Unfortunately, many facts given on Web pages are simply wrong, whether from carelessness, exaggeration, guessing, or other reasons. Often facts are wrong because the person creating that page's content did not check the facts. If you need a specific fact, such as the date of a historic event, look for more than one Web page that gives the date and see if they agree. Also remember that one Web site may be more authoritative than another. If you have a quotation in hand and want to find who said it, you might want to go to a source such as Bartleby.com (which includes very respected quotations sources), instead of taking the answer from Web pages of lesser-known origins.

For more details and other ideas about evaluating quality of information found on the Internet, the following two resources will be useful.

The Virtual Chase: Evaluating the Quality of Information on the Internet
www.virtualchase.com/quality

Created and maintained by Genie Tyburski, this site provides an excellent overview of the factors and issues to consider when evaluating the quality of information found on a Web site. She provides checklists and examples of sites that demonstrate both good and bad qualities.

Evaluating the Quality of World Wide Web Resources
www.valpo.edu/library/user/evaluation.html

This site from Valparaiso University provides a detailed set of criteria and also several dozen links to other sites that address the topic of evaluating Web resources. Links to exercises and worksheets on the topic are also included.

Retrospective Coverage of Content

It is tempting to say that a major weakness of Internet content is lack of retrospective coverage. This is certainly an issue for which the serious user should have a high level of awareness. It is also an issue that should be put into perspective. The importance and amount of relevant retrospective coverage available depends on the kind of information you are seeking at any particular moment and on your particular question. It is safe to say that no Web pages on the Internet were created before 1991.

Books, Ancient Writings, and Historical Documents

The lack of pre-1991 Web pages does not mean that earlier content is not available. Indeed, if a work is moderately well-known and was written before 1920 or so, you are as likely to find it on the Internet as in a small local public library. Take a look at the list of works included in the Project Gutenberg site and The Online Books Page (see Chapter 7) where you will find works of Cicero, Balzac, Heine, Disraeli, Einstein, and thousands of other authors. Also look at some of the other Web sites discussed in Chapter 7 for sources of historical documents.

Scholarly and Technical Journals and Popular Magazines

If you are looking for full-text articles from journals or magazines written several years ago, you are not likely to find them free on the Internet (and, for most journal articles, you are not even likely to find the ones written this week, last month, or last year). This lack of content is more a function of copyright and requirements for paid subscriptions than a matter of the retrospective aspect. The distinction also needs to be made here between free material and "for fee" material on the Internet. On a number of Internet sources (such as IngentaConnect and Google Scholar), you can find references to scholarly and other material going back several years. Most likely you will need to pay to see the full text, but fees tend to be very reasonable. Whatever source you use for serious research, whether it's the Internet or other, examine the source to see how far back back it goes.

Newspapers and Other News Sources

If, when you speak of news, you think of "new news," retrospective coverage is not an issue. If you are looking for newspaper or other articles dating back more than a few days, the time span of available content on any particular site is crucial. In 2000, many newspapers on the Internet contained only the current day's stories, with a few having up to a year or two of stories. Fortunately, more and more newspaper and other news sites are archiving their material, and you may find several years of content on the site. Look closely at the site to see exactly how far back the site goes.

Old Web Pages

A different aspect of the retrospective issue centers on the fact that many Web pages change frequently and many simply disappear altogether. Pages that existed in the early 1990s are likely to either be gone or have different content than they did then. This becomes a significant problem when trying to track down early content or citing early content. Fortunately, there are at least partial solutions to the problem. For very recent pages that may have disappeared or changed in the last few days or weeks, a search engine's "cache" option may help. For Web pages in their databases, the major search engines have stored a copy. If you find the reference to the page in search results, but when you try to go to it, the page is either completely gone or the content that you expected to find on the page is no longer there, click on the "cached" option and you will get to a copy of the page as it was when the search engine last indexed it. Even if you found the page elsewhere initially, search for it in a search engine, and if you find it there, try the cache.

For locating earlier pages and their content, try the Wayback Machine.

Wayback Machine—Internet Archive

www.archive.org

The Wayback Machine provides the Internet Archive, which has the purpose of "offering permanent access for researchers, historians, and scholars to historical collections that exist in digital format." It allows you to search more than 55 billion pages and see what a particular page looked like at various periods in Internet time. A search yields a list of what pages are available for what dates as far back as 1996 (Figure 1.4). As well as Web pages, it archives moving images, texts, music, and other audio. Its producers claim it is the largest database ever built.

Figure 1.4

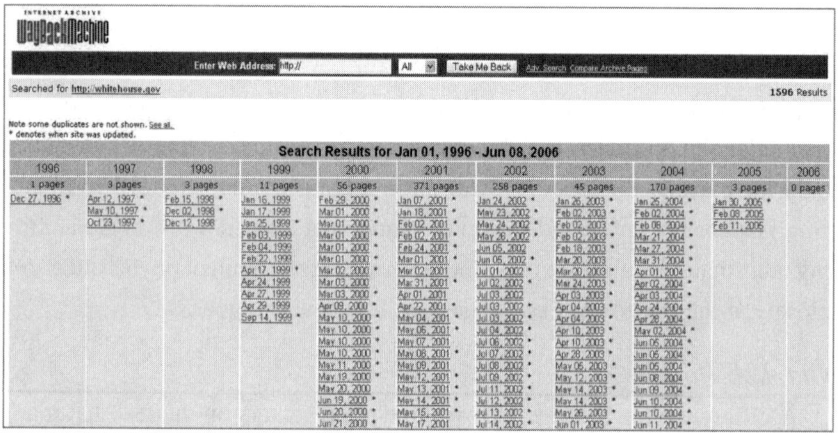

Wayback Machine search results showing pages available for whitehouse.gov

CONTENT—THE INVISIBLE WEB

No matter how good you are at using Web search engines and general directories, there are valuable resources on the Web that search engines will not find for you. You can get to most of them if you know the URL, but a search engine search will probably not find them for you. These resources, often referred to as the "Invisible Web" or "Deep Web," include a variety of content, including—and most importantly—databases of articles, data, statistics, and government documents. The "invisible" refers to "invisible to search engines." There is nothing mysterious or mystical involved.

Knowing about the Invisible Web is important because it contains a lot of tremendously useful information—and it is large. Various estimates put the size of the Invisible Web at from 200 to 500 times the content of the visible Web. Before that number sinks in and alarms you, keep in mind the following:

1. The Invisible Web contains very important material.

2. For the information there that you are likely to have a need for and the right to access, there are ways of finding out about it and getting to it.

3. In terms of volume, most of the material may be meaningless except to those who already know about it, or to the producer's immediate relatives. Much of the material that can't be found is probably not worth finding.

To adequately understand what this is all about, one must know why some content is invisible. Note the use of the word "content" instead of the word "sites." The main page of an Invisible Web site is usually easy to find and is covered by search engines. It is the rest of the site (Web pages and other content within the site) that may be invisible. Search engines do not index certain Web content mainly for the following reasons:

1. The search engine *does not know about the page*. No one has submitted the URL to the search engine and no pages currently covered by the search engine have linked to it. (This falls in the category, "Hardly anyone cares about this page, you probably don't need to either.")

2. The search engines have *decided not to index* the content because it is too deep in the site (and probably less useful), the page may change so frequently that indexing the content would be somewhat meaningless (as, for example, in the case of some news pages), or the page is generated dynamically and likewise is not amenable to indexing. (Think in terms of "Even if you searched and found the page, the content you searched for would probably be gone.")

3. The search engine is *asked not to index* the content by the presence of a robots.txt file on the site that asks engines not to index the site, or specific pages, or particular parts of the site. (A lot of this content could be placed in the "It's nobody else's business" category.)

4. The search engine *does not have or use a technology that would be required* to index non-HTML content. This applies to files such as images and, to a lessening degree, audio and video files. Until 2001, this category included file types such as PDF (Portable Document Format) files, Excel files, Word files, and others that began to be indexed by the major search engines in 2001 and 2002. Because of this increased coverage, the Invisible Web may be shrinking in proportion to the size of the total Web.

5. The search engine cannot get to the pages to index them because *it encounters a request for a password or the site has a search box* that must be filled out in order to get to the content.

It is the last part of the last category that holds the most interest for searchers—sites that contain their information in databases. Prime examples of such sites would be phone directories, literature databases (such as Medline), newspaper sites, and patents databases. As you can see, if you can find out that the site exists, then you (without going through a search engine) can search its contents. This leads to the obvious question of where one finds out about sites that contain unindexed (Invisible Web) content.

The best way to find out about these sites is to find a good specialized directory (resource guide) that covers your area of interest. In such a directory, you will find reference to the major Web sites in that subject area, including Web sites that contain databases (see Chapter 3 for the discussion of specialized directories).

In the past, there were multiple sites that contained collections of links to major Invisible Web sites. What were the best known have been discontinued or have not been updated because of the difficulty of adequately keeping up. The following site, however, is a directory of searchable databases and does provide another way of finding Invisible Web sites for a broad variety of subject areas. For more information on what the Invisible Web is, why things are invisible, etc., you may also want to check out the excellent book by Chris Sherman and Gary Price, *The Invisible Web: Uncovering Information Sources Search Engines Can't See* (CyberAge Books, Medford, NJ, 2001).

TIP:

On virtually every site, look for a site index and a search box. They are often more useful for navigating a site than the graphics and links on its home page.

CompletePlanet

completeplanet.com

The site claims "70,000 searchable databases and specialty search engines," but a significant number of the sites are such things as company Web site searches, university catalogs, and art gallery catalogs, and many are not necessarily "invisible." It does list a lot of useful resources, but the content on the CompletePlanet site also emphasizes how trivial much Invisible Web material can be.

COPYRIGHT

Because of the serious implications of this topic, this section could extend for thousands of words. Because this chapter is about basics, however, a few general points will be made, and the reader is encouraged to go for more detail to the sources listed next, which are much more authoritative and extensive on the copyright issue. For those in large organizations, particularly an educational institution, you may want to check your organization's site for local guidelines regarding copyright.

Copyright—Some Basic Points

Here are some basic points about copyright:

1. For the U.S., "Copyright is a form of protection provided by the laws of the United States (title 17, U.S. Code) to the authors of 'original works of authorship,' including literary, dramatic, musical, artistic, and certain other intellectual works" (www.copyright.gov/circs/circ1.html#wci). As stated on the official U.K. Intellectual Property site, "Copyright gives the creators of a wide range of material, such as literature, art, music, sound recordings, films and broadcasts, economic rights enabling them to control use of their material in a number of ways, such as by making copies, issuing copies to the public, performing in public, broadcasting and use online. It also gives moral rights to be identified as the creator of certain kinds of material, and to object to distortion or mutilation of it" (www.intellectual-property.gov.uk/faq/copyright/what.htm). Other countries will have similar definitions and descriptions according to their own legal definition of copyright. Regardless of the country,

copyright (and any failure to acknowledge it appropriately) has legal, moral, and economic implications and repercussions.

2. Assume that what you find on a Web site is copyrighted, unless it states otherwise or you know otherwise, for example, based on the age of the item. See the site for the copyright office in your own country for details about the time frames for copyrights. (In the U.S., of considerable use for Web page creators is the fact that "Works by the U.S. Government are not eligible for U.S. copyright protection" (www.copyright.gov/circs/circ1.html#_wwp). You should still identify the source when quoting something from a site, even if the material is not under copyright.

3. The same basic rules that apply to using printed material apply to using material you get from the Internet, the most important being: For any work you write for someone else to read, cite the sources you use.

For more information on copyright and the Internet, see the following sources.

U.S. Copyright Office
lcweb.loc.gov/copyright

The official U.S. Copyright Office site has copyright information (for the U.S.) directly from the horse's mouth.

The U.K. Patent Office—Copyright
www.patent.gov.uk/copy

The copyright section of the U.K. Patent Office site describes in detail, but also in a very readable fashion, what both the creators and users of copyrighted material need to know. (For other countries, do a search for analogous sites.)

Copyright Web Site
www.benedict.com

This site is particularly good for addressing, in laypersons' language, the issues involved in the copyright of digital materials. It also provides background and discussion on some well-known legal cases on the topic.

Copyright and Fair Use in the Classroom, on the Internet, and the World Wide Web

www.umuc.edu/library/copy.html

This page, from the University of Maryland, is an example of an institutional site that provides practical guidelines—in this case, in the educational context—for use of copyrighted material on Web sites and elsewhere.

CITING INTERNET RESOURCES

The biggest problem with citing a source you find on the Internet is identifying the author, the publication date, and so forth. In many cases, the information just isn't there or you have to really dig to find it. Basically, when citing Internet sources, you need to give as much of the typical citation information as you would for a printed source (author, title, publication, date, etc.), add the URL, and include a comment such as "Retrieved from the World Wide Web, October 15, 2003" or "Internet, accessed October 15, 2003." If your reader isn't particularly picky, just give the information about who wrote it, the title (of the Web page), a date of publication if you can find it, the URL, and when you found the material on the Internet. If you are submitting a paper to a journal for publication, to a professor, or including it in a book, be more careful and follow whatever style guide is recommended. Since the details of exactly how you will write the latter kind of citation will vary both with the particular style (MLA, APA, Chicago, etc.) and with the type of publication (articles, books, newsletters, stand-alone Web site page, etc.), it is not feasible to provide examples here. Fortunately, many style guides are available online. The following two sites provide links to popular style guides online.

Journalism Resources—Guide to Citation Style Guides

bailiwick.lib.uiowa.edu/journalism/cite.html

Karla Tonella provides links to more than a dozen online style guides.

Style Sheets for Citing Resources (Print & Electronic)

www.lib.berkeley.edu/TeachingLib/Guides/Internet/Style.html

This site provides a compilation of guidelines based on the following well-known style guides: MLA, APA, Chicago, and Turabian.

KEEPING UP-TO-DATE ON INTERNET RESOURCES AND TOOLS

For those who want to be alerted to the more valuable resources that become available online, the following sites will be useful. Also, numerous specialized sites that cover specific areas or tools (such as science or search engines) will be mentioned throughout the following chapters. All the sites listed here provide free e-mail alerting services and also provide archives of past content.

ResourceShelf

www.resourceshelf.com

This site, compiled and edited by Gary Price, provides extensive updates on new resources. He also produces a Weblog ("blog") newsletter that is extremely useful for being alerted to new sites, particularly those in the Invisible Web.

FreePint

www.freepint.com

This U.K.-based site, which was created by William Hann, provides:

- A free e-mail newsletter with tips on Internet searching and reviews of Web sites
- FreePint Bar: Forums where subscribers can post Internet-related research questions and comments
- Resources including book reviews, lists of events, and the Free Pint Portal that bring together current and archived Free Pint articles and book reviews, etc.

ResearchBuzz

www.researchbuzz.com

This site by Tara Calishain covers news on a broad spectrum of Internet research tools and provides articles, archives, and a weekly newsletter.

Internet Resources Newsletter

www.hw.ac.uk/libwww/irn

Produced by the Heriot-Watt University Library, "the free, monthly newsletter for academics, students, engineers, scientists and social scientists" contains descriptions and reviews of new, useful Web sites, and other Internet-related news, reviews, press releases, etc.

The Internet Scout Project

scout.wisc.edu

The Internet Scout Project produces the Scout Report, published since 1994, which provides well-annotated reviews of new sites, with both a weekly general report and also specialized mailing lists in the areas of life sciences, physical sciences, mathematics, engineering, and technology.

CHAPTER 2

GENERAL WEB DIRECTORIES AND PORTALS

General Web directories are Web sites that selectively catalog and categorize the broad range of sites available on the Web, usually including sites that are only likely to be of interest to a large number of users. Although they have quite a bit in common with Web search engines, general Web directories, such as the Yahoo! Directory, also differ tremendously from search engines. This chapter addresses where these tools fit, when they should be used, and when they should not be used.

General Web directories serve unique research purposes and in some cases may be the best starting point, even though their databases may include far less than 1 percent of what search engine databases cover. This chapter looks at their strengths, weaknesses, and special characteristics.

STRENGTHS AND WEAKNESSES OF GENERAL WEB DIRECTORIES

Strengths

✔ Selective
✔ Classified (categorized)
✔ Easily browsed
✔ Good for general questions
✔ Most have some searchability

Weaknesses

✔ Relatively small database compared to Web search engines
✔ May not have sites addressing very specific topics
✔ Typically less search functionality than most search engines
✔ Paid inclusion may affect quality
✔ Tend to index only the main pages of sites

SELECTIVITY OF GENERAL WEB DIRECTORIES

The two most distinguishing characteristics of these tools (especially in contrast to Web search engines) are their *selectivity* and their *classification* (categorization) of sites. By selectivity, we mean that each site included in the directory is reviewed by a human being and included on the basis of some measure of quality. The underlying characteristic generally looked for is that the site must contain significant content and the content should be of interest to a fairly large number of people. Impinging on the decisions of the directory's editors is the issue of paid inclusion. For some directories, inclusion of a site is influenced by the payment of a fee. In the case of Yahoo!, noncommercial Web sites technically do not have to pay to be included, but may pay to get a site considered for inclusion. No matter how important, relevant, and useful they may be to you, commercial sites will probably not be found in the Yahoo! Directory unless these sites have paid a fee. For any site, chances of being included in the Yahoo! Directory in a timely fashion is greatly increased by the payment of a fee. In contrast, Open Directory does not accept any fees for inclusion.

A third characteristic of these tools is that typically only the main page of a site is indexed (in contrast to Web search engines, which may index all pages of a site). Web sites rather than Web pages are what is included in general Web directories. One impact of this distinction is that if a term is not on a site's main page, a directory will probably not identify that site as relevant for your search. Furthermore, directories are less likely to index every word even on the main page and may list and search only a brief description.

CLASSIFICATION OF SITES IN GENERAL WEB DIRECTORIES

General Web directories typically organize sites into about a dozen broad categories, with each of those categories broken down into additional levels of hierarchy. This categorization can be the most important reason to go to a directory. It allows browsing down through the levels of the classification hierarchy and can provide valuable direction for a searcher who is not quite sure how to narrow down a broad topic.

Different directories use different classification schemes, which may influence a user to choose one over another. Yahoo! has a major category for

Government, but in Open Directory, government sites are scattered among other categories. Both of these, however, do use cross-references (indicated by an "@" sign), which means that you are not totally reliant on having to have chosen exactly the correct category in which to begin your browsing.

Searchability of General Web Directories

All major directories have a search box on their main page, which causes confusion with Web search engines. (Technically, almost any Web site that has a search box does indeed have a search engine behind it, but that's not what is generally meant by Web search engine.) By entering a term in a directory's search box, you will usually be searching the directory's database. This brings us to two issues: (1) the size of the database, and (2) how much search functionality is offered.

Size of Web Directory Databases

Whereas major Web search engines can contain as many as several *billion* records (Web pages), directories typically have a few *million* or a few thousand records (sites). This is good news and bad news: good because it is reflective of the high degree of selectivity, bad because you are missing out on the vast majority of Web content that is out there.

Search Functionality in Web Directory Databases

Directories usually provide less than search engines in terms of search functions. The major Web directories automatically AND all of the terms you enter. Most allow you to use quotation marks to search for phrases and use a minus sign or the NOT operator to exclude a term. Some provide an advanced search page, and some even provide search functions not available in major search engines. Remember that the main thrust of these tools is browsing, not searching.

When to Use a General Web Directory

When all of these factors are combined, they point to some fairly obvious situations in which starting with a directory is your best bet:

1. For a general question—in other words, when you don't have something very specific in mind—a general Web Directory is the place to go. You're headed to Tblisi for the first time, and you just want to look around on the Web to see what information is available about the city. What defines "general" vs. "specific"? As a rule of thumb, you might think in terms of the number of concepts involved. One or two concepts such as "Tblisi" or "Tblisi museums" is fairly general, and you might want to head for a directory rather than a search engine. Three concepts is getting more specific than a general directory is able to support, for example, "Tblisi art museums." In addition, if a single term itself is very specific, such as "cyclopentanecarbaldehyde," don't count on a directory.

2. This is basically a corollary of the previous point: Start with a general Web directory when you know you need to get more specific than what you have in mind at the moment and you need to browse to help narrow your search.

THE MAJOR GENERAL WEB DIRECTORIES

Two very large general Web directories and a few directories that are smaller and more selective but not subject-specific make up the major general Web directories category. We'll look here at the two largest and some additional representative, well-known, more selective sites. Specialized directories that focus on particular subject areas will be discussed in Chapter 3.

Yahoo! Directory

dir.yahoo.com

The Yahoo! Directory is the best-known general Web directory, although it is probably smaller than Open Directory. For Yahoo! users, it is important to clearly distinguish the Yahoo! Directory from the Yahoo! Web search. Yahoo! got started as a directory rather than as a search engine, and in its first years, the main Yahoo! page was primarily a directory, with the list of categories dominating the page. By 2001, the emphasis had moved in the direction of a "portal," with a lot more resources on its main page besides just the directory. In 2004, Yahoo!'s marketing emphasis moved to the search function when

Yahoo! began offering its own general Web search databases in order to compete with Google. By mid-2006, the directory function was, to say the least, "downplayed," with the directory categories not shown at all on the main page or even directly linked to. (Hopefully, Yahoo! will continue to at least maintain the directory, but as with many other Internet companies, the user's fate rests in the hands of whichever Silicon Valley marketing whiz is currently in charge.) To get to the Yahoo! Directory, the easiest way is to go directly to dir.yahoo.com.

Browsing Yahoo!

Yahoo! has categorized the sites in its directory into more than a dozen major categories on the Directory home page, each typically with three to six sublevels, for example:

Home > Science > Mathematics > Geometry >
Computational Geometry > Trigonometry

A fairly full understanding of the capabilities Yahoo! provides when browsing can be gotten by a close examination of a directory page. Figure 2.1

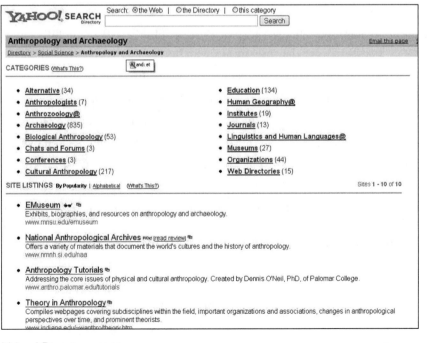

Figure 2.1

Yahoo! Directory page

shows a page that resulted from clicking on the Social Science category, and from there, on Anthropology and Archaeology.

Note the following points:

1. There is a search box that allows you to search the Web, the Directory, or just within the current category. The "just this category" choice is a very powerful tool. If you are looking for "graphics" sites (from the "graphic arts" side rather than from the computer and Web side), you might start by browsing from "Arts and Humanities" to "Design Arts" to "Graphic Design." At that point, because more than 1,000 Yahoo! listings are included at that level, you might use the search box to search just in the current category to avoid bumping into many irrelevant sites.

2. Near the top of the pages, Yahoo! reminds you where you are in the directory (Directory > Social Science > Anthropology and Archaeology). The preceding levels are clickable here, allowing you to go back up one or more steps.

3. The Categories section of the pages shows what additional subcategories are available and how many listings are in each. The @ sign indicates that this is a cross-reference for a category primarily found elsewhere in the hierarchy. In this example, if you click on Anthrozoology, you will be taken to a page from the Biology category.

4. "Site Listings" lists the sites classified at this current level of specificity. Clicking on them will take you to the actual site. In some cases, they are broken down by "By Popularity" and by alphabetical listing. "Sponsor Results" found here are ads.

5. Inside Yahoo! listings (not shown in Figure 2.1) takes you to potentially relevant Yahoo! resources such as News, Finance, and Health.

Yahoo!'s Advanced Directory Search Page

Yahoo! provides an Advanced Directory Search page that enables you to use simple Boolean ("all of these words," "any of these words," or "none of these words"), search by a specific phrase, limit to a specific category, limit to when updated, apply the SafeSearch limit (to avoid adult content), and specify how many results are shown per page.

Yahoo! Directory RSS Feeds

If you would like to be alerted to new entries in Yahoo! Directory categories, you can take advantage of the "New Additions via RSS Feeds" section on the Directory's main page. (RSS Feeds are discussed in detail in Chapter 9, but briefly, RSS [Really Simple Syndication] is an HTML format by which news providers, Web sites, Weblogs, and others can easily distribute their content over the Internet.) With this feature, you can have Yahoo! automatically notify you, through your personalized My Yahoo! portal or any other RSS reader, of new additions in any of more than 30 directory categories/subcategories.

Yahoo! Kids

Yahoo! Kids (kids.yahoo.com) is the popular version of Yahoo! built for kids ages 7 to 12. The directory portion of the site contains age- and content-appropriate sites, along with a number of other references and other features to use at home and in the classroom.

Open Directory Project

dmoz.org

Open Directory Project (Open Directory) is the largest of the general Web directories (with more than 4 million sites) and differs from Yahoo! in several significant ways: (1) Instead of paid editors, Open Directory uses volunteers (more than 75,000 of them of them); (2) it is pure "directory" and does not position itself as a portal or general Web search engine; and (3) its database is used for the directories that you will find on many other sites, including Google. Google's implementation of Open Directory is different enough that it is treated separately later in this chapter.

Browsing Open Directory

Open Directory divides its site into 16 top-level categories, and each is further categorized by several additional levels, such as:

Top: Society: Government: Finance: Central Banks: Supranational

The World category is particularly unique in that it provides directory access to Web sites in more than 70 languages. The subcategories found there will differ.

Figure 2.2

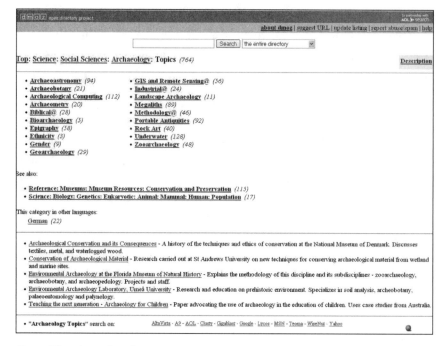

Open Directory directory page

A look at an example of a directory page (as with Yahoo!) can identify some of Open Directory's most important aspects (Figure 2.2). The most significant features are:

1. A search box that gives the option of searching the entire directory or just the current category.

2. A reminder, under the search box, of where you are in the subject hierarchy, each section being clickable, allowing you to move back up the hierarchy easily.

3. The subject hierarchy is followed by a list of the subcategories and usually a "See also" list of categories. The latter points to other sections in the Open Directory, as does the @ sign that occurs after some of the subcategories.

4. Following that will be the listings of the sites themselves, with brief annotations.

5. If the directory database contains articles on this topic in languages other than English, you will see a listing for "This category in other languages."

6. Unique to Open Directory is the "Descriptions" link in the upper right-hand corner of the page. Clicking on this will take you to a "scope note" defining what kinds of things are placed in this category.

7. At the bottom of the pages are links to search engines and even to Yahoo!. Clicking the links will cause the name of the current category to be searched in these tools.

Searching Open Directory

The Open Directory database can be searched using either the search box found on the main page, at the top of directory pages, and at the bottom of search results pages. Search syntax is a bit more sophisticated than that offered by Yahoo!:

- Multiple terms are automatically ANDed. *Eastern Europe* will get only those items containing both terms (capitalization is ignored).
- The automatic AND can be overridden by use of an OR (capitalization not required), e.g., *cycling OR bicycling*.
- You can specify a phrase using quotation marks, e.g., *"Native American."*
- A minus sign or "andnot" will exclude a term; e.g., *vienna -virginia* will eliminate records containing the term "virginia" from the listing of Web sites but not from categories.
- Prefixes can be used to limit results to records that have a particular term in the title, URL, or descriptions, for example, *t:austria*, *u:cam*, or *u:cam.ac.uk*.
- You can use right-hand truncation. *german** will retrieve german, germany, and germanic.
- Various combinations of these functions can be used in combination. However, if you are looking for that degree of specificity, consider using a search engine instead of a directory.

Primarily because of the lack of related portal features, Open Directory search results pages are simpler than those from Yahoo! (Figure 2.3).

Figure 2.3

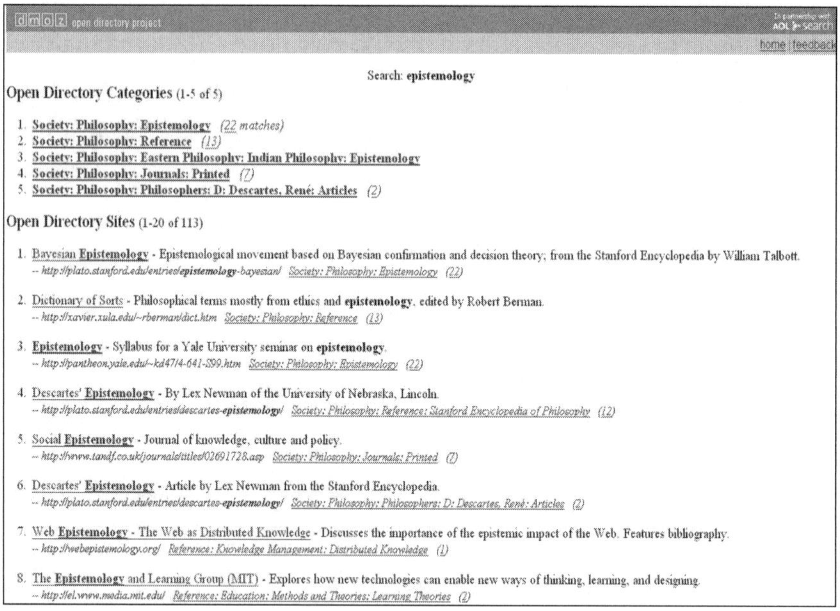

Open Directory search results page

Open Directory search results pages contain the following details:

- Category headings containing the term you searched for or that were identified through the Web sites identified by the search. The number of sites in the category is also shown.
- Sites where the title of the site or the annotation contained your term(s). The category in which the term occurred is also shown and is clickable so it can take you to that category.
- As when browsing through categories, links to search engines are given at the bottom of search results pages. Clicking on any of these links will cause you to be switched to that engine, and your search will be executed there. Another Open Directory search box will also be found at the bottom of search results pages.

Open Directory's Advanced Search Page

The link to the advanced search page, found on Open Directory's main page beside the search box, takes you to a page where you can limit your search to a particular category, to "categories only" or "sites only," or to sites that fall in the categories of Kids and Teens, Kids, Teens, or Mature Teens.

Google's Implementation of Open Directory

For its Web directory, Google uses the Open Directory database. To get to it, click the More link above Google's search box, then on Directory, or go directly to www.google.com/dirhp. You will find that the layout of directory and results pages in Google is almost identical to the pages you see when using Open Directory at dmoz.org with a couple of important exceptions:

1. Whereas the dmoz.org site ranks retrieved records by relevance, Google's results are ranked by the same popularity-based approach as is the Google Web search.

2. Searching is done using the same syntax as Google's Web search:
   - OR to "OR" terms
   - Quotation marks for phrases
   - -term to exclude a term

OTHER GENERAL WEB DIRECTORIES

Other general Web directories are available, although none as large as the two just discussed. Most of the others specialize in some way, and the dividing line between general and specialized is a bit hazy. Some directories are general in regard to subjects covered, but specialized with regard to geographic coverage, such as the numerous country-specific directories. Those directories that are specialized by subject are covered in the next chapter. Here, though, we will look at two more directories that are general with regard to subject coverage, but that are much more selective and, hence, much smaller. Others fall in this category, but these two are certainly among the best and are representative of the genre. Additional directories, which are "general" in subject area but "specialized" in that they focus on *academic* material (INFOMINE, Resource Discovery Network, and BUBL Link), are discussed in Chapter 3.

Librarians' Internet Index

lii.org

The highly respected Librarians' Internet Index is a collection of tens of thousands carefully chosen resources selected on the basis of their usefulness to public library users. Provided by the Library of California, it is well annotated, easily browsable, and also searchable.

Browsing Librarians' Internet Index

The contents of the site are divided into 14 top-level categories, each usually having from 12 to 50 subcategories, some of which have an additional level of subcategory. The moderately lengthy annotations also provide links to the sometimes multiple categories in which they were placed, and the date the annotation was created.

Searching Librarians' Internet Index

A search box appears on most pages. The search automatically ANDs your terms, but you can use an OR between terms, and you can truncate using an asterisk (e.g., *transport**). A spell-checker kicks in for terms that appear to be misspelled. An advanced search page allows you to search by the following fields: description, title, subject, author, publisher, URL, indexer initials, and category. Advanced search also allows a Boolean AND, OR, and NOT, by use of pull-down windows, and here stemming (truncation) is automatic unless you check the "No Stemming" box.

Librarians' Internet Index also provides a free subscription to weekly e-mail updates on new sites added.

Internet Public Library

www.ipl.org

The Internet Public Library (IPL), from the University of Michigan School of Information, contains 40,000 well-organized "librarian-approved resources," including ready reference resources, books, magazines, newspapers, and other special collections (for topics such as Weblogs, science fairs, and Native American authors). IPL also offers a free "ask a question" reference service. The types of resources included do indeed parallel a "public library" collection, with a broad range of topics but also a special emphasis on resources for children, teens, and teachers.

Browsing Internet Public Library

The IPL provides 10 subject areas (each with from six to 30 subcategories), plus sections of links for Ready Reference, Reading Room (magazines and newspapers online), KidSpace, TeenSpace, Special Collections, and Searching Tools. Annotations are provided for each item.

Searching Internet Public Library

To search the site, you can use either the search box on the main page or the advanced search form found under the Search this Site link on the menu. In either the main search box or the advanced search form, you can use multiple terms, but they are ORed, rather than ANDed. (If you search for the terms *physics history,* you will get all of the physics records plus all of the history records.) The advanced search form enables you to limit your retrieval to one or more of the following: Subject Collections, Magazines, Newspapers, KidSpace, TeenSpace, Associations on the Net, Pathfinders, IPL Resources. Search results are organized into those categories.

Where to Find Other General Directories

Unfortunately, most lists of searching tools do not adequately distinguish between search engines and directories and lump the two species together. Keeping that in mind, one place to go for a list of regional (continent or country-specific) tools is Search Engine Colossus (www.searchengine colossus.com).

Most Important Things to Remember About Directories

1. Web directories are most useful when you have a general rather than a specific question.
2. The content of directories is selected by humans who evaluate the usefulness and appropriateness of sites considered for inclusion.
3. Directories *tend* to have one listing per Web site and do not index individual pages.

GENERAL WEB PORTALS

Portals, or gateway sites, are sites that are designed to serve as *starting places* for getting to the most relevant material on the Web. They typically have a *variety of tools* (such as a search engine, directory, news, etc.) all on a single page so that a user can use that page as the "start page" for his or her browser. Portals are often personalizable regarding content and layout. Many serious searchers choose a portal, make it their start page, and personalize it. Thereafter, when the searchers open their browsers, they have in front of them such things as news headlines in their areas of interest, the weather for where they are or where they are headed, stock performance, and so on.

The portal concept goes considerably beyond the idea of general Web directories as we have been discussing them. However, this chapter seemed the appropriate place to discuss them for two reasons: (1) General Web directories (such as Yahoo! Directory and many of the sites that make use of Open Directory) are often presented in the context of a portal; and (2) general portals embody the concept of getting the user quickly and easily to the most relevant Web resources. In addition, when specialized directories are discussed in Chapter 3, we will see that their directory and portal natures meld so tightly that it is not feasible to try to separate them in that discussion. Hence, this chapter seemed the place to discuss general portals.

In addition to Yahoo!, well-known general portals include AOL (aol.com), Netscape (netscape.com), Lycos (lycos.com), and Excite (excite.com). Most countries have their own popular general portals, for example, the French portal Voila! (www.voila.fr).

General portals usually exhibit three main characteristics: *a variety of generally useful tools*, positioning as a *start page*, and *personalizability*.

General Web Portals as Collections of Useful Tools

In line with the "gateway to Internet resources" idea, general portals provide a collection of tools and information that allows users to easily put their hands on information they frequently need.

Instead of having to go to different sites to get the news headlines and weather, or to find a phone directory, general Web directory, search engine, and so forth, a portal can put this information—or a link to this information—right on your start page. General portals usually include some variety of the following on their main pages:

- A general Web directory
- A Web search engine
- News
- Weather
- Stock information

- White pages
- Yellow pages
- Sports scores
- Free e-mail
- Maps/directions
- Shopping

- Horoscope
- Calendar
- Address book
- Chat, message boards, newsgroups

General Web Portals as Start Pages

Most general portals are designed to induce you to choose their site as your browser's start page. Because at least part of their support comes from ads, you will find some ads on the page, but the portal producer knows that the useful information must not be overpowered by ads or no one will come to the page. The overall thrust is to provide a collection of information so useful that it makes it worthwhile to go to that page first.

General Web Portals—Personalizability

Most successful general portals make their pages personalizable, allowing the user to choose which city's weather appears on the page, which stocks are shown, what categories of headlines are displayed, and so on. If you look around on the main pages of these sites, you will usually see either a "personalize" link or a link to a "My" option, such as My Yahoo! or My Netscape, that will allow you to sign up and personalize the page or direct you to your personalized page if you have already done so. A sign-in link will do likewise.

Yahoo!'s Portal Features

A look at Yahoo! offers a good idea of the types of things most general portals can do. Yahoo! is undoubtedly one of the best of the general portals, particularly with regard to personalization features. As a matter of fact, a case could be made that for the serious searcher, Yahoo!'s personalized portal (My Yahoo!) is more important than the Yahoo! Directory (and with the disappearance of the directory from Yahoo!'s home page, Yahoo!'s designers seem to agree).

TIP:

To make a chosen

page your

browser's start

page:

Internet Explorer: From the main menu bar, select Tools > Internet Options. Then under the "General" tab, enter the URL (including the http://) in the Address box.

Firefox: From the main menu bar, select Tools > Options > General > Home Page. Then enter the URL (including the http://) in the Location box.

Netscape: From the main menu bar, select Edit > Preferences. Then under the "Navigator" section, enter the URL (including the http://) in the Home Page box.

Yahoo! has a number of portal features on its main, nonpersonalized page (yahoo.com). Some of them, such as news headlines, are displayed directly on the page along with links to more than 30 other portal features. Some of these links lead to a section such as Autos, Real Estate, and Finance. Many of these sections are more specialized portal pages provided by the site with, again, a collection of tools and links specific to the topic of the channel. Other links on Yahoo!'s main page take you to a phone directory, maps, groups, and more. The best way to understand a portal such as Yahoo! is to lock yourself in your office and not leave until you have clicked on every link on the page. (Skip the ads, though.)

My Yahoo!

An example of a personalized general portal page (My Yahoo! at my.yahoo. com) is shown in Figure 2.4. Yahoo! provides one of the most personalizable general portals, with possibly the widest variety of choices. It also provides personalized versions for most of its 32 country or language-specific versions.

Some Popular General Portals

The following sites all exhibit the three characteristics of general portals to varying degrees and with varying content. Determining which is the best for any individual probably depends on what content is available on the portal and how it is presented. Try more than one before deciding. Most of the better-known general portals have dozens of options to choose from (many, many more if the portal allows you to enter any RSS feed you wish). Such items as "Word of the Day" and "Pregnancy Watch" may or may not necessarily be of interest to you. Your personal stock portfolio is handled very differently by various portals, and what data the portal displays and how it displays that data may make the difference in your choice. A portal may

Figure 2.4

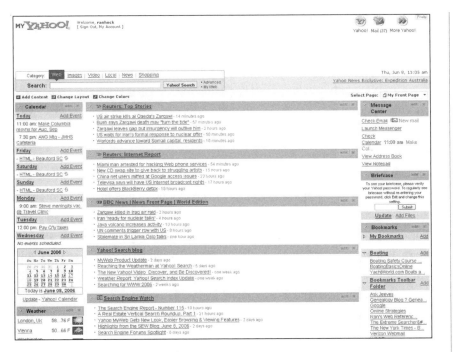

My Yahoo! personalized portal page

allow very detailed specification of what categories of headlines are displayed, or only very general categories, and so on. The following portals are among the best known in the U.S. For non-U.S. portals, take a look at the "World" section of Open Directory (dmoz.org/world), choose your country, and then search for the term "portal" in the relevant language.

Other Selected Examples of General Portals

Excite (excite.com) - Once the best and still used by many people.

Lycos (lycos.com) - Minimal personalization.

AOL (aol.com) - Mentioned here mainly because it was the first popular general portal; parts are available only to AOL subscribers.

MSN (msn.com) - Widely used largely because it came pre-installed on so many computers. For those of you who can't get enough of Bill Gates, here's one more opportunity to have him around.

Netscape (netscape.com) - Very good content, very clean design, and very personalizable. Netscape was acquired by AOL in 1999.

Other Resources Relating to General Directories and Portals

Traffick: Frequently Asked Questions about Portals
www.traffick.com/article.asp?aID=9#what

This site provides a concise but quite informative overview and history of the Web portal concept.

SUMMARY

Remember that general Web directories provide sites that are evaluated and selected by human beings. This, along with the fact that all sites are placed in categories to allow browsing, makes these tools a good starting place when you want selected sites, when you want only a few sites, and when your question has a general rather than a specific nature. Take advantage of one of the general, personalizable portals as starting places so you can go to your own selection of frequently needed information.

CHAPTER 3

SPECIALIZED DIRECTORIES

For some immediate expertise in Web resources on a specific topic, there is no better starting point than the right specialized directory, or portal. Also known as resource guides, metasites, cyberguides, Webliographies, or just plain "collections of links," these sites bring together selected Internet resources on specific topics. They provide not only a good starting place for effectively utilizing Internet resources in a particular area, but also, very importantly, a confidence in knowing that no really important tools in that area are being missed. The variety of theses sites is endless. They can be discipline-oriented or industry-oriented; they may focus on a specific kind of document (e.g., newspapers or historical documents) or take virtually any other slant toward identifying a useful category of resources.

If the producer of the site adds some valuable content to the collection of links, such as news headlines or lists of events, you not only have a specialized directory, but a specialized portal or gateway, making it even more useful as a starting point.

STRENGTHS AND WEAKNESSES VS. OTHER KINDS OF FINDING TOOLS

Strengths

✔ Specialized
✔ Very selective
✔ Provide some immediate "Web expertise"

Weaknesses

✔ Relatively small
✔ Variable quality and consistency
✔ Most are browsable but not searchable

HOW TO FIND SPECIALIZED DIRECTORIES

There are at least a couple ways to identify systematically a specialized directory for a particular area of interest. Some easy and reasonably effective ways are: Yahoo!'s "Web Directories" subcategory; searching for them in search engines; keeping an eye out for them in professional journal articles and books; and using directories of directories.

Using Yahoo!

Yahoo! lists thousands of specialized directories. As a matter of fact, it has lists of one or more specialized directories for almost 800 categories, ranging from semiconductors to storytelling to sumo. The trick to finding them in Yahoo! is simple: Look for the Web Directories subcategory either by browsing through the Yahoo! categories list or by putting your subject and the phrase *Web directories* in Yahoo!'s Directories search box. (This can also be done in Open Directory using the subcategory "Directories," but you will find significantly fewer results. Only about 200 categories in Open Directory list this subcategory.)

Using Professional Publications

Keep an eye out for articles that discuss Internet resources for specific areas in professional publications (printed and online): journals such as *ONLINE* and *Searcher*, and Web sites for searchers such as FreePint (freepint.com). A book by Nora Paul and Margot Williams titled *Great Scouts: CyberGuides to Subject Searching on the Web* (CyberAge Books, Medford, NJ, 1999) focuses on specialized directories and lists more than 500 sites.

Using Directories of Directories

Directories of directories are valuable sources for locating topic-specific information. The following two sites contain collections of specialized directories (and may contain other content as well).

The WWW Virtual Library

www.vlib.org

Perhaps the best-known catalog of Web directories, The WWW Virtual Library, started by none other than Tim Berners-Lee, founder of the Web, contains an excellent selection of specialized directories arranged by category. In one sense, it is one large directory with individual sections maintained by a large number of volunteers, but because the format of each section is also very independently done, The WWW Virtual Library is indeed a collection of individual directories. The quality of the individual directories tends to be quite high.

Search Engine Guide

www.searchengineguide.com

Although this site does not adequately distinguish between search engines and directories, if you use the search box under the Internet Search Engines link or browse the categories listed there, you will find a useful collection of specialized directories.

Using Search Engines

You may be successful in finding a specialized directory in your area by searching a term for your area AND the word "resources," for example, *geology resources.* You may want to be more specific by using the phrase, "Internet resources," for example, *geology "internet resources."* You can also try using "metasite" in addition to or instead of "resources." For industry portals, search for the industry plus the word "portal," for example, *"electronics industry" portal.* If you would like to get a site that provides a list of printed resources for a subject, as well as Internet resources, use the word "pathfinder." Many libraries provide pathfinders that are guides to the literature and to Internet resources in their library. Even if you don't have access to the library that produced it, the guide can provide reminders of printed tools you might want to track down.

WHAT TO LOOK FOR IN SPECIALIZED DIRECTORIES AND HOW THEY DIFFER

Many areas have a variety of directories. If you want to find the best, several factors must be considered. An excellent specialized directory does not have to be strong in all of these facets, but, depending on your need, you might want to focus on a few particular aspects. They tend to differ mainly in these terms:

- Size – Sometimes large is good; sometimes fewer sites to focus on is good.
- Categorization/Classification – Especially if the number of sites included is large, it is helpful to have them divided into useful categories.
- Annotations – A large portion of specialized directories (including many very good ones) do not have annotations describing the sites they list. Annotations, however, can be very useful by providing a quick overview of what the sites cover and any special characteristics of the sites.
- Searchability – A fairly small portion of specialized directories provide a search box to save users from having to browse. If the directory is large, this can be quite useful.
- Origin – Who (or what organization) produced the site is sometimes a good indication of the quality you might expect from the site. Unfortunately, many sites do not give a clear indication of who produced them, and you may have to rely on the URL for a clue.
- Portal features – If, in addition to the collection of links, other features are included, the site can be especially powerful. Look for such things as news headlines, lists of events (conferences, etc.), professional directories (e.g., a list of members if it is a site produced by an association), directories of companies in that area, and so on.

SOME PROMINENT EXAMPLES OF SPECIALIZED DIRECTORIES

The examples of specialized directories included here are mentioned for a variety of reasons: Some were chosen simply because they are sites that most serious searchers should be aware of; some demonstrate particularly good or unique characteristics of a specialized directory; some are very wide-ranging (as well as having other values as a specialized directory). In some categories, such as Government, more than one is listed to provide contrasts between sites. (Sometimes multiple directories are listed for an area because I just could not make up my mind which one to choose.)

Don't forget that effective use of a directory approach for identifying relevant sites can mean using a combination of the general Web directories covered in the previous chapter and the specialized directories covered here. In one sense, each section of a general directory such as Yahoo! Directory or Open Directory is itself a specialized directory.

General, Academic, and Reference Tools

The first two sites that follow provide an extensive collection of links to reference tools such as encyclopedias, dictionaries, and so forth. These directories, which vary in exhaustiveness and method of arrangement, are worth getting to know. The next three focus on a broad range of subjects, but their coverage is limited primarily to sites of interest in the academic/research setting. The last two included in this section—Project Gutenberg and the Library of Congress Gateway—provide links to books and library catalogs available online.

Refdesk

refdesk.com

This fairly extensive collection is actually arranged more as a portal with news headlines and other features, as well as links to valuable reference resources. (It was achieving a deserved status on its own, but got a boost when then-U.S. Secretary of State Colin Powell said something to the effect that it should be on the screen of every State Department employee.) Most of the "Reference Tools" are found toward the bottom of the page.

Internet Public Library Reference Ready Reference

www.ipl.org/div/subject/browse/ref00.00.00

From the School of Information at the University of Michigan and part of the broader IPL Web site mentioned in the previous chapter, this is a great collection of ready reference links, including almanacs, biographies, census data, dictionaries, encyclopedias, and other reference resources.

INFOMINE

infomine.ucr.edu

A well organized, categorized, and searchable collection of more than 40,000 links, this directory is specialized in that it focuses on "scholarly" Internet resources. Look here for sources that will be useful at the university level. For a specialized directory, the advanced search page has quite extensive searching capabilities. INFOMINE comes from the University of California, with contributions from librarians at a number of other universities.

BUBL LINK

bubl.ac.uk/link

This site, from University of Strathclyde, includes more than 12,000 resources, covering all academic areas. Part of its uniqueness is that the main categories used are based on the Dewey Decimal Classification, and it has a particularly strong focus on library and information science. It is very easily browsable, with indexes by subject, country, and type, and BUBL LINK also has good search capabilities on its advanced search page.

Intute

www.intute.ac.uk

Intute (formerly the Resource Discovery Network) contains more than 100,000 sites selected by more than 70 U.K. educational and research institutions. The collection is now arranged in four main categories: Science and Technology; Arts and Humanities; Social Sciences; and Health and Life Sciences. The entire collection can be searched using the search box on the main page or can be browsed (Figure 3.1).

Project Gutenberg

www.gutenberg.org

Want to read a good book? Come here. This is the site for a project that dates back to the early years of the Internet and aims to make available to the world all books that are out of copyright and in full text online. It leads to 19,000 books, from Cicero to the Bobbsey twins. All these books are in the U.S. public domain, no longer under copyright (therefore, almost all are from before 1923). For many of the books, the entire text is available in a single file, allowing a researcher to quickly find all references to a word in a text (by using the "Edit > Find in This Page" function of a browser). Using this approach (not just here but elsewhere), you can go to the text of *The Odyssey*, for example, and quickly, one-by-one, find every mention of Telemachus, if you are inclined to do such things.

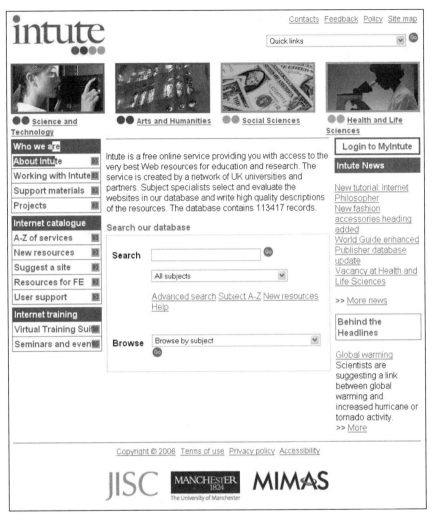

Figure 3.1

Intute

Library of Congress Gateway to Library Catalogs

lcweb.loc.gov/z3950/gateway.html

Going beyond just a "collection of links," this site uses a consistent interface to bring together the capability of searching (one at a time) the contents of the online catalogs for nearly 500 libraries in the U.S. and elsewhere. All of these are catalogs that use the Z39.50 standard for online library catalogs.

Social Sciences and Humanities

In addition to the more specific sites below, for a broader range of social sciences and humanities, use Intute (www.intute.ac.uk).

Tennessee Tech History Web Site

www2.tntech.edu/history

At first it looks like this site is simply about history and Tennessee Tech, but there's much more, with excellent large collections of resources for both history and historiography. Although anyone interested in history will find it valuable to browse most sections of this site, the most profitable part for many may be under the Internet Resources in History heading, and under that, the sections History Sites by Subject and History Sites by Time Period.

Best of History Web Sites

www.besthistorysites.net

Best of History Web Sites furnishes annotated and rated links to more than 1,000 history-related Web sites in categories such as Prehistory, Ancient/Biblical, Medieval, U.S. History, Early Modern European, 20th Century, World War II, Art History, General Resources, and Maps. There are also categories for Lesson Plans/Activities, Multimedia, and Research.

Virtual Religion Index

religion.rutgers.edu/vri

With a focus on scholarly sites, this directory site contains extensive links for the world's major (and minor) religions, and on the academic study of religion and religious issues.

Physical and Life Sciences

At present, there does not seem to be a single broad-reaching directory for the sciences in general. Your best bet for focusing on a specific science may be to try the techniques for finding specialized directories mentioned earlier, or try the appropriate section on sites such as INFOMINE. The following are some notable examples of science sites in specific areas.

ChemDex

www.chemdex.org

This site, from the University of Sheffield, contains more than 7,000 chemistry-related links. The links are arranged by 13 top-level categories and include both scholarly sites and links to chemical companies and suppliers. Go to "WebElements" for an outstanding online periodic table. Even if you have no connection with chemistry, you will find the site interesting and even fun, with contents ranging from the usual periodic table data for each element, to bond enthalpies, to cartoons about the element.

healthfinder

www.healthfinder.gov

From the U.S. Department of Health and Human Services, this site provides reliable health information aimed at consumers. It includes links that range from medical dictionaries to background on diseases to directories of physicians, hospitals, nursing homes, and a variety of other easily understandable resources.

MedlinePlus

www.nlm.nih.gov/medlineplus

MedlinePlus, from the U.S. National Library of Medicine and National Institutes of Health, is a portal that offers a combination of information provided directly on the site and an extensive collections of links. The Health Topics section contains more than 570 topics on conditions, diseases, and wellness. Other parts of the MedlinePlus site include Drug Information, Medical Encyclopedia, Dictionaries, News (health news from the past 30 days), Directories (doctors, dentists, and hospitals), and Other Resources.

Business and Economics

In addition to the specialized directories listed here for business-related information, be sure to look at the sites listed in Chapter 7 for company information. Some of the sites listed there, such as CorporateInformation, can also be considered specialized directories.

New York Times > Business > A Web Guide: Business Navigator

www.nytimes.com/ref/business/business-navigator.html

This bare-bones collection of business-related links provides categories for Markets (exchanges, etc.), Investing, Company Information (directories, news, etc.), Banking & Finance, Government (Federal Reserve, IRS, BLS, etc.), Business and Financial News, Business Directories, and Miscellany. Only about half of the 150 or so sites it includes are annotated (and just briefly), but the clarity, selectivity, and categories into which they are divided make it an easy and quick guide to critical business resources.

CEOExpress

ceoexpress.com

CEOExpress is a cluttered looking but rich site with a strong emphasis on business news sites (Figure 3.2). For a good understanding of what it can provide, spend three or four minutes browsing the unique arrangement of category links. The main site is free, but a paid subscription provides customization of the home page, e-mail, and other tools and benefits.

Virtual International Business & Economic Sources (VIBES)

library.uncc.edu/vibes

Divided into Comprehensive, Regional, and National categories, the 3,000 links on this site emphasize "full-text files of recent articles and research reports," "statistical tables and graphs," and other business-related directories.

Resources for Economists on the Internet

rfe.org

Edited by Bill Goff and sponsored by the American Economic Association, this site lists more than 2,100 resources categorized into 97 sections. These sections range from the obvious things of interest to economists, such as data, to less obvious but very useful categories, such as software and mailing lists. (If you need a break, check out the "Neat Stuff" section.)

I3—Internet Intelligence Index

www.fuld.com/Tindex

Produced by Fuld and Company, a leader in the competitive intelligence field, this directory provides well-organized and annotated links to more than 600 sites important to competitive intelligence researchers. To get to the list of sites from the URL above, click on the I3 link.

Government and Governments

Although some countries have single sites that provide links to sites for individual departments or ministries, many do not, and it is not always easy to identify the particular agency site you need. The first two sites that follow are directories that make this much easier by bringing together large collections of sites by country or other category. The second two sites are examples

Figure 3.2

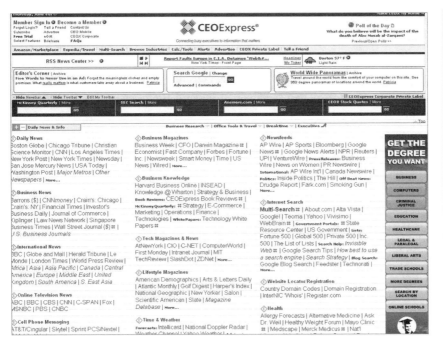

CEOExpress main page

of portals for specific countries, and the final site in this section is a resource guide for political parties worldwide.

Governments on the WWW

www.gksoft.com/govt

Although a bit slow in updating, this site contains links to more than 17,000 Web sites from governments (and multinational organizations) around the world, including sites for parliaments, law courts, embassies, cities, public broadcasting corporations, central banks, political parties, and the like. There are no annotations, but the names of the sites are translated into English.

Foreign Government Resources on the Web

www.lib.umich.edu/govdocs/foreign.html

Whereas the preceding site provides access by country, this site provides both a country index and a subject index, the latter with more than 30 headings, such as anthems, decolonization, economics, human rights, and others. There may be fewer sites for each country, but annotations are provided for the sites that are included. ("Foreign" for this site means "non-U.S.")

FirstGov.gov

firstgov.gov

This site, which is the official portal to U.S. government sites, contains links to state sites (Figure 3.3). The main divisions on the home page (for Citizens, Businesses and Nonprofits, Federal Employees, and Government-to-Government) allow browsing by who is seeking the information or who the information is for. The "By Organization" menu will take you to links arranged by branch of government and also provides an alphabetic index to agencies.

Directgov (U.K. Online)

www.open.gov.uk

As the official U.K. government portal site, this site provides links to U.K. public sector information. The main portions on the site are arranged by subject (Education and Learning, Home and Community, etc.) and by resources for specific groups of people (Parents, Disabled People, Over 50s, Britons Living Abroad, Caring for Someone, Young People). The Directories and the Guide to Government provide additional avenues to information from and about the government.

Political Resources on the Net

www.politicalresources.net

This is an excellent resource for quickly identifying the sites of political parties for any country. On the map on the home page, click on a continent and then the country. Links for international parties and other related resources are also provided.

Legal

FindLaw

www.findlaw.com

This very rich portal contains links to a broad range of legal subjects from lawyers and law firms to cases and codes. Don't expect it to turn you into an expert legal researcher, but if you are one, you are probably already making good use of this site. If you aren't one, it will point you in the right direction for many of the best legal resources on the Internet. Most of the legal resources are primarily for the U.S., but the International Lawyer Search covers more than 160 countries.

Figure 3.3

Businesses and Nonprofits category page at FirstGov.gov

Education

Kathy Schrock's Guide for Educators

school.discovery.com/schrockguide

This well-known directory for K–12 teachers and parents contains links to hundreds of sites, each with a brief annotation. You can browse by subject or you can search (either the entire site or the parents or teachers areas). Among other things, it is a good source for links to lesson plans.

Education World

www.education-world.com

Education World contains a browsable and searchable database of more than 500,000 education-related sites. The site itself is more portal than merely a directory and contains much original content by the producers of the site (such as articles and lesson plans) as well as the links to other sites.

Education Index

www.educationindex.com

Education Index contains more than 3,000 sites with annotations, arranged in 66 categories and covering all levels of education. You can browse either by subject area or by "Lifestage." The "Coffee Shop" section is a collection of online discussion groups.

Education Atlas

www.educationatlas.com

Education Atlas is a clearly organized resource guide containing 8,000 education Web sites arranged in four major sections (Early Childhood, K–12 Education, Higher Education, Teacher's Corner). It also has categories for various levels of education as well as for topics such as home schooling and Regional (international).

News

Kidon Media-Link

www.kidon.com/media-link

Although a number of sites serve as directories of newspapers and other news sources on the Internet, Kidon Media-Link is one of the most extensive and seems to have relatively few dead links, a problem with some of the other news directories. The site is arranged by continent, then country, and provides more than 18,000 links to newspapers, news agencies, magazines, radio, and TV sites (Figure 3.4). (Additional news resource guides can be found in Chapter 9.)

Figure 3.4

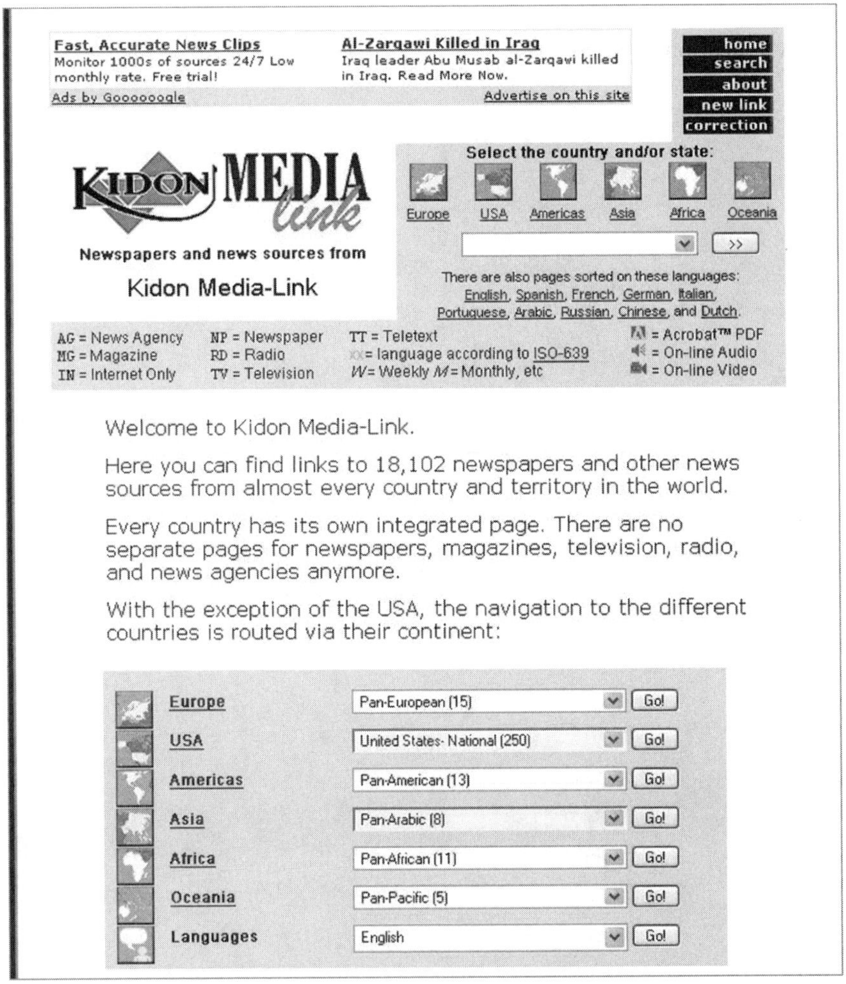

Kidon Media-Link main page

Genealogy

Cyndi's List of Genealogy Sites on the Internet

www.cyndislist.com

This is perhaps the best-known of the numerous genealogy directories with links to more than 250,000 sites. You can browse through the 180 categories or take advantage of the search box. Both beginners and experienced genealogists should find it useful.

SEARCH ENGINES: THE BASICS

General Web search engines, such as Google, Yahoo! Search, and Ask.com, stand in contrast to Web directories in three primary ways: (1) They are much larger, containing billions instead of a few million (or fewer) records; (2) there is virtually no human selectivity involved in determining what Web pages are included in the search engine's database; and (3) they are designed for searching (responding to a user's specific query) rather than for browsing, so they provide more substantial searching capabilities than directories.

For someone using Internet resources, a workable definition of a Web search engine is a service on the Web that allows searching of a large database of Web pages by word, phrase, and other criteria. There is actually some ambiguity involved when one speaks of "search engines." From a slightly more technical perspective, when we use a site such as Google, we are utilizing a "service" that facilitates searching of a database. In the narrower sense, the "search engine" is the program utilized by the service to query the database. Almost any site that provides a search box could be considered to have a search "engine." Here, when we speak of "search engines," we will really be referring to a service, such as the three just mentioned, that provides searching of a very large database of Web pages and may provide other services as well, such as translations, shopping, and others.

HOW SEARCH ENGINES ARE PUT TOGETHER

To take full advantage of search engines, it is useful to understand the basics of how they are put together. Four major steps are involved in making Web pages searchable by a search engine service. These steps also correspond to the "parts" of a search engine: the spiders, the indexing program and index, the search engine program, and the HTML user interface.

1. Spiders (a.k.a. crawlers) – These are programs used by the search engine services to scan the Internet to identify new sites or sites that have changed, gather information from those sites, and feed that information to the search engine's indexing mechanism. For some engines, popular sites (likely to have many links to them) are crawled more thoroughly and more frequently than less popular sites. Tied into this crawling function is a second way for Web pages to get identified—by the process of submitted URLs. A link on most search engines' sites will let anyone submit a URL, and with the exception of those pages that are identifiable as "spam" (pages that are designed to mislead the search engine and search engine users and/or illegitimately lead to high rankings) or pages that are unacceptable for other reasons, the pages will be indexed and added to the database.

2. The indexing program and the index – Once a new page is identified by the search engine's crawler, the page will typically be indexed under virtually every word on the page. Other parts of the page may also be indexed, such as the URL, metatags, the URLs of links on the page, and image file names.

3. The search "engine" itself – This is the program that identifies (retrieves) those pages in the database that match the criteria indicated by a user's query. Another important and more challenging process is also involved, that of determining the order in which the retrieved records should be displayed. This "relevance-ranking" algorithm usually takes many factors into account, such as the popularity of the page (as measured by how many other pages link to it), the number of times the search terms occur in the page, the relative proximity of search terms in the page, the location of search terms (for example, pages where the search terms occur in the title of the page may get a higher ranking), and other factors.

4. The HTML-based (HyperText Markup Language) interface that gathers query data from the user (the "search page") – The home page of the search service and advanced search pages are the parts we usually envision when we think of a particular search engine.

These pages contain the search box(es), links to the various databases that are searchable (images, news, etc.), and perhaps a number of other features.

How Search Options Are Presented

Exactly what search options are available varies from search engine to search engine. In any particular search engine, some available options are presented on the home page, but on the advanced search page, usually several more options are clearly displayed. Options are typically made available in one of two ways: (1) by means of a menu or (2) by the searcher directly qualifying the term when it is entered in the main search box.

An example of the menu approach is shown in Figure 4.1, where (in Yahoo!) a pull-down menu allows the term entered in the box to be qualified. In this example, the search is requesting that only those pages be retrieved that have the term "antioxidants" in the title of the page.

Figure 4.1

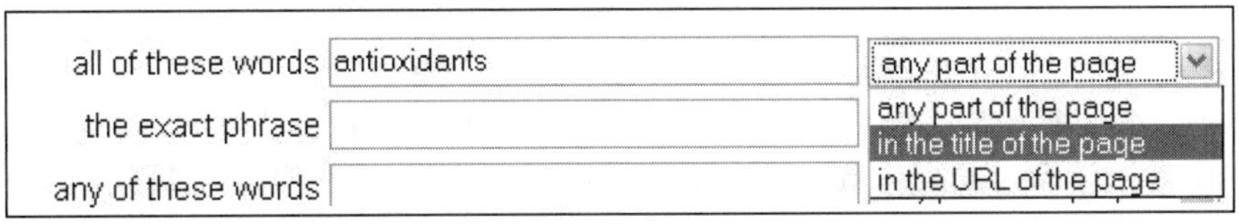

all of these words	antioxidants		any part of the page
the exact phrase			any part of the page / in the title of the page
any of these words			in the URL of the page

Example of the menu approach to qualifying a search term

Figure 4.2 shows an example of qualifying a term directly. Here (in Google) the "intitle:" prefix is inserted to do the same thing as shown in the menu example in Figure 4.1. (Whenever using prefixes such as this to qualify a term, be sure *not* to put a space on either side of the colon.)

Figure 4.2

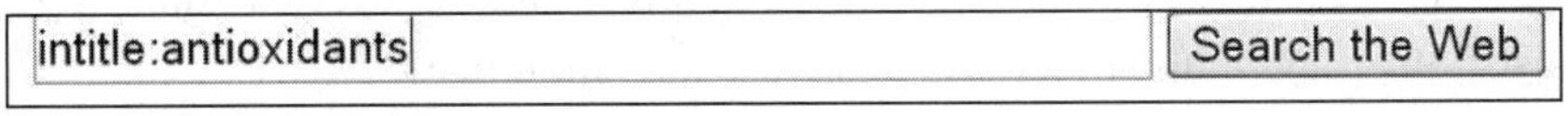

intitle:antioxidants	Search the Web

Example of using a prefix to qualify a search term

Usually you have a choice as to which approach to use. The menu approach is easier in that you do not need to know the somewhat cryptic prefixes. If you do know the prefixes, you may accomplish your search more quickly and easily.

TYPICAL SEARCH OPTIONS

A number of search options are fairly typical. These include phrase searching, language specification, and specifying that you retrieve only pages where your term appears in a particular part (field) of the record, such as the title, URL, or links. Now that major engines include more than just HTML pages, for some engines, you can also specify file type (Web pages, PDF files, Excel files, etc.). Every engine also offers some form of Boolean operations.

The following gives a quick look at why you might want to use (or not use) those options. Table 5.1 near the end of Chapter 5 identifies which options are available in which engines, and the profiles that follow provide some details for using the search options in the major engines. Expect occasional changes in exactly which options are offered by which engines.

Phrase Searching

Phrase searching is an option that is available in every search engine, and perhaps surprisingly, can be done the same way in all of them. To search for a phrase, put the phrase in quotation marks. For example, searching on *"Red River"* (with quotation marks) will assure that you get only those pages that contain the word "red" immediately in front of the term "river." You will avoid records such as one about the red wolves of Alligator River. When your concept is best expressed as a phrase, be sure to use the quotation marks. You are not limited to two words; you can use several. For example, to find out who said "When I'm good I'm very good, but when I'm bad I'm better," search for a few of the words together, such as *"when I'm bad I'm better."* (Search engines have limits on the number of words you can enter.)

Some engines automatically identify common phrases, and most engines give a higher ranking to pages that have your terms next to each other. To be sure, though, that you are only getting records with your terms adjacent to each other and in the order you wish, use quotation marks.

Title Searching

This is often the most powerful technique for getting to some highly relevant pages quickly. It may also cause you to miss some good ones, but what you do get has an excellent chance of being relevant. All the major engines have this option, and most of them let you search titles by either menu options or prefixes (see Figures 4.1 and 4.2).

URL, Site, and Domain Searching

Doing a search in which you limit your results to a specific site allows you, in effect, to perform a search of that site. Even for sites that have a "site search" box on their home page, you may find better results by doing a site search in a large search engine. If you want to find where on the FBI site the term "internship" is mentioned, use a search engine's advanced search page and specify the term "internship" in the search box and "fbi.gov" in the box that lets you specify the site (or domain or URL). Most engines will let you accomplish the same thing using a prefix. For example, in Google, Yahoo!, Windows Live, and Ask.com, you could search for:

> *internship site:fbi.gov*

Most engines allow you to be more specific and search a portion of a site, for example (in each of the four engines just mentioned):

> *internship site:baltimore.fbi.gov*

As well as specifying an exact site, you can, in most engines, just specify that you want a term to be somewhere in the URL by using the "inurl:" prefix, for example:

> *members inurl:aiip*

In many search engines, domain searching is identical to URL searching. The use of the term, though, points out that you can use this approach to limit your retrieval to sites having a particular top-level domain, such as gov, edu, uk, ca, or fr. This could be used to identify only Canadian sites that mention tariffs, or to get only educational sites that mention biodiversity.

Link Searching

There are two varieties of "link" searching. In one variety, you can search for all pages that have a hypertext link to a particular URL, and in the other, you can search for words contained in the linked text on the page. In the former, for example, you can check which Web pages have linked to your organization's URL. In the second, you can see which Web pages have the name of your organization as linked text. Either variety can be very informative in terms of who is interested in either your organization or your Web site. It can be very useful for marketing purposes, and can also be used by nonprofits for development and fundraising leads. Also, if you are looking for information on an organization, it can sometimes be useful to know who is linking to that organization's site.

This searching option is available in some search engines on their advanced page and/or on the main page with the use of prefixes. Engines may let you find links to an overall site or to a specific page within a site. If you want to search exhaustively for who is linking to a particular site, definitely use more than one search engine. In link searching, the difference in retrieval is even more pronounced than in keyword searching.

Language Searching

Although all of the major engines allow you to limit your retrieval to pages written in a given language, they differ in terms of which languages can be specified. The 30 or so most common languages are specifiable in most of those engines, but if you want to find a page written in Galician, not all engines will give you that option. If you find yourself searching by language, be sure to look at the various language options and preferences provided by the different engines, particularly if a non-Western character set is involved.

Searching by Date

Searching by date is one of the most obviously desirable options, and most major engines provide such an option. Unfortunately, it may not have much meaning. Through no fault of the search engines, it is often impossible to determine a "date created" or the "date of publication" of the content of the page. To get around this, engines may use the date when the page was last modified and, if that cannot be determined, it may assign the date on which the page was last crawled by the engine. When searching Web pages, keep this approximation in mind and do not expect much precision. (On other databases an engine may provide, such as news or groups, the date searching may be very precise.)

Searching by File Type

Now that search engines are indexing non-HTML pages, including Adobe Acrobat (PDF) files, Word documents, Excel files, and so on, there are times when you may want to limit your retrieval to one of those types. For example, if you wanted to print out a tutorial for Dreamweaver, you might prefer the more attractive PDF (Personal Document Format) over the format of an HTML page. If you want a nice "summary" of a topic, try a PowerPoint format. Collections of statistics on a specific topic can sometimes be easily identified by limiting your retrieval to Excel files. Specifying file type may not be required very often, but at times it will be very useful.

Boolean Search Options

In the context of online searching, "Boolean searching" basically means the following: the process of identifying those items (such as Web pages) that contain a particular combination of search terms. It is used to indicate that a particular group of terms must all be present (the Boolean "AND"), that any of a particular group of terms is acceptable (the Boolean "OR"), or that if a particular term is present, the item is rejected (the Boolean "NOT"). This is represented by the dark areas in the Venn diagrams shown in Figure 4.3.

Very precise search requirements can be expressed using combinations of these operators along with parentheses to indicate the order of operations.

Figure 4.3

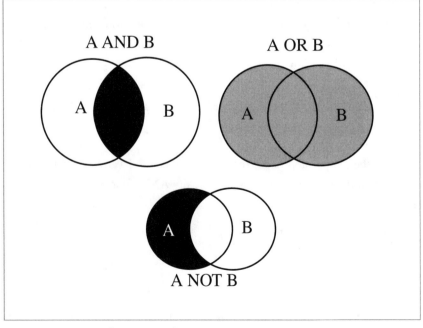

Boolean operators (connectors)

For example:

> *(grain OR corn OR wheat) AND (production OR harvest) AND oklahoma AND 1997*

The use of the actual words AND, OR, and NOT to represent Boolean operations has been downplayed in Web search engines and has been replaced in many cases by the use of menus or other syntax. Even if you have never typed the AND, OR, or NOT, you have probably still used Boolean. (One point here being that Boolean is "painless.") If you choose the "all the words" option from a pull-down menu, you are requesting the Boolean AND. If you choose the "any of the words" option from a menu, you are specifying an OR. Because all major search engines automatically AND your query terms (if you do not specify otherwise), any time you just enter two or more terms in a search box, you are implicitly requesting an AND (even if you do not realize it).

Varieties of Boolean Formats

As with title, site, and other search qualifications, Boolean usually provides two options for indicating what you want: (1) a menu option or (2) the option of applying a syntax directly to what you enter in the search box. Using the menu option can be thought of as "simplified Boolean" or "simple Boolean." An example of a Boolean menu option is shown in Figure 4.4.

Figure 4.4

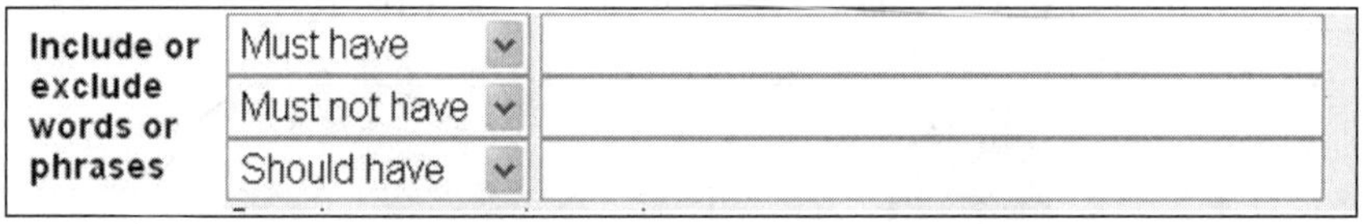

Include or exclude words or phrases	Must have ⌄	
	Must not have ⌄	
	Should have ⌄	

Menu form of Boolean options

With the syntax approach, the exact syntax used varies with the search engine. All major engines now automatically AND your terms, so when you enter:

> *prague economics tourism*

what you will get is more traditionally described as:

> *prague AND economics AND tourism*

Figure 4.5 shows an example of Boolean syntax (from Yahoo!'s main search page).

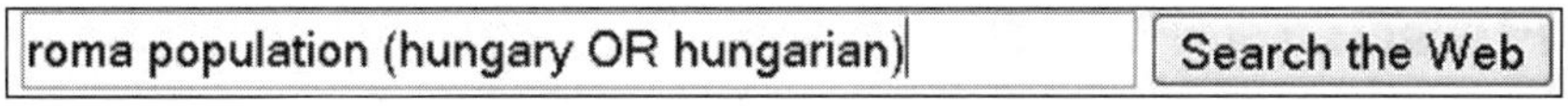

Figure 4.5

| roma population (hungary OR hungarian)| | Search the Web |

Example of Boolean syntax

Full Boolean

Even though most engines provide syntax to allow near-maximum Boolean capabilities, engines assert their independence by varying the particular syntax used for entering a Boolean expression. For example, Google uses an OR but does not use parentheses, while Windows Live and Yahoo! require the use of parentheses around ORed terms.

Table 4.1 shows how a typical Boolean-oriented search would be structured in the major search engines. For all practical purposes, a search engine might be considered to have "full" Boolean capabilities if it provides for all three Boolean operations (AND, OR, and NOT).

Boolean Syntax at Major Search Engines

Table 4.1

Search Engine	Boolean Pattern	Full Boolean	Expression
Ask.com	A B -D	No	endan gered species" maryland -rockfish
Google	A B OR C - D	Yes	"endangered species" maryland OR virginia -rockfish
Windows Live	A (B OR C) -D	Yes	"endangered species" (maryland OR virginia) -rockfish
Yahoo!	A B -D	Yes	"endangered species" (maryland OR virginia) -rockfish

Note: Since searches on Google ignore parentheses, the following will work in Google, Windows Live, and Yahoo!: "endangered species" (maryland OR virginia) -rockfish

SEARCH ENGINE OVERLAP

It is important to recognize that no single search engine covers everything. Due to differences in crawling, indexing, and other factors, each engine's database includes Web pages that the others do not. In a typical search, if you search a second engine, it can significantly increase the number of unique records you find. Searching a third and fourth engine will also often yield records not found by the first engines. Therefore, if you need to be exhaustive—if it is crucial that you find everything on the topic—do your search in a second and third engine. (At the end of this chapter, you will see why metasearch engines are *not* the solution to this problem.)

RESULTS PAGES

One of the most useful things a searcher can do is to take a few extra seconds to look not just at the titles of the retrieved Web pages, but for other things included on results pages and also at the details provided in each record. Most engines provide some potentially useful additional information besides just the Web page results. At the same time they search their Web database, they may search the other databases they have, such as news, images, video, and directories. You may find some news headlines that match your topic; a link to images, audio, or video on your topic; a directory category; and more.

One thing offered on search results pages by all of the major engines is a spell-checker. If you misspelled a word, or the search engine thinks you might have, it graciously asks something like "Did you mean?" and gives you a likely alternative. If it was indeed a mistake, just click on the alternate suggestion to correct the problem.

Watch out for Sponsor Results or Sponsored Links on results pages. These are the "ads" for Web sites and are there because the site has paid to appear on the search engine's results pages. Major engines keep these sponsor sites easily identifiable, for example, by putting them in a blue background or to the side of the page. When placed at the top of the results pages, though, they may send less experienced users to an ad while thinking they have gone to a regular search result.

Also look closely at the individual Web results records. In most search engines, results are "clustered," that is, only the first one or two records from any site will be shown, and there will be a link in the record leading you to "more from this site" or "Show more results from …". If you are not aware of these links, you may miss relevant records from that site.

One other option you will notice on search results for some engines is a "Translate this page" link. If a page is in French, German, Italian, Portuguese, or Spanish, or another language in some cases, you may see such a link attached to the record. Click on it to receive a machine translation of the page. As with other machine translations, what you get may not be a "good" translation, but it may be an "adequate" translation, in that it will give you a good idea of what the page is talking about. Also keep in mind that only "words" are translated. The translation program cannot translate words you see on a page that are actually "images" rather than "text." (Many "purists" flagrantly reject the use of these translation tools. That attitude, it can be argued, is analogous to saying I should never attempt to read a German newspaper or article because my own translation will have a lot of mistakes, that being totally ignorant of the content of the page is better than having just a general idea of what is being said.)

SEARCH ENGINE ACCOUNTS

For many features provided by the major search engines, you must have an account, particularly for using features that involve personalized services such as personalized portals, e-mail, search histories, etc. In most cases, to sign up for these free accounts requires your divulging only a bare minimum of "personal" information (sometimes just an e-mail address). (For any readers who may be intensely spamophobic, you may find it worthwhile to know that the author has accounts with all the major search engines and most minor search engines that offer accounts, and has yet to identify having gotten anything he regards as "spam" as a result of having signed up with them.) Considering the benefits these account provide, it is worth the few seconds it takes to sign up.

SPECIALTY SEARCH ENGINES

Numerous specialty search engines are available. Some are geographic (focusing on sites from one country), and some are topical (focusing on a particular subject area). To locate these, check out the following category in Open Directory (dmoz.org): Computers > Internet > Searching > Search Engines > Specialized.

METASEARCH ENGINES

Metasearch engines are services that let you search several search engines at the same time. With one search, you get results from several engines. (They should not be confused with "metasites," another term for specialized directories, which were discussed in Chapter 3.) Considering the usefulness of using more than one engine, the metasearch idea seems compelling—and it is indeed a great idea. However, the reality is often something else. You may find that you like a particular metasearch engine and have legitimate reasons for using it, but it is important to note some particularly important shortcomings.

First, though, it should be noted that this section addresses the free sites on the Web that allow the searching of multiple engines. There are metasearch programs (software) that can be purchased and loaded on your computer to help you search multiple engines. These "client-side" programs may do a more complete job, but they involve downloading (and eventually purchasing) a program and sometimes several more steps to get to your results. These programs go beyond what the free online metasearch engines do, and can effectively search a variety of Web search engines, sort out the results, allow further local searching, and perform a variety of related tasks. Copernic is among the most frequently noted among this group. If you need to repackage search results for a client, you may want to consider buying one of these programs.

Free metasearch engines on the Web are numerous. New ones frequently appear and older ones disappear just as quickly. Among the better known are Dogpile, Ixquick, Vivísimo, MetaCrawler, and Search.com. They can cover portions of a large number of search engines and directories in a single search and they can sometimes be useful in finding something very obscure.

However, each metasearch engine usually presents one or more (and sometimes all) of the following drawbacks:

1. They may not cover most of the larger search engines. If you have a favorite metasearch engine, see if it covers Google, Yahoo!, Windows Live, and Ask.com.

2. Most only return the first 10 to 20 records from each source. If record No. 11 in one of the search engines was a great one, you may not see it.

3. Most syntax does not work. Some metasearch engines may let you search by title, URL, and so on, but most do not. Some do not even recognize even the simplest syntax: the use of quotation marks to indicate a phrase.

4. Some present paid listings first.

Also, by now you know that on search engine results pages, the additional content presented (besides just the listing of Web sites) can often be very valuable. You lose this with metasearch engines.

If you find that a metasearch engine meets your needs, use it. However, they are not the solution for an exhaustive—or even a moderately extensive—search.

Search Engine Shortcuts

Several search engines, particularly Yahoo!, Google, and Ask.com, provide shortcuts for quick answers, including phone numbers, stock prices, calculations, conversions, etc. With these, you can just enter a brief statement in the main search box, click on search, and an answer will appear at the top of the results page. Some of these will be mentioned in Chapter 5, but for a fuller list, take a look at www.extremesearcher.com/shortcuts.

Mashups

Wikipedia describes a mashup as "a website or web application that seamlessly combines content from more than one source into an integrated experience." Mashups are an excellent example of the increasing variety of things search engines can do, what you can do with search engines, and the different kinds of Web experiences provided by the "Web 2.0." In one sense, mashups are hypertext taken to another level, with data from one source being integrated with (not just linked to) data from another source. Though mashups can refer to the mixing of lots of different kinds of data on the Web, mashups first received public attention thanks to Google and Yahoo!. By means of APIs (Application Program Interfaces) provided by Google and Yahoo!, a broad range of data that was coded as to an exact geographic location (geo-coded) was integrated with maps and aerial images, producing exciting new ways to find and visualize that data.

There are thousands of mashups publicly available, although most deal with specific interests. For example, maps can display property for sale or rent, crime data, earthquakes, historical sites, disease outbreaks, and soccer fields in Phoenix, Arizona. To explore mashups, check out the following sites that provide collections of links to mashups.

Google Maps Mania

googlemapsmania.blogspot.com

Click on the Mashups and Tools Index link to find a directory of hundreds of Google-based mashups.

Yahoo! Maps Application Gallery

ws1.inf.scd.yahoo.com/maps/applications.html

This site contains examples of how developers have applied their data using the Yahoo! Maps API.

DESKTOP SEARCH PROGRAMS

All the major Web search engines (and other companies as well) provide a desktop search program that you can download for free. Once downloaded, it will index the contents of your computer, which you can then use to literally "instantly" search almost all of your files for any particular term or combination of terms.

For the desktop search programs provided by Google, Yahoo!, Windows Live, and Ask.com, all have fast search speed (virtually instantaneous), and all index hundreds of basic file types (documents, images, text, PDFs, etc.). None search every word of every file on a computer. They differ in how many and exactly which file types are indexed, which e-mail clients are indexed, how much control you have over what gets indexed, what searching options are provided, whether they provide quick previews of the files in your desktop search results, how they are integrated into your Web searches, whether your network drives are indexed, and whether they provide an enterprise version (for your entire organization to use). For a typical user, any of these desktop versions will do a good job and indeed do a much better, and astoundingly faster, job than the file search that has come with Windows operating systems (at least up through Windows XP). If there is any consensus among reviewers of the four desktop programs mentioned here, the favorites are from either Yahoo! or Google. The biggest strength of Google's desktop search program is that it integrates desktop search results automatically into every search (unless you don't want it to), while Yahoo!'s program provides more searchability and sortability of results and a full preview for most files. Give one or both a try. It can save you hours when finding lost files.

KEEPING UP-TO-DATE ON WEB SEARCH ENGINES

To keep up-to-date with what is happening in the realm of Web search engines, take advantage of the sites listed in the section "Keeping Up-to-Date on Internet Resources and Tools" in Chapter 1. Look at Search Engine Watch—the best-known search engine news site on the Web—as well.

Search Engine Watch

searchenginewatch.com

Search Engine Watch, which provides up-to-date news and reports in a clear and readable style, is a valuable resource for both the search engine user and Web site developer. Access to much of the content on the site is free, but more in-depth material is available for a small subscription fee. A free biweekly newsletter is also available. For those who want to get updates on a daily basis, Search Engine Watch also provides SearchDay, a daily e-mail newsletter.

SEARCH ENGINES: THE SPECIFICS

Chapter 4 provided an overview of search engines, how they work, and their common features. This chapter, however, provides detailed profiles of each of the top search engines. The descriptions give an overview of the service, and a look at the features on the home page and advanced page and notable additional features.

For some features, such as news and image databases, only a brief mention is given in the profile because the subject is covered in detail in a relevant chapter elsewhere in the book. As you use these engines, expect to occasionally find new features, new arrangements of home pages, and other changes. For updates, occasionally check www.extremesearcher.com, the companion Web site for this book.

The engines presented here are the four most popular among serious searchers. (If you look at many published lists of "most popular" search engines, you will often see AOL Search listed among the top five. It is not discussed here because AOL is still the "Internet on training wheels," with limited search functionality, no advanced search page, and typical search results that are much smaller than those found with the engines discussed in this chapter.)

See Table 5.1 at the end of the discussion on the major search engines for an outline of which options are available in which search engines.

GOOGLE (GOOGLE.COM)

In about four years, Google went from being the new kid on the block to being the favorite search engine for the majority of search engine users. For the most part, its own popularity stems from using the popularity of a Web site as a major ranking factor, its simplicity for the casual user, and its vigorous efforts to increase both the size of its database and the provision of additional features and types of content. In ranking records, it puts emphasis on the popularity of a Web page, measured by how many other pages link to that page and the popularity of those linking pages. (Web pages are known by the friends they keep.) Google was the first major engine to provide a "cache" feature to let you go to a cached copy of the page as it looked when last indexed by Google. Besides Web page searching, Google is now also the best source for newsgroup searching (with a Usenet collection dating back to 1981, plus Google's more recently introduced user-created groups). It also provides excellent image, news, and shopping databases (yellow pages), as well as an increasing number of "non-search" services including e-mail, satellite images, and maps. Google's Web database contains more than 8 billion records.

Google's Home Page

One of the reasons Google is so popular is its insistence on a simple, uncluttered home page (Figure 5.1). Even though the home page is simple, exploring the few links on the page will uncover several features. The home page includes the following:

- Search box – Enter one or more words. The minus sign in front of a term will NOT that term, and ORs can be used, as well as several prefixes such as "intitle:". Google will ignore small, common words unless you insert a plus sign immediately in front of them (e.g., +*the*), or if they are part of a phrase within quotation marks.
- Links to Google's databases:
  - Web database (the default)
  - Images – Leads to one of the largest image search databases on the Web

Figure 5.1

Google's home page

- Groups – Allows searching of more than 800 million Usenet postings back to 1981, plus other groups that are created by Google users
- News – Covers 4,500 English-language news sources going back 30 days
- Froogle – Google's shopping database
- Maps – A "yellow pages" and maps search for the U.S., Canada, and the U.K. that also provides driving directions and satellite images
- More – Links to other Google services, such as Desktop Blogs and Photos
- Advanced search link
- Language and display preferences:
  - Language search and interface preferences
  - Safe Search option (adult content filter)
  - Number of results per page
  - Option to have results opened in new window
- Language tools:
  - Limit retrieval to a specific language or country of origin
  - Translate a specific Web page between English and nine languages (Arabic, Chinese, French, German, Italian, Japanese, Korean, Portuguese, or Spanish) or between French and German
  - Choice of having the Google interface in any one of 120 languages
  - Link to the Google country-specific versions for 139 countries
- "I'm Feeling Lucky" – Takes you to the page that Google would have listed first in your results (mostly a gimmick)
- Various special options – Includes links for information on advertising, the company, and sometimes a featured service; the About Google link leads to special Google offerings and tools and Google's help screens
- Personalized Home/Sign In – If you have signed up for Google's personalized page, search history, or other services, use the link at the top of the page to sign in or sign out, go to your account, etc.

Figure 5.2

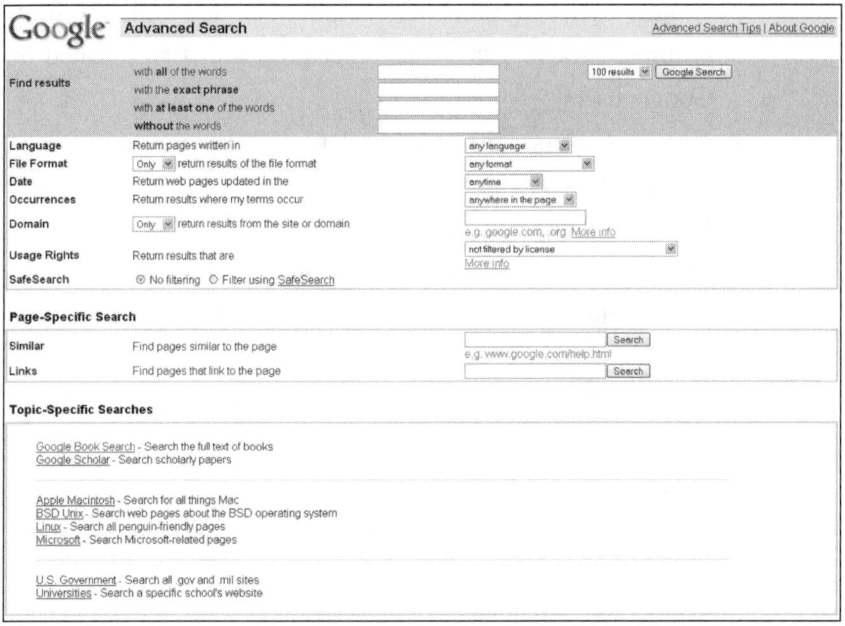

Google's advanced search page

Google's Advanced Search

As with other engines, many Google searches can be completed by putting one or two terms in the home page search box. If you need enhanced capabilities, Google's advanced search page provides all the common field search options (title, domain, link, language, and date) as well as some less common ones (Figure 5.2).

You will find the following on Google's advanced search page (in roughly this order):

- Boxes to perform simple Boolean combinations ("all the words," etc.)
- Choice of 10, 20, 30, 50, or 100 results per page
- Choice of searching for documents in all languages or one of 35 languages
- Option to retrieve only a specific file format (PDF, xls, doc, ps, PPT, rtf)
- Date restriction (anytime, last three months, last six months, last year)

- Window to limit retrieval to title, text, or URL fields, or within the links on the page
- Box for limiting to (or excluding) a particular site or domain
- Usage Rights menu to limit retrieval to material that can be used, shared, modified, etc., above and beyond "fair use," without infringing on copyright (this material has a Creative Commons [creativecommons.org] license)
- A filter option to block adult content
- "Page Specific Search" for pages that are *similar* to the URL on a particular page you entered in the box
- "Page Specific Search" for pages that link *to* a particular page (enter the URL of the page of interest)
- Links to "Topic-Specific Searches":
  - Google Book Search – Searches full-text books
  - Google Scholar – Searches scholarly papers
  - Apple Macintosh – Searches for Mac-related pages
  - BSD Unix – Searches Web pages about the BSD operating system
  - Linux – Searches Linux-related pages
  - Microsoft – Searches Microsoft-related pages
  - U.S. Government – Searches all .gov and .mil sites
  - Universities – Searches pages from selected universities

Search Features Provided by Google

By using the menus on the advanced page and prefixes on the main page, Google provides field searching for all of the commonly searchable Web page fields (title, URL, link, language, date), plus searching by file format and for "similar" pages.

Boolean

On the home page, Google automatically ANDs all of your words. You can also use a minus sign to NOT a term, and you can use one or more ORs (the OR must be capitalized).

Example: *warfare chemical OR biological -anthrax*

This search expression would find all records that contain the word "warfare" and those that contain either "chemical" or "biological" but would eliminate all records containing the word "anthrax."

On Google's advanced search page, simple Boolean is done by use of the "with all the words," "with at least one of the words," and "without the words" boxes.

Title Searching

Searches can be limited to words appearing in the page title in one of two ways. First, on the advanced search page, you can enter your terms in the search boxes, then choose "in the title of the page" from the pull-down menu under the Occurrences section of the page.

Second, on the home page, you can use the prefixes "intitle:" or "allintitle:". The "intitle:" prefix specifies that a single word or phrase is included in the title.

Examples: *intitle:online*   *intitle:"online strategies"*

Use "allintitle:" to specify that all words after the colon be in the title, but not necessarily in that order. For example, the following would retrieve titles with both words somewhere in the title, not necessarily in the specific order:

allintitle:nato preparedness

These prefixes can be combined with a search for a word anywhere on the page.

Example: *summit intitle:nato*

You cannot use a combination such as the one just mentioned using the menus on the advanced search page because your single menu choice will apply to all terms you enter in the search boxes.

URL, Site, and Domain Searching

If you want to limit retrieval to pages from a particular URL, it can be done in a way parallel to title searching. You can do it either using menus on the advanced search page or using prefixes on the home page. On the advanced search page, enter a URL or part of a URL in the search boxes, then choose "in the URL of the page" from the Occurrences section.

On the home page, you can use the "inurl:" or "allinurl:" prefixes.

Examples: *inurl:bbc inurl:"bbc.co.uk"*
allinurl:bbc co uk

On the advanced search page, you can also use the Domain box to search for part or all of a URL (*uk, edu, ford.com*). To do a site search for a specific topic, enter terms for your topic in the search boxes and the URL in the Domain box. A site search can be done on Google's home page as follows:

hybrid inurl:ford.com

The prefix "site:" is almost identical to the "allinurl:" prefix, but using "site:" requires a search term as well.

Example: *hybrid site:gm.com.*

Link Searching

To find pages that link to a particular site, use the Links box in the Page-Specific section of the advanced search page by entering the URL in the box, or perform the search on Google's home page by using the "link:" prefix. For example, to find pages that link to the Modern Language Association site, search for:

link:mla.org

Language Searching

To limit retrieval to a particular language, use the Language menu on the advanced search page. The default is "all languages," but you can choose any one of 35 languages. If you want a particular language as your default choice, use Google's Preferences page. On that same page, you can also request that the Google search pages appear in one of 120 languages (including Bork! Bork! Bork!, Elmer Fudd, and Klingon, as well as "real" languages).

Searching by Date

The Date window on the advanced search page allows you to limit results to pages that are new in the last three months, six months, or year. Keep in mind that date searching is only an approximation, because the origination date or last updated date is often not clearly identified on most Web pages.

Searching by File Type

By using the File Format menu on the advanced search page, results can be limited to or exclude any of the following formats: Adobe Acrobat files

(.pdf), Adobe Postscript files (.ps), Microsoft Word files (.doc), Microsoft Excel files (.xls), Microsoft PowerPoint (.pdf), and rich text format (.rtf).

On Google's home page, you can accomplish the same thing by using the "filetype:" prefix. For example, if you want a 1099 IRS tax form to print out, search for:

1099 IRS form filetype:pdf

Searching for Related (Similar) Pages

You can search for pages that are similar to a particular page by using the Similar box in the Page-Specific section of Google's advanced search page. Enter the URL of the page in the box or use the "related:" prefix on Google's home page.

Example: *related:searchenginewatch.com*

Searching by Other Prefixes

The following prefixes can be used on Google's home page to search for specific information.

cache: Enter a URL after the colon to get Google's cached version of the page.

Example: *cache:www.aps.org*

info: Enter a URL after the colon to get basically the same information that is shown on a results page when the record for that site is retrieved.

Example: *info:cyndislist.com*

stocks: Enter one or more stock symbols after the colon to get links to stock quotes.

define: Search the collection of glossaries that Google has found on Web sites. This is particularly useful for word definitions that will not be found in standard dictionaries, such as slang, neologisms, and technical terms.

Example: *define:spam*

safesearch: Used for the intention of removing adult content.

Example: *safesearch:underwear*

allinanchor: Use this prefix (followed by one or more words) to find pages that have links containing those terms.

Example: *allinanchor:extreme searcher*

numrange: Allows you to find any pages that contain a number that is within the range you specify.

Example: *american pottery numrange:1900..1920*

Actually just using the range, with the two periods but without the prefix, also works just as well.

Example: *american pottery 1900..1920*

You can do a less-than or more-than search by leaving out the first or last number.

Example: *skyscraper height numrange:1000.. ft*

"Wildcard" Words

Google allows the use of one or more asterisks for "wildcard" *words* (not to be confused with "truncation," which is for wildcard *characters* within or at the end of a word). You can use the asterisk for unknown words in a phrase search. The use of *each asterisk insists on the presence of one word.*

Example: *"erasmus * rotterdam"*

That search will retrieve "Erasmus Universiteit Rotterdam" and "Erasmus von Rotterdam." It will not necessarily retrieve any "Erasmus Rotterdam" records.

Example: *"erasmus * * rotterdam"*

That search will retrieve "Erasmus University of Rotterdam" but not necessarily the "Erasmus Universiteit Rotterdam" records.

If you want "Franklin Roosevelt" and "Franklin D Roosevelt" as well as "Franklin Delano Roosevelt," search for:

*"Franklin Roosevelt" OR "Franklin * Roosevelt"*

Caution: The above does not always work. Google's own documentation says that "red * blue" will search for "the words red and blue separated by one or more words," but that actually seems to be less correct.

Calculator

For a quick arithmetic calculation, you can use the Google search box. Enter *46*(98-3+32)*, and Google provides the answer. For addition, subtraction, multiplication, division, and exponents use +, -, *, /, and ^ respectively. You can also nest using parentheses, for example, *15 (14+43)*.

Metric-Imperial Conversions

From the main search box, you can easily convert measurements between metric and imperial systems for all common units of length, volume, mass, and temperature.

> Examples:
> *32 feet to meters*
> *30 km to miles*
> *8 liters to quarts*
> *68 f to c*

Google Results Pages

On Google results pages, it pays to look closely at the entire page and also at the content of the individual records (Figure 5.3).

Figure 5.3

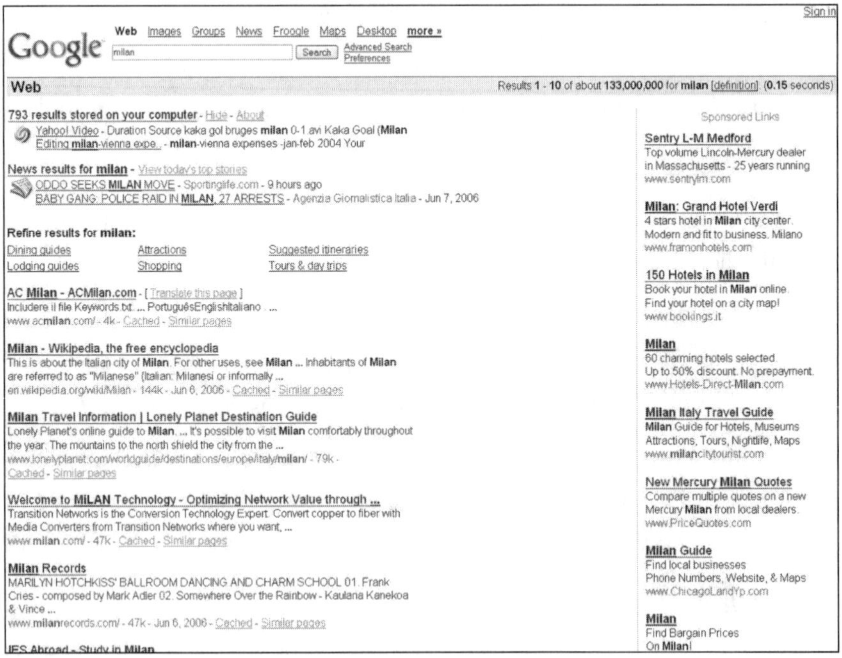

Google results page

On the line where Google reports your results, for example,

Results **1 - 10** of about **133,000,000** for <u>milan</u>

look for underlined terms. Depending upon the nature of the terms, clicking on them will lead to dictionary definitions, encyclopedia articles, maps, local time, a currency converter, statistics, etc. from more than 60 reference tools included in Answers.com.

Google also searches its news database whenever you do a Web search. If your topic has been in the news recently, at the top of your results list you may see up to three headlines and a link to more. Click on them to go to the news stories. In addition to links for news, you will sometimes find links near the top of the page with suggestions for refining your search, an image from an image search on the topic, etc. If you are using Google's Desktop Search, Google will automatically search your computer and list the results of that search above the Web search results.

If Google "thinks" you may have misspelled a word, you will see a "Did you mean" message, with a suggested alternative spelling.

A few additional parts of individual records are also worthwhile examining (Figure 5.4).

Figure 5.4

Spontaneous Human Combustion
SHC Cases, **spontaneous human combustion**, **shc**, fire from heaven, ablaze,bursting into flame, Krook,bleak house,csicop fails to debunk,wick effect.
www.alternativescience.com/**spontaneous-human-combustion**-burning-issue.htm - 17k - Cached - Similar pages

---

Example of an individual record in a Google search result

By clicking the Cached link in the record, you will be directed to a cached copy that Google stored when it retrieved the page. This feature is especially useful if you click on a search result and the page is not found, or it is found, but the terms you searched for do not seem to be present. If this happens, go back to the Google results page and click on the Cached link.

Clicking on "Similar pages" will lead to pages with similar content ("More like this"). Take advantage of this capability to find related pages that may be difficult to find otherwise.

If you encounter a record for a page that is in Arabic, Chinese (Simplified), French, German, Italian, Korean, Japanese, Spanish, and

Portuguese, you will see a link to "Translate this page." Click on that link for an English translation of that page.

If your search results include any Adobe Acrobat, Adobe Postscript, Excel, PowerPoint, Word, or Rich Text Format files, a link will be available to view those records as HTML. Click on "View as HTML" to see an HTML version of the page as "translated" by Google.

On search results pages, you can simply click on any of the links above the search box to have the same search done in those additional databases (Images, News, etc.).

Other Searchable Google Databases

In addition to the Web database of more than 8 billion pages, Google also provides searching for images, groups, news, shopping (Froogle), maps (yellow pages), a phone directory (white pages), Web directory, books, journal articles, satellite images, shopping catalogs, and stock price databases. The image, groups, news, shopping, and maps databases are accessible by clicking the appropriate link above the search box on Google's main page (and on many other Google pages). The others can be accessed by the "more" link on Google's main page. The exceptions are the phone directory and stocks databases, which are accessed directly from Google's main search box. Because the Google images, groups, news, and shopping databases are discussed in some detail in the chapters that follow, they are only mentioned briefly here.

Images

Google claims that it has the largest searchable image collection on the Web, with billions of images. Details on image searching are covered in Chapter 8.

Google Groups (Newsgroups)

Google provides access to the Usenet collection of newsgroups, going back to 1981 and containing more than 800 million messages. In 2005, Google added user-created groups. More details on Google groups are available in Chapter 6.

News

Google's news search is reachable by the link on Google's home page or directly at news.google.com. It covers about 4,500 news sources and is updated continually. Records are retained for 30 days. Read more about news searching in Chapter 9. Also in the news category, Google provides a search of Weblogs (blogsearch.google.com). Expect the blog search to at some point be integrated with Google's main news search or Web search.

Froogle

Froogle, Google's shopping engine, contains product pages that Google has identified by crawling the Web for product sites as well as catalog pages submitted by merchants. For more details on Froogle, see Chapter 10.

Google Maps (Local Search)

The "local" searches provided by various search engines all allow you to locate businesses in or near a particular city or other location, plus get road maps and driving directions. In the case of Google, its map search combines a search of a yellow pages database, information it has found from crawling the Web, and its maps and satellite images databases, to provide not just names, phone numbers, and addresses of businesses, but also an accompanying (draggable) road map with the locations of the businesses shown, with options to get driving directions and a satellite view of the location, or a hybrid view that combines the satellite view and streets (Figure 5.5). Google Maps covers the U.S., the U.K., and Canada, and you can probably expect other countries to be added.

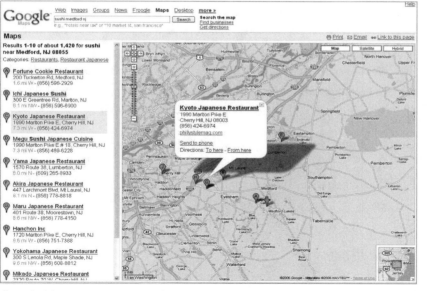

Figure 5.5

Google Maps result

To find businesses, enter the topic (e.g., restaurants, hotels, pet massage) and the location. For location, you can enter a city or ZIP code, post code, or postal code. You can also be more specific as to the location, for example, *london hotel near westminster*. Results show both a list and the map, with the results list being ranked by distance from the location. Above the results listing, you are usually also shown categories (e.g., Hotels & Inns, Hotel Booking Agents) to enable you to narrow your search.

Phone Book and Address Lookup

A phone book lookup for U.S. phone numbers and addresses can be done on Google, directly from the home page search box. For a business, type a business name and either city and state or ZIP code. For individuals, give the first name or initial, the last name, and either state, area code, or ZIP code. It will also work without either the first name or initial if the last name is not very common. As with all phone directory sites on the Web, do not expect perfect results all the time.

You can also do a reverse lookup just by entering the phone number in the search box, with or without punctuation. Include the area code.

Web Directory

Google uses Open Directory for its browsable and searchable Web directory database (found at google.com/dirhp). Whereas it once was listed prominently on Google's home page, it has been demoted to just being listed under the "more" link. For details on Open Directory itself, see Chapter 2. Although Open Directory category pages and results pages look slightly different depending on if you are searching its own site (dmoz.org) or through Google, the content, arrangement, searchability, and browsability are virtually the same. The biggest difference is that when you search the directory through Google, results are ranked by Google's ranking algorithm.

Google Book Search

Through arrangements with publishers and several major libraries, Google Book Search provides bibliographic information on and, in some cases, full text access to a large collection of both new and old books. Google Book Search is discussed in some detail in Chapter 7.

Google Scholar

Google Scholar covers "peer-reviewed papers, theses, books, preprints, abstracts and technical reports." The availability of this scholarly material on

Google is a result of agreements with publishers, associations, universities, and others, allowing Google to index databases that search engine crawlers usually cannot penetrate ("Invisible Web" material). For more on Google Scholar, see Chapter 7.

Google Earth

One of the most exciting, useful, and fun new search engine offerings to come along in quite a while is Google Earth (Figure 5.6), which is a searchable database that provides aerial views of places throughout the entire planet. Google Earth is also notable because it represents effective integration of a variety of trends and technologies, including nontextual content search and retrieval (in this case maps and images), streaming data, "local search," and sharing.

Google Earth is a combination of a downloadable program and online data that provides satellite and aircraft imagery and allows users to integrate and superimpose their selection of an impressive array of related data.

Once the program has been downloaded, Google Earth's main page presents a control console and an image of the Earth. Click on an area of your

Figure 5.6

Google Earth

choice, and then zoom in on exactly what you want to see—your own back-yard, Maui, or Timbuktu. You can also zoom directly to your destination by typing in an address. At an "altitude" of your choice, you can have Google Earth superimpose roads, railways, schools, parks, hotels, restaurants, and other landmarks as well as political boundaries, statistics, driving directions, and more. You can tilt and rotate your image and "fly" over an area, and for 38 major U.S. metropolitan areas, you can see 3D images of buildings and terrain. You can add your own placemarks and annotations and even share these with others.

Images (all taken within the past three years) are available for the entire world, with higher resolution versions for most major U.S., Canadian, U.K., and European cities. Road maps are available for the U.S., Canada, the U.K., and Western Europe. Google Maps search features are provided for the U.S., Canada, and the U.K. For the lower resolution sites, such as remoter parts of the world, the resolution will enable you to at least see major geographic features and towns. The higher resolution sites allow you to identify something the size of a car or better. More powerful versions, Google Earth Plus and Google Earth Pro (with higher resolution, GPS device support, etc.), are also available for an annual subscription fee.

Catalog Search

Google's Catalog Search, a database of published merchant catalogs, con-tains catalogs of thousands of merchants (catalogs.google.com). The main page has a subject directory that allows you to browse by category, a search box, and a link to an advanced catalog search. You can search the entire col-lection, a category, or an individual catalog by using the advanced search. You can also view an actual image of every catalog page or just a portion for a particular product. The timeliness of the catalogs on Google has occasion-ally been an issue.

Stock Search

Enter a ticker symbol for a U.S. company in Google's main search box for current stock quotes and you'll get links to more information about the stock and the company from a half-dozen finance and market-related sources (MSN Money, Market Watch, etc.). This information, which will appear above the regular Google search results, is an example of search engine "shortcuts" discussed in Chapter 4.

Google Toolbar

The Google Toolbar is a free downloadable feature that allows you to add the Google search box and additional features as a toolbar on Internet Explorer or Firefox browsers. Go to the "more" link on the home page to find out about what the Google Toolbar provides, including:

- Google Search – With the toolbar showing, the search box always appears on your browser screen.
- Search Site – Allows you to search only the pages of the site currently displayed.
- PageRank – Allows you to see Google's ranking of the current page.
- Page Info – Use this to get more information about a page, similar pages, and pages that link to a page; you also get a cached snapshot.
- Highlight – Highlights your search terms (each word in a different color).
- Word Find – Allows you to find search terms wherever they appear on the page.
- Spell Check
- AutoFill – Automatically fills out forms on a Web page.
- Translate – Hold the cursor over a word for an instant translation (Chinese, Japanese, Korean, French, Italian, German, or Spanish).
- Your choice of buttons for a variety of Google services.

The Google Toolbar can be customized to include most of the features on the regular Google home page (and in several languages).

Google Answers

Google Answers is a service in which users can ask questions that are then answered by other users who have signed up as researchers. First, submit a question, and pay a 50-cent fee, plus an amount that you are willing to pay for the answer (from $2 to $200). Researchers then bid to answer your question. For more information, see the Google Answers FAQs (answers.google. com/answers/faq.html). Be aware that no special qualifications are required for a person to become a researcher for this service.

Other Google Features and Content

The folks at Googleplex, Google's headquarters, let no grass grow beneath their thousands of computers. While on the one hand some Google announcements receive inordinate attention, others receive relatively little press and even less attention from the majority of Google users. Informal polling shows that many Google users have not even clicked on more than one or two of the links on Google's home page to see what is there, and even many very experienced searchers have not taken time to fully explore everything Google offers. The following Google offerings described include some of the more significant features and some content that may be easy to miss. These can be found either with the "more" link above the search box on Google's homepage or with the "About Google" link at the bottom of Google's home page (some of these are still in Beta mode):

- Alerts – This feature enables you to be automatically notified of news stories on topics of your choice or new or changed Web pages. These are discussed in Chapter 9.
- Gmail – This is Google's free e-mail service, providing standard e-mail functions and virtually unlimited storage, and comes with an integrated chat, instant messenger, and voice message function (Talk).
- Talk – This is Google's own instant messaging service and includes a voice call option.
- Personalized home page – This is Google's attempt at a personal portal, with your choice of sections, including weather, Gmail, horoscope, movies, word-of-the-day, quotes-of-the-day, bookmarks, and a selection of news sources. You can also have as one of your sections Google's Search History, which records (when you wish) your searches and sites you have visited. (Compare Google's Personalized Page to Yahoo!'s My Yahoo!.)
- Finance – This is a finance portal page that provides stock information, news, and a personal stock portfolio. (Compare this to Yahoo!'s Finance section.)
- Google Labs – This is where Google provides a demonstration of a variety of projects on which it is working, which may or may not be destined for "prime time."

- Calendar – This is a personal online calendar that you can view by day, week, month, or next few days, share with others, have multiple calendars, get e-mail reminders, import events from other calendars, send invitations for events, and more.
- Blogger – This program lets you create a Weblog of your own and search other Weblogs.
- Picasa – This free downloadable program allows you to edit, organize, and share photos stored on your computer.
- Google APIs – APIs (Application Program Interfaces) are interfaces with which an application program can communicate and interact with another program. Google provides such interfaces so that a developer can integrate its own data with a Google program, most notably Google Maps and Google Earth. This function lets users create mashups (discussed in Chapter 4).
- Mobile – Google provides several services for mobile devices, including search, SMS (short-message-services, or text messaging) for search shortcuts, Gmail, Google Local, and more.
- Video – Google's video search (video.google.com) is discussed in Chapter 8.

YAHOO! (YAHOO.COM)

Yahoo! has made dramatic changes in recent years, moving away from the directory function to the search function. In 2004, Yahoo! created its own new Web page database to challenge Google's database. Yahoo! also has extensive databases for images, video, audio, local, news, and shopping, as well as providing a search of the directory. The My Yahoo! feature provides the best general portal on the Web, and Yahoo! has a broad collection of additional content accessible from its main page. In addition to the search box and search-related links on Yahoo!'s main page (yahoo.com), Yahoo! also provides a minimalist Yahoo! Search page (search.yahoo.com; see Figure 5.7). The size of Yahoo!'s Web database is about the same magnitude as Google's, but for both, the significance of the numbers is largely overshadowed by the search functions that can be applied to the databases.

Figure 5.7

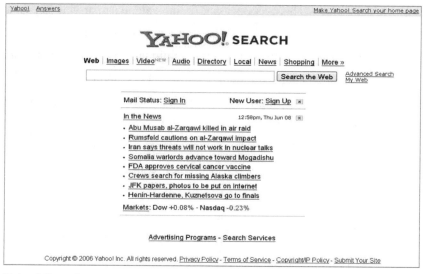

Yahoo! Search page

Yahoo!'s Home Page

The Yahoo! home page is in the format of a general portal, with sections for search, news, and weather, and links to more than 40 Yahoo! services and sections. The search section at the top of the main page is virtually the same as on the streamlined Yahoo! Search page and on personalized My Yahoo! pages. The Yahoo! Search page includes the following:

- Search box – AND is implied between terms and you can use ORs, minus for NOT, parentheses for nesting, and any of several prefix qualifiers.
- Advanced Search link – Leads to a page with additional search qualifications (language, country, date, domain, etc.).
- My Web link – Yahoo!'s personalized search history records, organizes, tags, and shares searches.
- Links above the search box provide access to searches of alternate databases:
  - Images – A search of billions of images that Yahoo! has found by crawling the Web
  - Video – A search of millions of videos found by crawling the Web or from submission by video producers
  - Audio – A search of millions of audio files

- Directory – A search of the contents of the Yahoo! Directory (discussed in Chapter 3)
- Local – A yellow pages search by type of business and location that provides a listing of matching businesses, maps, driving directions, and more
- News – A search of more than 7,500 news sources from around the world
- Shopping – Yahoo!'s product search with descriptions, photos, prices, ratings, and comparisons
- More – A link to more than a dozen other Yahoo! services

Yahoo!'s Advanced Search

Yahoo! offers extensive and easy search functionality on its advanced search page (Figure 5.8), including the following:

- Boxes to perform simple Boolean combinations ("all the words," "any of the words," or "none of the words")
- Pull-down windows for limiting to title or URL
- Date restriction (anytime, last three months, last six months, last year); as with date searching in other search engines, this is not really reliable
- Options to limit to a particular top-level domain or a specific domain
- Creative Common option for identifying copyright-free or shareable materials only
- File Format option to retrieve only a specific file format (HTML, PDF, Excel, PowerPoint, Word, RSS/XML, and text)
- SafeSearch filter for blocking adult content
- Country origin option to limit to 27 countries
- Language option to limit to 37 languages
- Subscription content inclusion from nine major database providers
- Choice to specify the number of results per page (10, 15, 20, 30, 40, 50, 75, and 100)

Figure 5.8

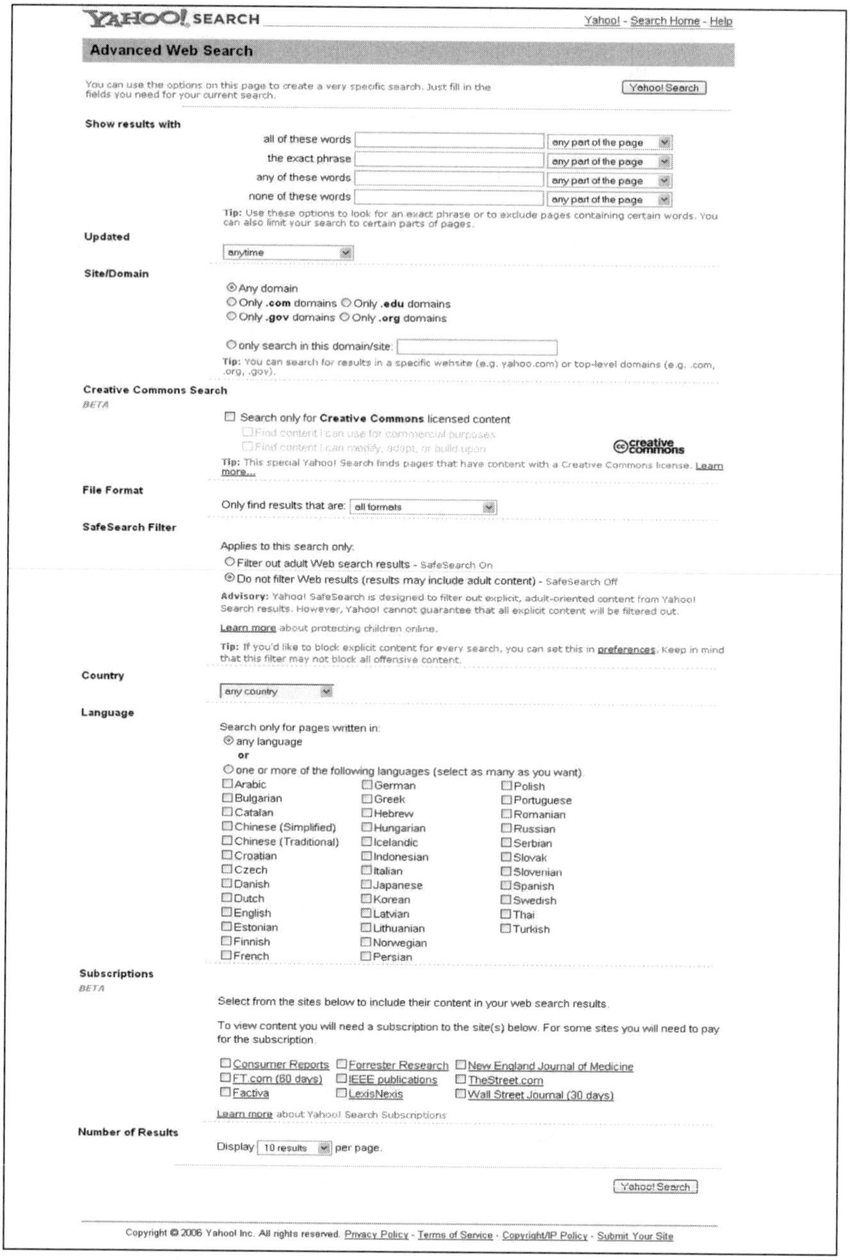

Yahoo!'s advanced search page

Search Features Provided by Yahoo!

Yahoo! offers a good collection of limiting and other search features both on its advanced search page and from its main search box.

Boolean

When you enter multiple terms (e.g., *national debt*) in Yahoo!'s main search box, an AND is implied and you will only get back pages that use all of the terms. To OR two or more terms, place OR between the terms. In Yahoo!, you also need to add parentheses around your alternate terms. You can also use a minus sign in front of a term as a NOT to exclude pages that contain that term.

Example: *(oil OR petroleum) reserves kuwait –war*

On Yahoo!'s advanced search page, you can use simple Boolean by means of the search boxes at the top of the page ("all of these words," "any of these words," or "none of these words").

Title Searching

To limit your retrieval to only those pages where your terms appear in the title of the page, either use the "in the title of the page" option in the Occurrences section of the advanced page or use the "intitle:" or "allintitle:" prefixes in Yahoo!'s main search box.

Examples:
intitle:"gross national product"   *intitle:roosevelt*

Use "allintitle:" to specify multiple words in the title, but not necessarily in that order:

allintitle:depression history

This can be combined with one or more terms not necessarily in the title:

hook car door handle intitle:"urban legends"

URL, Site, and Domain Searching

With Yahoo!, you can limit your retrieval to pages from a particular site or kind of site by using the advanced search page or by use of the "site:", "url:", "inurl:", and "hostname:" prefixes.

On the advanced search page, use the Site/Domain radio buttons to limit your search to .com, .edu, .gov, or .org top-level domains. For other domains, put the top-level domain extension (uk, fr, mil, etc.) or combinations of these (e.g., co.uk) in the text box there. In that box, you can also specify a particular site (e.g., cruisemates.com).

In Yahoo!'s main search box, you can use the "site:", "url:", "inurl:", and "hostname:" prefixes. All of these can be combined with subject terms or other prefixes such as "intitle:".

The "site:" prefix finds all pages from a domain and its subdomains; you can also use it to limit to a top-level domain (edu, com, org, mil, fr, ca, etc.).

> Examples:
>
> *site:chrysler.com*
>
> *site:chile.chrysler.com*
>
> *human cloning intitle:ethics site:edu*

Use the "inurl:" prefix for searching a part of a URL:

> *inurl:worldbank*

The difference between the "hostname:" and "site:" prefixes is a bit esoteric and relates to subdomains (you may want to put this on your list of things to forget about). The "hostname:" prefix is used to get pages from a very specific domain or subdomain and exclude others.

> Examples:
>
> *site:autos.com* would get both *chrysler.com* and *chile.chrysler.com*
>
> *hostname:chrysler.com* gets precisely and only *chrysler.com* (not the records from subdomains such as *chile.chrysler.com*).
>
> *hostname:chile.chrysler.com* would not get just plain *chrysler.com*

The "url:" prefix is used to find the Yahoo! record for a specific site and requires that you enter the "http://" part of the address:

> *url:http://onstrat.com*

Link Searching

To do a link search in Yahoo!, use the "link:" prefix. Be aware that in Yahoo!, you must include the "http://" part of the address.

> Example: *link:http://www.fas.org*

You may want to try variations on the address, for example:

> *link:http://fas.org OR link:http://www.fas.org*

Language Searching

Use the Language checkboxes on the advanced search page to search any of 37 languages. Toward the bottom of Yahoo!'s main page, you will find links to the Yahoo! International sites for more than two-dozen countries or continents, with each country site in the language or languages of that country.

Searching by Date

Keep in mind that date searching for Web pages is usually unreliable. But if you want to try it, use the Update window on the advanced search page to limit the pages that Yahoo! identifies as updated in the last three months, last six months, or last year.

Searching by File Type

The File Format pull-down menu on the advanced search page lets you narrow your search to one of the following document types: Word (.doc), Excel (.xls), PowerPoint (.ppt), XML (.xml), and text (.txt). In results pages, you will recognize these file types by PDF or other designations at the end of file names.

Searching by Country

Yahoo!'s advanced search page lets you limit your search results to those that are identified as coming from any one of more than 27 countries. The results are "approximate" and will both miss some pages and misidentify others.

Creative Commons

Creative Commons licenses provide means by which copyright owners can easily grant some of their rights to the public, yet at the same time retain some of their rights. (For details, see the Creative Commons Web site at creativecommons.org.) Using the Creative Commons section of Yahoo!'s advanced search page, you can search specifically for materials with a Creative Commons license and which you can therefore more freely and easily use in your own publications, etc. You can more specifically narrow your search to content that you can use for commercial purposes or content that you can "modify, adapt, and build upon."

Subscriptions

The Subscriptions section of the advanced search page allows users to simultaneously search multiple selected databases that ordinarily require a subscription in order to access the database's content (which typically consists of news or journal articles). Unless you have a subscription through Yahoo!, the farthest you will usually get is to a bibliographic description of the items, and perhaps an abstract. Some of the services, though, allow you to purchase selected articles online without a subscription. If you do have a subscription to one or more of these services and are already logged into your account with the provider (perhaps, for example, through a university's network), you will be taken directly to the content. Otherwise, you will be prompted to log in with your account information. On the advanced search page, choose which subscriptions you wish to search by clicking the appropriate checkboxes. Yahoo!'s Subscriptions search started with databases from ACM, Consumer Reports, Factiva, Forrester Research, FT.com, IEEE, LexisNexis, the *New England Journal of Medicine*, TheStreet.com, and the *Wall Street Journal*. In most cases, the content represents just a portion of the offerings from these services.

Conversions

To find measurement conversions easily, use Yahoo!'s main search box and enter the word "convert" followed by your requested conversion.

> Examples:
> *convert 238.5 miles to kilometers*
> *convert 3 mi to in*
> *convert 19 c to fahrenheit*

It works for most common units of length, weight, temperature, area, and volume. You can usually use the full term or abbreviations and either singular or plural units (inch or inches).

Calculator

For a quick calculation, enter your problem in Yahoo!'s search box instead of pulling up a calculator.

> Example: *46*56.98*

For addition, subtraction, multiplication, division, and exponents use +, -, *, /, and ^ respectively. You can also nest using parentheses, e.g., *15*(14+43)*.

Stock Search

Stock quotes, charts, and news are available by entering the ticker symbol in the Yahoo! search box. The stock information will be shown at the top of the results page. The main Yahoo! site (yahoo.com) provides quotes for U.S. markets. Use other country sites (e.g., uk.yahoo.com) for markets in those countries.

My Web

Yahoo!'s My Web provides the ability to save items you select from your searches, and to go back and work with them again—sort of a fancy bookmarking service, where you can share your bookmarks with others. To use this, click on the My Web link that you find on your My Yahoo! page and elsewhere. (You must be logged into your Yahoo! account to use My Web.)

Once signed up and logged in, on search results you will see an additional option in each retrieved record to save the result. My Web also allows you to add tags to your items (for searching them later), to share your saved results with others, and to import and export your bookmarks to or from your browser. Since items you save are saved on the Yahoo! computers, you can access them from wherever you find yourself.

Yahoo! Results Pages

Records on Yahoo! search results pages are listed (ranked) according to the relevance to the search terms (Figure 5.9).

In addition to the expected parts of a results listing—a title that links to the page, a snippet of text showing search terms that matched, and the URL of the page—you may also find the following, depending on the record (Figure 5.10):

- Cached – Clicking on this link will take you to an archived version of the page. Use this when you encounter a Page Not Found message or when the word for which you searched is no longer on the current page.
- More from this Site – Yahoo! only shows one (the highest ranked) page from any site; to see the other matching pages from any site, click on this link.
- Save – If you are using Yahoo!'s My Web feature, this will save that page to your collection of saved pages.

Figure 5.9

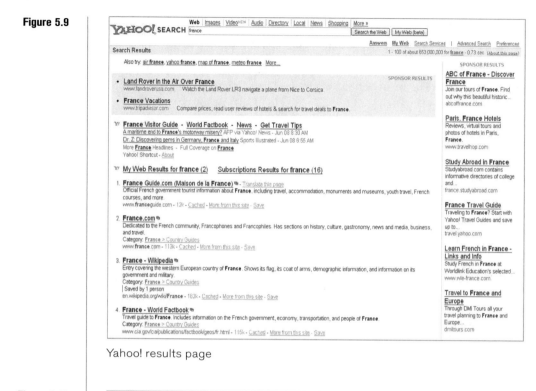

Yahoo! results page

Figure 5.10

1. **UNDERSTANDING THE GHOST DANCE**:
   UNDERSTANDING THE GHOST DANCE: PRAYER FOR AN NEW WAY. AI did not know
   then how much was ended. ... the sacred tree is. dead.@ Black Elk. **Ghost Dance** Websites:
   ...
   www.unc.edu/courses/2002fall/anth/010/006/oct29.html - 29k - Cached - More from this site -
   Save

Example of an individual record in a Yahoo! search result

- Translate This Page – If a page is in French, German, Italian,
  Portuguese, or Spanish, clicking this link will result in a machine
  translation of the page.
- View as HTML – When you retrieve a page that is in Adobe
  Acrobat, PowerPoint, or Word format, there will be a "View as
  HTML" link, from which you can view an HTML equivalent of
  the page (which may be quicker, but probably not as pretty).
- RSS/View as XML – If a site listed in your results is one that
  offers an RSS (Really Simple Syndication) news feed, you will

see this link. Clicking on it will show you a page with the XML code for the news feed page. The URL of that page is what you need if you want to subscribe to that feed. (For more on RSS, see Chapter 9.)

Remember, you can click on any of the tabs above the search box on search results pages and have your same search done in those additional databases (Images, Audio, etc.).

Just above your Web page results listings, you may also find a number of other related items, depending upon your topic. These may include:

- Also Try – This section lists other searches that have been done that used one or more of your search terms. This section can be useful to see ways to narrow your search.

- Did You Mean – If Yahoo! feels you misspelled one of your search terms, this feature suggests an alternate spelling.

- News – At the same time Yahoo! does your Web search, it also automatically checks its news database; if there are matches for your search terms, you may receive up to three headlines, plus links to additional stories.

- Inside Yahoo! – Though Yahoo! is no longer calling this "Inside Yahoo!," the term still describes some links that may appear near the top of results pages. These lead to other places in Yahoo! that may be relevant to your search. For example, when you search for a city or country, you may see links to a visitor guide. Search for the name of a car to get links to relevant parts of Yahoo!'s Auto section. Search for a breed of dog to get links to Yahoo! Pets. A search on an actor may lead to that actor's page in Yahoo!'s Movies section, photos, and DVDs and videos. A search on a disease may lead to a link to a page on that disease from Yahoo!'s Health section. Other topics will lead to other Yahoo! places.

- Subscription Results – If you have set the Preferences page to search any of the subscription databases, then any time your search terms match items in those databases, your subscription results will be shown on search results pages above the regular results.

Other Searchable Yahoo! Databases

Yahoo! also provides access to several major additional databases via the links above the search box on its main page: Images, Video, Audio, Directory, Local, News, and Shopping. (The choice of databases changes fairly frequently.) In addition, there are at least a score more databases that can be found within the various Yahoo! sections on Yahoo!'s main page: The Autos section has databases of new and used car prices; the Health section has databases of Diseases & Conditions and Drugs; HotJobs is an employment database; Yahoo! Classifieds is a large database of classified ads; the Movies section has databases of old and new films, reviews, actors, etc.; and Yahoo! Travel has Yahoo!'s implementation of the Travelocity database as well as a database of destinations, and so on. The major offerings are described in the following section very briefly since they are covered in more detail in later chapters. The best way to get to know what searchable databases Yahoo! offers is to start with Yahoo!'s main page and spend time browsing the links you find there.

Images

Yahoo!'s image database is about the same size as Google's. See the section on searching images in Chapter 8.

Video

Here you can search the millions of videos that Yahoo! has identified by crawling Web pages, plus video gathered directly from video publishers. Use the Video link above Yahoo!'s main search box to begin your search or go to video.yahoo.com. For more details on Yahoo!'s video search, see Chapter 8.

Audio

Yahoo!'s audio search service, which is accessible from the Audio link above the Yahoo! search box, provides a search of millions of audio files, including music, newscasts, interviews, speeches, podcasts, sound effects, and e-books. It can also be used as a music comparison-shopping site to let you choose from a number of music providers. To search, just enter some terms (subject, artist, album, etc.) in the search box. For more details, see Chapter 8.

Yahoo! Directory

You can search Yahoo!'s traditional Web directory by clicking on the Directory link and entering your search terms in the search box. A search will yield a list of any matching categories and matching sites.

Local

Yahoo!'s Local search, available from a link above the main Yahoo! search box, features a directory of U.S. businesses. (If you access Yahoo! from one of its international sites, check the main page to see if Yahoo! has a similar service for your country.)

To search for a business, enter a name or type of business (Saks, Blockbuster, plumber, pizza, interpreter, etc.) and either a ZIP code or the name of a city and a two letter postal code for a state. Yahoo! will retrieve a list of matching businesses with the name, phone number, and address of the business, a rating (by Yahoo! users), and the distance from your own default location (which you can select by using the "make this my default Yahoo! location" link beneath the search box). Links are also provided for maps, driving directions, transferring information to your mobile phone, and saving information to My Web. The category links let you click to get all local businesses under that category. Click on one of the names in the results listings to get more detailed information, including a business Web address (if there is one) and a customizable map that you can make larger and that shows nearby ATMs, hotels, parking, public transportation, restaurants, and other services and facilities.

On the left side of the main results page, a map with the locations of all of the matching businesses will be shown along with options to refine your search by distance from your location, by neighborhood (for larger cities), by category, and by rating.

The Yahoo! Local site (local.yahoo.com) has browsable business directory categories specifically for your default location, a map, a list of upcoming local events, and user-recommended restaurants and other businesses.

News

The Yahoo! news search covers 7,000 news sources in 35 languages. This is discussed in detail in Chapter 9.

Shopping

Yahoo! Shopping is one of the Web's largest and easily searchable online shopping sites with millions of products and tens of thousands of merchants (see Chapter 10).

Yahoo! Groups

Yahoo! Groups, which are all created by Yahoo! users, provides a very powerful communication tool. The content of "public" groups (those that the groups creator decides can be public) is searchable and is an excellent place to gather advice and opinions. To get to Yahoo! Groups, click on the Groups link on the Yahoo! main page or go to groups.yahoo.com.

People Search

Yahoo!'s People Search is a directory of U.S. and Canadian phone numbers, mailing addresses, and e-mail addresses. The main People Search page provides information for the U.S., but you will find a link on that page for a similar search in Canada. (For other countries, check the country-specific Yahoo! site for a "People" section.) Although you can search by first name, last name, city, and state, only the last name is required, which means you may not have to know the state in which a person lives. With the advanced e-mail search, you can search by name, city/town, state/province, former e-mail address, name variants (SmartNames), as well as organization and type. To get to People Search, use the link on the main Yahoo! page or go to people.yahoo.com.

Yahoo! Toolbar

The free downloadable Yahoo! Toolbar, available for Internet Explorer and Firefox, provides very easy access to most Yahoo! services regardless of what Web page is showing in your browser window, plus added features such as anti-spy software. Among the things the toolbar provides are:

- Search box – Available at all times with a pull-down menu for searching the alternate Yahoo! databases (Images, Audio, Video, etc.)
- A choice of buttons for more than 70 Yahoo! services and sections such as Mail, News, My Yahoo!, Notepad, Calendar, Briefcase, etc.
- Anti-spy software
- Translate This Page – Translate the current page into English
- Pop-up blocker (Internet Explorer version only)
- Highlight – Highlight your search terms on the page (Internet Explorer version only)

- "Smart Tools" – Highlight any text on the Web page in your browser window and a Yahoo! Icon appears (for Internet Explorer 6.1 and higher, and eventually other browsers); click it and search your highlighted text, save it to My Web, e-mail it, IM it, copy it, or translate it

Other Yahoo! Features and Content

Here are just a few additional services that can be accessed through Yahoo's main page (yahoo.com):

- Address Book – Store addresses and related information for use with Yahoo! Mail, Yahoo! Groups, or the calendar, or for just finding a phone number or address. For the latter, it can be your "traveling" address book.
- Auctions – Bid on and buy items for sale by individuals and companies as well as sell your own items.
- Autos – Research new/used cars and prices as well as buy and sell cars.
- Calendar – Enter events and tasks, have e-mail reminders sent to you, list and print events, tasks, and calendar pages in a variety of ways, and even share your calendar.
- Finance – Access a broad range of statistics, advice, news, background, tools, and services related to finance and investing, along with a personal portfolio option.
- GeoCities – Build Web pages in a few minutes using probably the best-known free Web site building service.
- Health – Find a range of information on issues, diseases, and conditions, including a medical encyclopedia, a drug guide, health news, expert advice, information on clinical trials, and health news.
- Mail – Sign up for Yahoo!'s robust Web-accessible e-mail service, one of the most-used free e-mail services in the world.
- Messenger – Send instant messages.
- Mobile – Download a tailored version of various Yahoo! services to mobile devices such as cell phones. These services include

Messenger, Mail, News Alerts, and other alerts, games, photos, and some Web searching.

- Movies – Find reviews, showtimes, trailers and clips, biographies, filmographies, news, and more—about new movies and old, about what's in the theaters and what's on DVD and video.

- Y! Music – Purchase and download music online, and locate information, interviews, and videos about musicians, groups, and recordings. Yahoo!'s LAUNCHcast provides customizable Internet radio "channels" for almost all musical genres.

- Photos – Store photos on Yahoo!, arrange them in albums, share albums with friends, and have high-quality prints mailed to you.

- Travel – Make reservations for airlines, trains, autos, vacation packages, and cruises, and find country and city guides.

- Yahoo! Kids – Check out Yahoo! Kids, "The Web Guide for Kids," a well-respected safe place for younger kids to find their way to selected Web sites with the Yahoo! Kids directory, and play games, find homework resources, and much more.

- Y!Q – Click on this purple icon (particularly in the News section) to do a Web and news search of that topic in a separate pop-up window.

WINDOWS LIVE (LIVE.COM)

After a long period of promises, in 2004 MSN delivered its "new" MSN Search with a new interface and a crawler of its own (rather than, as previously, using someone else's). Analogous in more ways than one to Microsoft's Millenium Edition of its operating system, the delivery of MSN Search was fairly quickly followed, in late 2005, by release (in Beta mode) of Windows Live (live.com), Microsoft's "new" new Web search engine. By late 2006 MSN Search was no longer available, replaced by Live. Windows Live has a different look and feel than MSN Search and conveys a "Web 2.0" approach, with the use of newer Web programming techniques. Its main page is designed as a portal page, but one that starts out with minimal content (barely more than the search box) and provides an Add Stuff link by which users add to the page the content they wish, choosing from categories such as

Figure 5.11

Live Search page

News & Weather, Sports, Entertainment & Media, Finance & Technology, and others. Each of those categories has multiple options from which to select.

Though the Windows Live interface looks very different than its predecessor, and includes features and content that MSN Search did not, the searchability of Live is very similar. A Search Only link on the regular Live page takes you to the Live Search page and a link there will take you back to the "personalized" page.

Live Search Page

The very simple Live Search page (Figure 5.11) provides the following features, but be aware that in its early stages the interface tends to change fairly often:

- Search box – In the search box, terms you enter are automatically ANDed and you can use OR, NOT, and several prefixes.
- Links to other databases – News, Images, Local, QnA, and More can be searched by using the links below the search box.
- Options – Use this to set your language preferences and click on the Change Your Search Settings link to get more choices, including:
  - Display – Language in which you would like the search interface to appear (40 choices)
  - Results – How many results per page, maximum number from any site (1, 2, 3)

- SafeSearch (adult content filter) on or off
- Default location for local search and other geographically significant searches
- Default language of search results (can limit your search results to one or more of 38 languages)

Live's Advanced Search

If you click on the Advanced Search link found on Live results pages, you are provided with a menu of advanced options (Figure 5.12). You can use this to easily, one step at a time, build additional qualifications into your search. The options include:

- Search Terms – A menu provides simple Boolean options for the terms you enter, including "All of these terms," "Any of these terms," "None of these terms," as well as "This exact phrase."
- Site/Domain – To include only, or exclude, a specific site or top-level domain (.com, .edu, uk, fr, etc.).
- Links to – Limits your search to only those pages that link to a specific site.
- Country/Region – Limits your search to pages from any one of 92 countries.
- Language – Limits your search to any one of 38 languages.
- Results Ranking – Allows you to modify, by use of "sliders," the ranking of the results by increasing or decreasing the emphasis on how recently the page was updated, how popular the page is, and the degree that you want an exact match with your search terms.

Figure 5.12

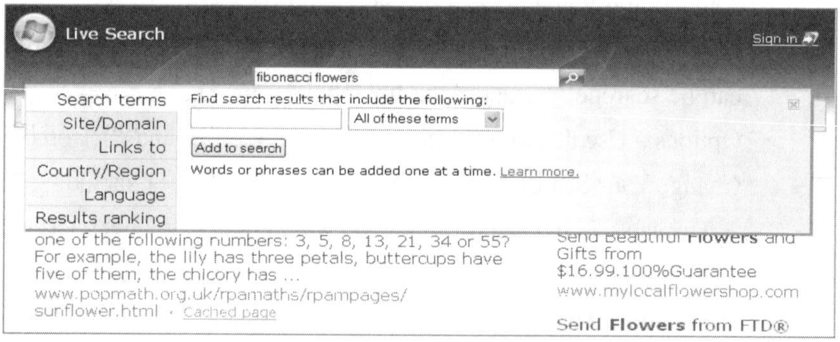

Live's advanced search page

Search Features Provided by Live

Boolean

All terms you enter are automatically ANDed. You can use the OR connector, but must be sure to include your ORed terms in parentheses. To exclude words, you can either use NOT or a minus sign in front of the word. (To facilitate copying and pasting a query into another engine, you may prefer to use the minus for the NOT.)

Example: *muskrats (recipe OR recipes) –baked*

Title Searching

To limit to pages that have your term in the title, you must use the "intitle:" prefix. You can use this with quotation marks for a phrase. To specify multiple words without insisting on a specific phrase, re-use the prefix.

Examples:
intitle:handel
intitle:"Georg Frideric Handel"
intitle:handel intitle:biography

Site, Domain, and URL Searching

To find all pages that Live has indexed for a particular site, or for subdomain of a site, use the "site:" prefix. Use this in conjunction with a term in order to do a "site search."

Examples:
site: fujifilm.com
site:phototips.fujifilm.com
shadows site:phototips.fujifilm.com

This can also be used to limit your retrieval to a specific top-level domain.

Example: *esters saponification site:edu*

The advanced search also provides a Site/Domain search option. Live has a "url:" prefix, but it only retrieves the one record for that specific URL.

Link Searching

To find pages that link to a particular site or page, use either the "Links to" section of the advanced search menu or the "link:" prefix.

Example: *+link:freepint.com*

Language Searching

The easiest way to search for items in a particular language is to use the Language portion of the advanced search menu. You can use the "language:" prefix if you know the two-letter code for the language.

Example: *biographie clemenceau language:fr*

Searching by Date

Live does not have a date searching feature. If, though, you are looking for more current material, try using the Results Ranking section of advanced search and maximizing the "Updated Recently" slider. This may enable you to get the more current material closer to the top of your results list.

Searching by File Type

You can search by file type by using the "filetype:" prefix.

Example: *photoshop tutorial filetype:pdf*

This works for html, txt, PDF, doc, xls, and ppt files.

Searching by Other Prefixes

In addition to the prefixes just covered, the following can be used in Live Search:

country/region – Enter "loc:" or "location:" followed by 2-letter country code

Example: *Fledermaus location:de*

contains – Use to find pages containing a link to a particular filetype

Example: *Janice Joplin contains:mp3*

in the Anchor (link) – Use to find pages that have a particular word in the text of a link

Example: *Texas restaurants inanchor:dallas*

in the Body – Use this if for some obscure reason you want to identify pages that have a term in the body of the pages (as opposed to the title, etc.)

Example: *inbody:frog*

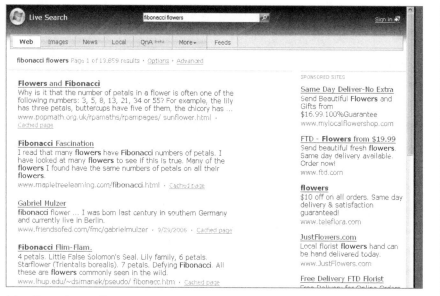

Figure 5.13

Live Search results page

Live Results Pages

As with results pages for other engines, Live Search results are ranked by relevance. Individual Web page results listings include the page title, a brief description or snippet of text, the URL, and a link to a cached version of the page (Figure 5.13). Some records will also show a date. If more than one matching page from any site has been found, you will be shown two records from the site and a Show More Results link to see any additional pages.

Other Searchable Live Databases

News

Live Search's news search covers more than 4,800 news sources world-wide, plus blogs, and is based on the MSNBC News site's NewsBot search.

Images

An image search in Live produces significantly smaller numbers of results than does a similar search in Google or Yahoo!, but the results are displayed in a more innovative manner. Results are not shown page by page, but continuously as you move the scroll bar down. The slider on images search results pages allows you to see many more (smaller) thumbnails on a single screen. When you click on an image the original page shows up on the right side of the screen and a continuous scrolling list of thumbnails for other image results are shown on the left.

Local

The Local Search for Live is substantially more robust than was the local search in MSN Search, incorporating the MSN Virtual Earth product (Microsoft's answer to Google Earth). Live Local provides road maps and aerial views for the entire world, plus driving directions, yellow pages information (for the U.S., the U.K., Canada, and additional locations), and Traffic Reports (for selected locations). You will find other features such as the Scratch Pad to collect maps and locations and the Location Finder, which will attempt to identify your current location based on your IP address. For a number of U.S. areas you will also find excellent "Birds Eye" views, taken from planes and providing more detailed photos with more "perspective."

QnA

Live's QnA search is a database of questions and answers, provided by Live users. If you don't find your question already in the database, submit it for other users to answer.

Feeds

The feeds search in Live provides a search of RSS feeds. This serves as a way to add a feed to your Live main page and also a very easy way to read the current feed from the sources the search identifies. (Click the right arrow beside the name of the feed.)

Academic

Live Academic Search provides a search of journal publications from a number of leading scholarly publishers (and from the Web). Depending upon the source, you will get bibliographic citations, abstracts, and in some cases the article.

Other Live Features and Content

Phone Book and Address Lookup

If you enter the name of a person and address (e.g., *Phineas Bluster Doodyville VA*) in the search box, you can search for phone numbers of individuals (as well as businesses).

Stock Search

Enter a ticker symbol in the search box and get current quotes, links to company news, etc.

Calculator

As with other engines, you can use Live Search's main search box as a calculator. For addition, subtraction, multiplication, division, and exponents use, respectively, +, -, *, /, and ^. Parentheses can be used to nest operations, e.g., *(12+2.1-1)^2.*

The Evolving Windows Live

The features and content just described are the major offerings of the first stages of Windows Live. A number of other features are built in or planned, particularly connections with other Microsoft services such as Hotmail (plus a new generation Web mail service) and Windows Messenger, and features such as a browser toolbar, desktop search, and shopping. With Windows Live, Microsoft is also building in PC services (Windows Live OneCare and Windows Live Safety Center) with virus scanning, firewalls, tune-ups, file backups, and system checkups. Keep checking to see which of these services really get delivered. If Microsoft really does deliver on all (or even most) of what it is promising, Windows Live will be much more of a search engine "contender" than was MSN Search.

ASK.COM (ASK.COM)

Ask.com, formerly known as Ask Jeeves, has an interesting history going back to 1996. In its early days, it was not a "search engine" but rather a "question and answer" site, utilizing stored collections of answers and algorithms that made an attempt at understanding the question and then finding the probable answer. This approach changed significantly and when it purchased the Teoma search engine technology in 2001, Ask Jeeves was very obviously moving into the more standard search engine arena. Its transition was complete when, in 2006, it changed its name to Ask.com, retired the butler, and completely re-designed its interface. It provides, in addition to its Web search, a good collection of additional databases (images, etc.) and features. As well as the U.S. site, Ask.com also has sites for Germany (Ask Deutschland; de.Ask.com), Spain (Ask España; es.Ask.com), Japan (Ask

Figure 5.14

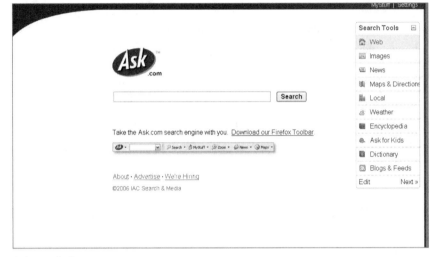

Ask.com's home page

Japan; Ask.jp), and the U.K. (Ask UK; uk.Ask.com). Each of those has a similar Web search function and contains some, but not all, of the other features discussed here.

Ask.com's Home Page

Simplicity and focus on the search box is the theme of Ask.com's home page (Figure 5.14). Links to nine or so additional databases and features are shown under Search Tools on the side of the page, with a link there to another list with about the same number. If you don't see the Advanced Search link in the first list, click Next and you will find it in the second list. The following items are found on the home page or on the second page of the Search Tools menu:

- Search box – The terms you enter are ANDed unless you specify otherwise. You can also use an OR, a minus sign for a NOT, and prefixes to qualify a term.
- Link to Ask for Kids, a kid-friendly search engine provided by Ask.com.
- Under Search Tools:
  - Images database
  - News – Search news, plus browsable news categories of news and

news photos from thousands of news sources provided to Ask.com from multiple news aggregators.

- Maps & Directions - Get maps and driving directions for the U.S. and Canada.
- Local (Yellow Pages service)
- Weather – Get weather reports and forecasts around the world.
- Encyclopedia – Search Wikipedia.
- Shopping – Search and browse for products.
- Desktop – Use Ask.com's downloadable desktop search program.
- Bloglines – Click on this link to get to the Bloglines site (owned by Ask.com) where you can use the Bloglines RSS reader plus search or browse for Weblogs and search Weblog postings.
- Advanced Search
- Currency Conversion – Get conversions for 180 currencies.
- Dictionary – Search the American Heritage Dictionary.
- Mobile Content - Search for ringtones, wallpapers, and games for your mobile devices.
- Movies – Shop for and get information about movies.
- My Stuff – If you have signed in to Ask.com, use this link to get to the search history page, where you can store a record of Web pages and images you have selected, search them, see the list of searches you have saved, arrange your saved items in folders, plus add your own descriptive tags to them.
- Stocks – Search for U.S. stock quotes.
- Thesaurus – Search Roget's II: The New Thesaurus.
- Unit Conversions – Convert from one measurement unit to another (some people may find this easier to use than the conversion programs from other search engines because it gives you pull-down menus for measurement options).
- White Pages – Search for phone numbers and addresses of people in the U.S.

The Edit button at the bottom of the Search Tools list lets you change the order of the tools listed and move features that are on the second page of tools to the first page.

Ask.com's Advanced Search

If you don't see the link to the advanced search page, look at the second page of the Search Tools. The advanced search page (Figure 5.15) provides the following options:

- Menu and search boxes – To perform simple Boolean ("must have," "must not have," and "should have"), with an Add an Entry button to get additional boxes
- Location of words or phrases – To limit retrieval to occurrence of your words in the page title or in the URL
- Language – To specify one of seven languages (Dutch, English, French, German, Italian, Portuguese, Spanish)
- Domain or site – To narrow your search to a domain (uk, edu, mil, etc.) or to a specific site (e.g., temple.edu)
- Geographic Region – To limit retrieval to pages from one of six regions of the world
- Date page was modified – By time frame (last week, last month, etc.) or before or after a specific date, or within a specific date range

Figure 5.15

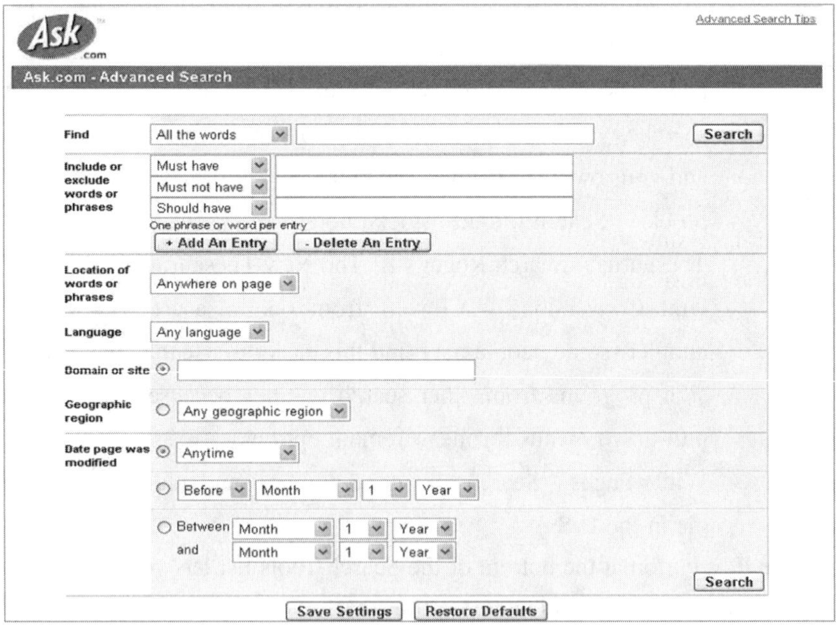

Ask.com's advanced search page

Buttons at the bottom of the advanced search page permit you to save your settings or change your settings back to the default settings.

Search Features Provided by Ask.com

By the use of options previously discussed on its advanced search page or by the use of prefixes, Ask.com provides a number of ways to refine your search.

Boolean

As with other search engines, all terms you enter in the main search box are automatically ANDed unless you specify otherwise. You can also use an OR, and a minus sign for NOT.

> Example: *concrete OR cement deterioration –bridges*

Using more than one OR or combining an OR with an additional term may or may not produce meaningful results. Look for this to improve.

Title Searching

For higher precision, you can limit your retrieval to items where your term occurs in the title. Use the Location of Words or Phrases menu on the advanced search page or use the "intitle:" prefix on the main page.

> Examples:
> *intitle:chrysanthemums*
> *symbolism intitle:chrysanthemums*

URL, Site, and Domain Searching

To limit to sites with a particular term somewhere in the URL, you can use either the "inurl:" or "site:" prefixes. To limit retrieval to a specific site or to pages that come from a particular top-level domain (com, fr, org, etc.), use the "site:" prefix. The latter, though, cannot be used by itself, but must be used along with another term or terms.

> Examples:
> *inurl:nato*
> *NATO site:de*
> *nonproliferation site:un.org*

Language Searching

By use of the advanced search page, you can limit to pages that are in Dutch, English, French, German, Italian, Portuguese, or Spanish. Alternatively, in the main page search box you can use the "lang:" prefix with the two letter code for those languages (en, nl, en, fr, de, it, pt, es).

Example: *goethe lang:de*

Calculator

You can perform calculations right from the main search box, as with other major engines. For addition, subtraction, multiplication, division, and exponents use +, -, *, /, and ^ respectively. You can also nest using parentheses, for example, *15(14+43)*.

Ask.com Results Pages

Though Ask.com's searchability and collection of databases is certainly respectable, its search results pages definitely go beyond the ordinary (Figure 5.16). For example, in a search on *cloning*, Ask.com produces the following on its search results page:

- Above the regular search results list, an excerpt from, and link to, an encyclopedia article (from Wikipedia). A pull-down menu is

Figure 5.16

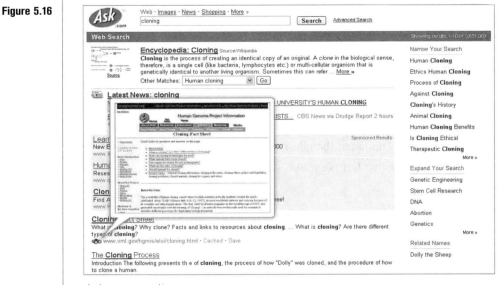

Ask.com results page

attached that provides links to "Other Matches" from the encyclopedia (human cloning, therapeutic cloning, etc.).

- The list of Web search matches contains the usual page title, snippet of text, and URL, plus (as is now pretty standard) a link to a cached copy of the page. If you are signed in, there will be a Saved link to add the site to your saved results on My Stuff.

- Along with each record you will see a binoculars icon, Ask.com's most unique results page offering. Just hold your cursor on the icon and you will see a pop-up window with a preview of the actual page.

- To the right of the results listing is a list of suggested narrower topics (Narrow Your Search), broader topics (Expand Your Search), and related names (in this case, Dolly the Sheep).

Other topics yield additional output, such as related news headlines.

Other Searchable Ask.com Databases

Though most of the things listed under Search Tools on Ask.com's main page are searches of various databases, following are those that probably deserve a bit more description.

Images

Ask.com's image search is designed very similarly to that of both Google and Yahoo!, but as with the Web databases, Ask.com's image database is substantially smaller. However, particularly because of the challenges each engine faces in identifying relevant indexing terms for images, even a smaller image database can provide good results and can be a very worthwhile image search tool.

Maps & Directions

Ask.com's Maps & Directions search offers maps and driving directions for the U.S. and Canada. In addition to draggable and zoomable maps showing streets, political boundaries, and physical features such as lakes and forests, Ask.com also provides aerial views and topographic map views.

Local

Ask.com's Local search is a U.S. business directory, which is searchable by type of business (or business name) and city or ZIP code. Results can be sorted by relevance, distance, or ratings. Content comes primarily from Citysearch, but Ask.com also provides maps and driving directions.

Shopping

Ask.com's Shopping search, which is powered by PriceGrabber.com, offers browsing of 20 main categories and a search function (on either the entire catalog or specific product categories). Click on a specific product listing to find a comparison price page, view product details, read user reviews, and check user discussion groups on the product.

Preferences Page

In addition to allowing you to re-order the Search Tools list, the Preferences page allows you to modify several other settings. To get to the Preferences page, click the Edit button on the Search Tools menu. Under the General tab of that page, you can change your location (for uses with Local search, weather, etc.), specify how many results per page you would like, request that your clicked results open in a new window, apply the adult content filter, make Ask.com the default search engine in your browser, and specify the default Ask.com site (U.S., U.K, etc.).

Ask.com Toolbar

The downloadable Ask.com Toolbar has the Ask.com Web search box, plus your choice of a button for any of the Ask.com Search Tools, links to save Web pages and images to My Stuff, a link to search the current site in your browser window, and quick stock quotes lookup for up to five stocks.

ADDITIONAL GENERAL WEB SEARCH ENGINES

The Web search engines covered in this section are additional engines that the serious searcher should be aware of. For these, most searchers may not want to absorb the level of detail provided for the four engines just covered, but should be aware of special features these provide or at least of their existence. The "special features" point applies particularly to the first one, Exalead. The others are listed here, to some degree at least, for "historical" purposes.

Table 5.1 Major Search Engines Features

	Ask.com	Google	Live	Yahoo!
Boolean	*term term*	*term term*	*term term*	*term term*
	(Defaults to an AND)	(Defaults to an AND)	(Defaults to an AND)	(Defaults to an AND)
	-*term* (for NOT)	-*term* (for NOT) OR	-*term* (for NOT)	-*term* (for NOT)
	term OR *term*	*term* OR *term*	(*term* OR *term*)	(*term* OR *term*)
Stemming		Some automatic stemming		Some automatic stemming
Title field	intitle:term	intitle:*term*	intitle: *term*	intitle:*term*
		allintitle:*term1 term2*		allintitle: *term term*
		(menu – Occurrences window)		
URL field	site:*term*	inurl:*term*	inurl: *term*	inurl:term
	inurl:*term*	allinurl:*term1 term2*	site:*term*	site:*term*
		term1 site:*term2*		hostname:*term*
		(Domain " window menu)		url:http://term
"Links to" a site		link:*term*	link:*term*	link:http://*term*
		("Links" textbox*)*	linkdomain:*term*	
File type		filetype:*extension*	filetype:*extension*	("File Format" window
		("File Format" window menu)		menu)
Language	lang:xx	Choice of 35 languages on	Choice of 12 languages	Choice of 37 languages on
	Choice of 7 languages on	Advanced Search page	in Advanced Search	Advanced Search page
	Advanced Search page		menu	
			lang:xx	
Media search	Images	Images, Video	Images	Images, Audio, Video
Also shown on	Links to cached pages	Links to cached pages	Links to cached pages	Links to cached pages
results pages	Encyclopedia	Similar pages link	News Headlines	Shortcuts, etc.
	News Headlines	Translation option		Link to cached page
	Related Topics	Link to definitions, etc.		Translation option
	Save to My Stuff	News Headlines		Link to definitions, maps
		My Search History link		News Headlines
				My Web, Search History

Exalead (exalead.com)

When new Web search engines appear, most searchers can probably ignore them unless they provide two things: (1) unique and useful features, and (2) a database of competitive size. Although the size of Exalead's rapidly growing Web database does not yet match the major engines, for a lot of searches, the uniquely powerful features it provides will more than make up for the size of the database (Figure 5.17).

Exalead provides all the basics expected of a search engine, including an advanced search page with Boolean and limiting by title, language, file format, domain, date, and country. In the main search box, AND is implied, and you can use OR, NOT (or "-"), and the "title:", "site:", "lang:", and "date:" prefixes. It is, however, in Exalead's special search options that its search really excels, with truncation, proximity, and more.

Perhaps the most important of these options is truncation (searching on the stem of a word to get all of the variant endings). From the main search box, add an asterisk to search on a word stem (e.g., *bank**). Enter NEAR between two terms to insist that the terms be within 16 words of each other. On the advanced search page, menus offer the truncation and NEAR options, and a separate search method menu also provides the following types of matches: exact, phonetic ("sounds like"), approximate spelling, and automatic stemming. (The latter only applies when you are searching two or more terms.)

As well as search features, Exalead has a good collection of features on its results pages, including very effective search results "categorization." On the side of results pages are lists of Related Terms, Related Categories (and subcategories), Web Site Location, and Document Type. Click on any of the headings there to narrow your search by that criterion. To the right of each search result there is a thumbnail image of the page. Click on a thumbnail and the page opens in a window within the results page. Icons at the top of results pages allow you to view just text results, just thumbnails, or both.

At the top of results pages are links that will take your search to Exalead's large audio and video databases. Exalead should definitely be in the toolbox of "power searchers."

Figure 5.17

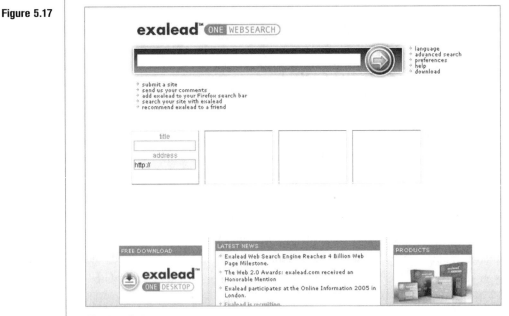

Exalead's home page

HotBot (hotbot.com)

HotBot is one of the oldest Web search engines, and was once one of the most powerful, with some pioneering and unique features. After years of neglect and downgrading, it has virtually nothing left of its former glory and the site is merely a watered-down interface for the Google, Ask.com, and Live Search Web databases.

Lycos (lycos.com)

Lycos, once a major contender on the search engine scene, positions itself as a portal rather than a search engine. It is a good portal with a good collection of resources, including news, multimedia, and other specialized searches; job listings; phone directories; weather; and other features. Its search is done using Ask.com's Web database and search technology.

WiseNut (wisenut.com)

WiseNut came on the scene in 2001 with a lot of fanfare. It peaked shortly thereafter. WiseNut's most outstanding feature is its "WiseGuide Categories" that appear on results pages and are generated based on semantic relationships of words in your search. These categories do allow easy and effective narrowing of search results by subject. WiseNut does not have an advanced mode.

AltaVista (altavista.com) and AlltheWeb (alltheweb.com)

Once among the top three or four search engines, AltaVista and AlltheWeb are now part of Overture, which was purchased by Yahoo! in 2003. AltaVista's unique and powerful search technology (including truncation and the NEAR connector) has been discontinued, and the databases of both have been replaced with Yahoo!'s database and search technology.

VISUALIZATION SEARCH ENGINES

Visualization engines provide a very different "look"—literally—at search results.

Instead of the traditional linear, textual list of retrieved items, results are shown on a map that displays conceptual connections spatially. Visualization continues to be an area of extensive research, and several sites demonstrate various visualization approaches. The type of conceptual and visual mapping done by these sites can be especially useful for a quick exploration of the concept possibilities, directions, and terminology for a particular search. Consider it for competitive intelligence and other searches where you need to start by understanding relationships rather than just browsing lists of results. Among the leaders in this area are KartOO, Grokker, and TouchGraph. Each uses the content of one or more of the larger search engines' databases.

KartOO (kartoo.com)

KartOO provides a visualization approach that displays linkage patterns found between the Web sites identified by a search on a particular subject. To search, enter one or more search terms in KartOO's search box (including, if you wish, OR, NEAR, *, and a variety of prefixes such as "title:", "domain:", etc.). On results pages, you will see a map with each site represented by a "page" icon. The map actually consists of two layers. The underlying layer has areas for commonly occurring ("associated") terms that were identified when KartOO analyzed the retrieved records. The top layer of the map shows the pages that were ranked highest. When you hold your cursor over one of the page icons, you will see lines to the related terms for that page. Hold your cursor over the URL and on the left of the screen you will see a description of the site. If you hold your cursor over a term on the map, lines will be displayed connecting that site to the most closely associated pages.

In addition to the map itself, when you first do a search, you will see, on the left of the screen, a helpful list of related topics and terms that KartOO identified. Click on any of those and KartOO will create a map for that topic. The essence of KartOO is in the maps, but if you look around you will see several additional choices: for restricting by language, lists of past searches, a natural language search option, additional "pages" of results, and much more.

Grokker (grokker.com)

Grokker is designed to be sold as an enterprise tool, but a free version is also available; you can enter a search which is then performed using the Web databases of Yahoo!, the ACM Digital Library, and/or Amazon. With the enterprise version, you choose the information sources to include. Search results are categorized and displayed in either an outline or a (more exciting) map format. As a result of a Grokker search, you will see a collection of circles in the map format containing buttons that look like various sizes of pastel-colored candies (Figure 5.18). The circles represent top-level categories and the round buttons are subcategories. Clicking on categories and subcategories leads to squares representing individual documents. Hold your cursor over a button to see the name of the subcategory or over a square to see document details. Click a circle or button to examine its contents, or click outside the circle to zoom back to the higher level. By clicking on a category, a list of retrieved records appears in the panel on the right side of the Grokker screen.

Use the tabs on the left of the screen to switch between the map view and the outline view, which shows top-level categories and the number of retrieved documents. Clicking on the arrow to the left of a category will display subcategories.

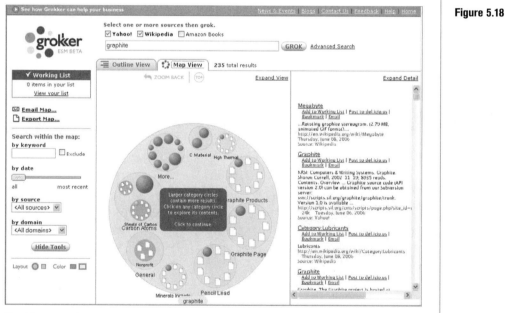

Figure 5.18

Grokker results page

TouchGraph (touchgraph.com)

TouchGraph offers a dynamic and interactive display of the relationships between Web sites. Searches can use the databases of Amazon, Google, or LiveJournal (which covers Weblogs). For the TouchGraph Google search, enter a URL (in contrast to KartOO and Grokker where you enter a subject term). For Amazon and LiveJournal searches, you enter subject terms. The results are displayed by a network of lines connecting the various nodes (Web sites). From each, site lines radiate to sites to which they link. Hold your cursor over a node to highlight the links from that node. When you do so an Info button will display that you can click to get a pop-up window with more detail about the site. Other URLs can be added to see how relationships to them fit in with your first site. You can choose to label nodes by title, by URL, or as points, while taking advantage of several other controls that modify how results are displayed.

CHAPTER 6

GROUPS, NEWSGROUPS, FORUMS, AND THEIR RELATIVES

WHAT THEY ARE AND WHY THEY ARE USEFUL

Groups, newsgroups, discussion groups, lists, message boards, and other online interactive forums are tools that are often under-used resources in the searcher's toolbox. Particularly for competitive intelligence (including researching and tracking products, companies, and industries) and for other fields of intelligence (including security, military, and related areas), newsgroups and their relatives can be gold mines (with, analogously, the product often difficult to find and to mine).

Groups, mailing lists, and a variety of their hybrids represent one aspect of the interactive side of the Internet, allowing Internet users to communicate with people having like interests, concerns, problems, and issues. Unlike regular e-mail, where you need the address of specific persons or organizations in order to communicate with them, these channels allow you to reach people you don't know and take advantage of their knowledge and expertise. This chapter outlines the resources available for finding and mining this information and some techniques that can make it easier.

A major barrier to understanding these tools is the terminology. Though "discussion groups" is probably the most descriptive term applied to most of this genre, a variety of other terms are used. "Newsgroups," which was the first term used, usually has little to do with "news," and mailing lists are definitely not to be confused with the junk mail you receive in either your e-mail or traditional mailbox. "Newsgroups," narrowly defined, usually refer to the Usenet collection of groups that actually originated prior to the Internet as we now think of it. "Groups," more broadly defined, includes newsgroups and a variety of other channels, variously referred to as groups, discussion groups, bulletin boards, message boards, forums, and even (by dot.com marketers, primarily) as "communities." In this chapter, the term "groups" will be used to refer to all of the incarnations just mentioned.

In terms of the type of communications channels they provide, it would not be unrealistic to include Weblogs in this chapter. However, the Weblog phenomenon is different enough to be addressed separately and is covered later in this book (see Chapter 11). "Groups" can be thought of as primarily a "communal," participatory, democratic, experience, whereas Weblogs are usually exclusively controlled, top-down, by an individual (with, however, some participatory possibilities).

Many groups provide both an online forum and a "mailing list" service. The biggest distinction between these two services lies in how the information gets to you. On the forum side, messages are posted on computer networks (e.g., the Internet) for the world to read. Usually anyone can go to a group and read its content and, usually, anyone can post a message. Mailing list content goes by e-mail only to individuals who subscribe to the list. With groups, you have to take the initiative each time to go get the messages; with mailing lists, the messages come automatically to you. One further important distinction is that messages that appear in groups are usually more fully archived and, therefore, more retrospectively available than the content of mailing lists.

Both groups and mailing lists can be moderated or unmoderated. With unmoderated groups (and lists), your posting appears immediately when you submit it. If the group or mailing list is moderated, your posting must pass the inspection of someone who decides whether to approve the posting, and, if approved, then submits it for publication to the list. Among other things, this means that moderated groups and lists are more likely to have postings that really are directly related to the subject.

GROUPS

Collections of groups originate from, and are found in, a variety of online collections, including the grandparent of all groups, Usenet; in commercial portals such as Yahoo!; and on professional association sites, among others. The next few pages will give an overview of the nature of these various collections and how you can most easily access them and participate.

Usenet

Usenet is the original and still best known collection of groups, created in 1979 at the University of North Carolina and Duke University by Jim Ellis,

Tom Truscott, Steve Bellovin, and Steve Daniel. Usenet (a "users' network," originally spelled USENET) started as a collection of network-accessible electronic bulletin boards and grew quickly both in terms of use and geographic reach. Not only does Usenet predate the Web, it predates the Internet as most of us know it today. With the popularization of the Internet and the Web, however, Usenet access is now, for all practical purposes, through the Internet, and most users use Web-based interfaces rather than the older specialized software known as news readers. (If you bump into any Usenet old-timers, be sure to let them know that you know that Usenet is not "part" of the Internet, but it is accessible through the Internet.)

Usenet groups are arranged in a very specific hierarchy, which at first glance appears a bit arcane. The hierarchy consists of 10 main top-level categories and thousands of other top-level hierarchies, based mainly on subject, geography, and language. Each hierarchy is further broken down (otherwise, they wouldn't be "hierarchies").

> Examples:
> *sci.bio.phytopathology*
> *rec.crafts.textiles.needlework*

The main top-level hierarchies are:
- alt. For "alternative," as in alternative lifestyle or alternative press. This is the "anything goes" category, and the creation of a new group in this category does not require the clearly defined nominating and voting process that is required for other hierarchies.
- biz. Business
- comp. Computers
- humanities. Humanities
- misc. Subjects that don't fit neatly into the other main categories
- news. Formerly primarily news relating to Usenet, but now that plus a variety of odds and ends
- rec. Recreation (sports, games, hobbies, etc.)
- sci. Science
- soc. Social sciences
- talk. Political and social issues, among others

The messages within each individual group are arranged by "threads"—series of messages on one specific topic consisting of the original message, replies to that message, replies to those replies, and so on. Users can post messages to either the original message or to any of the replies, or they can start a new thread.

Accessing Usenet Groups through News Readers

Until probably the late 1990s, most Usenet access was through an Internet Service Provider (ISP), and messages were read and posted by means of special software called news readers or through such software built into browsers such as Netscape. ISPs received newsfeeds from the computers that hosted Usenet groups and made that content available to the ISP's customers. Coverage (those groups that were stored by the ISP) was usually selective, due to the large volume of Internet traffic. If your ISP did not provide access to the group in which you were interested, you usually merely had to ask and the ISP would add the group. Although this process still happens, many ISPs today no longer support this direct form of Usenet access.

News readers are very similar to e-mail programs, allowing you to both read and post messages. You select from your ISP's list those groups to which you wish to subscribe, and when you wish to view postings to a group, or post a message yourself, you click on the name of the list in your news reader and recent postings are delivered to your computer. ("Subscribe" here means that you wish for that group to be on the list of groups for which your ISP sends you messages. For most groups, there is no official membership.)

The preceding paragraph will probably best be treated as history, but it is useful because you will still run across news readers and, to be conversant in Internet terminology, you should probably know what they are. However, most people who don't have a lot of time on their hands will probably be better off getting their Usenet access by means of the Web through their browser.

Web access to Usenet newsgroups first became widely available through a site called Deja News, which was created in 1996 and later became "deja.com." It was great—until the people responsible for its design and marketing began to miss the point and decided to make it into a shopping site, with the newsgroup access relegated to a minor position. Deja.com went out of business and can now best be remembered as an early pioneer of the dot.com bust.

To the rescue comes none other than almost-every-serious-searcher's favorite site, Google. In 2001, Google bought Deja's remains, began loading the archive, and quickly added the capability to not just search Usenet postings but to post messages as well. By the end of the year, it had made a 20-year archive of Usenet postings available. By 2002, the argument could be made that Google provided the easiest and most extensive capabilities ever for both the average user and the serious researcher to access and participate in newsgroups.

Other Groups

Although Usenet is the best-known collection of groups, it is not the only one. Groups can be found on commercial sites and portals such as Yahoo!, Delphi Forums (www.delphiforums.com), and ezboard (www.ezboard.com). You will also find a lot of specialized groups on association and club sites, such as the Utah Cycling Association, the Institute of Electrical and Electronics Engineers (IEEE), and the Welsh Rugby Union. These Web-based groups vary considerably in terms of the appearance of the interface, but they all function in about the same way. You can read, post, follow threads, and so on. Unlike Usenet, however, you usually have to sign up to use these groups and are required to identify yourself, although often your e-mail address is about all you need to do so. On sites such as Yahoo! Groups, you must sign up for a Yahoo! password, and on most association sites, you must be a member of the association to participate in the discussions.

Resources for Locating and Using Groups

The following resources (and others) can be used to locate *groups* of interest or messages on specific topics:

- Google Groups Search – For searching Usenet groups and postings and the newer Google Groups, which are not a part of Usenet
- Google's Web Search – For locating some non-Usenet groups
- Yahoo! Groups – Only for groups on the Yahoo! site, but there are hundreds of thousands of them
- Delphi Forums – More than 100,000 active forums on the Delphi Forums site
- ezboard – Another provider of forum services

- Big Boards – A resource guide for locating very large message boards and forums (www.big-boards.com)

Also, don't hesitate to simply use a search engine search to find a group. Searching on your topic and the term "forum" usually works well, as in the first example below, but if you want a more inclusive search do as in the second example:

> Examples:
> *physics forums*
> *"multiple sclerosis" (forum OR "discussion group" OR "message board")*

Sites of Associations Related to Your Topic

Look on the site of an association related to your search topic for an indication of a "forum," "discussion," or similar term suggesting the presence of a group. This tip also applies to locating mailing lists.

Using Google to Find Groups and Messages

At present, Google (google.com) is, by far, the best tool for finding, accessing, and using the Usenet collection. It contains not just current postings, but Usenet archives going back to 1981. In 2004, Google launched its own, user-created groups, mimicking to a significant degree the types of groups offered by Yahoo!. Google Groups total more than 1 billion messages. As with the rest of Google, the online documentation for Groups is quite good. The following is a quick overview and some highlights.

Browsing the Hierarchies

From the main Google Groups page (click on the Groups tab on Google's main page to get to it, or go directly to groups.google.com), you can use the Browse Groups Categories to browse through the eight main top-level hierarchies, or by Region, Language, Activity level, or number of members. A Browse All of Usenet link takes you to an alphabetic listing of Usenet-only groups.

As you browse throughout the levels, you will see links to additional lower levels in the hierarchy and also specific groups at that level. Clicking on the latter will take you to the messages threads for that group.

Figure 6.1

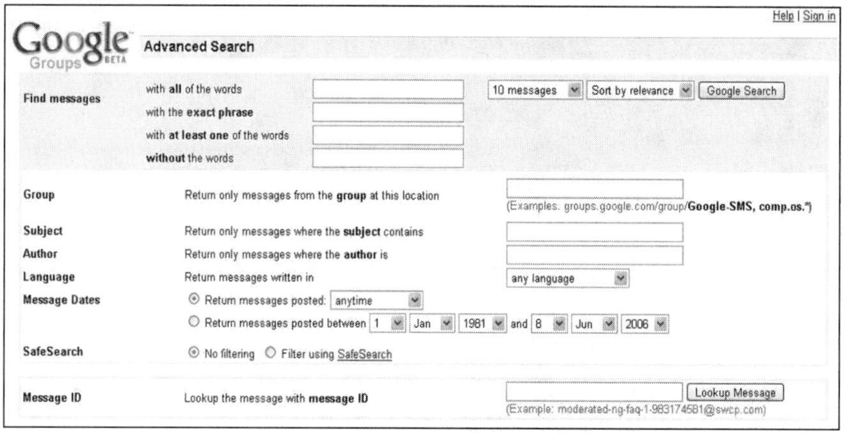

Google Groups advanced search page

Searching for Groups and Messages

When you use the main search box on the main Google Groups page, Google will retrieve all groups that have your term(s) in the group name, plus any threads containing that term. Those groups with your term in the group name will be shown at the top of the results. When browsing, you will see the main search box but also a second group search box that allows you to search just within the current level of the hierarchy. On pages for specific groups, there is a search box to search just the contents of that group. The Groups advanced search page (Figure 6.1) allows you to specify the following attributes:

- Simple Boolean expressions:
    - Use the "with all of the words" box to specify a Boolean AND
    - Use the "with at least one of the words" box to specify an OR
    - Use the "without the words" box to eliminate records that contain a particular word (NOT)
- Messages from a specific newsgroup only
- Subject, author, language, date or date range, message ID
- Safe Search Filter

Search results are ranked by relevance, but you can click the Sort by date link on the results page to view the newest first.

Figure 6.2

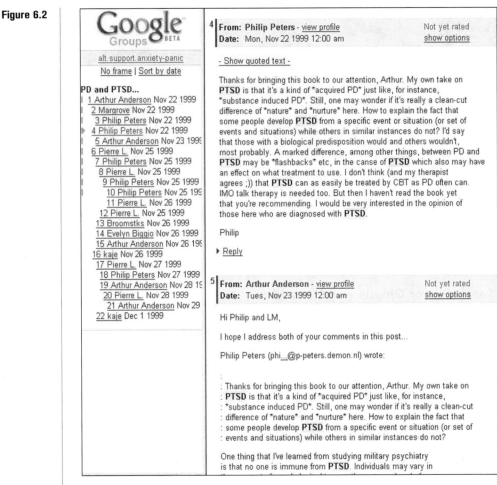

Message thread at Google Groups

Viewing Messages

Either browsing or searching will lead you to a list of threads, showing for each the thread title (linked to the entire thread), an excerpt of text around retrieving words, a link to the group in which it was found, a date, and the number of messages and authors in the thread. Click on the subject of the thread to see the individual messages. When you are viewing the messages, you will see all the messages in the thread (10 at a time). You will also usually see a convenient hierarchical list of the individual messages on the left of the screen (Figure 6.2). If not, click on the View as Tree link above the message. Click on the name of the group shown for any thread and you will be led to all threads for that group.

Posting Messages

To post a message, browse through the hierarchy until you find a group of interest. At the top of the list of messages in the group you are viewing, you will see a link that will enable you to start a new message in that group. When viewing a message, a link at the bottom of a message enables you to post a reply. To either start a new message (thread) or reply to a message, you will be required to register with Google. After clicking on the Post New Message or Reply link, you will be presented with a form to fill in, including your e-mail, the name you wish to use when posting, and a password of your choice. There is also a fairly long Terms agreement. Google will respond with a confirmation e-mail; click the confirmation link presented there, and you are ready to go. It is a good idea to read the "Posting Style Guide" that you will find linked on message pages. (Note: When you do a search and click on a message, the posting option will not appear. You must either browse the hierarchy or click on a group link somewhere.)

Starting a Group

Participating in discussions on Usenet is easily done, but starting a new group on a topic of your own choice is a long, complicated, and usually not feasible process. On the other hand, starting a group of your own on Yahoo! and elsewhere can be quick and easy. It was therefore natural for Google to begin offering an easy-to-use groups feature to go along with the Usenet groups.

To create your own group in Google, first sign in with your Google user name and password. Then click on the Create a New Group link on the Google Groups page. Follow the next several steps, which include naming your group, providing a description, and selecting the level of public access and subscription type. Options for access levels include: "Public," where anyone can read the archives and join the group; "Announcement-only," where anyone can read and join but messages can only be posted by moderators; or "Restricted," where only those you invite can participate and the archives are not searchable by others. Subscription-type options include the following: No e-mail (access only available on the Web); E-mail (e-mail messages are automatically sent to members for each new posting); Abridged E-mail (daily e-mail summaries sent); or Digest E-mail (all messages sent in a single e-mail daily). This can all be done in as few as a couple minutes and is quite simple. The result is a group with varying levels of public access, archives, and searchability, and depending upon the subscription type you choose, something that can be more of a "mailing list" than a group. However, until Google adds further functionality, the variety of things that can be done with the non-Usenet Google groups is quite limited compared to Yahoo! Groups.

Using Web Search to Identify Non-Usenet Groups

Although it doesn't advertise the fact, Google's Web search actually picks up over 24 million postings from non-Usenet, non-Google groups. It doesn't work perfectly, but you can locate some of these groups messages in Google by using this trick: As part of your search, use the phrase "next thread." Because that phrase is present in many messages from other groups, it will locate messages from a variety of sources that have been indexed by Google because of the existence of a group on a Web site.

Using Yahoo! to Find Groups and Messages

After Google, the second place to look to find groups is Yahoo! (groups.yahoo.com, or look for the Groups link on Yahoo!'s home page). If you want to create a group of your own, for free and with powerful options, the first place to look is Yahoo! Groups. Yahoo! Groups is actually a hybrid of groups and mailing lists, because for each group you can receive messages either at the Yahoo! Web site or by e-mail. Yahoo! allows you to search or browse through the groups, post messages, and create groups of your own. There are hundreds of thousands of Yahoo! groups, some with thousands of members and many with only a single member. (Join one of the latter and brighten someone's day.) There are more than a dozen "duct tape" groups alone.

Searching or Browsing for Groups

You can find Yahoo! groups of interest by either browsing through the 16 categories on the main Groups page or by using the search box there. Be aware that a search there only searches names of groups and their descriptions, not individual messages. Yahoo! does automatically truncate, though, so a search for "environment" will also retrieve groups that have "environmental" in their title or description. Terms you enter in the search box are automatically ANDed. Unlike regular Yahoo!, you cannot use "-word" to

Figure 6.3

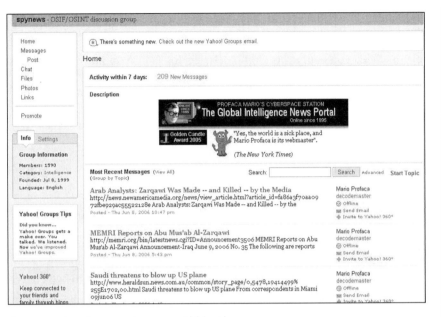

An example of a group's page at Yahoo!

exclude a word. Also, unlike almost every other search box you will find on the Internet, you cannot search a phrase by using quotation marks.

Whether you use the search box or browse the categories to find groups on Yahoo!, the listing of groups that results will contain the name of the group, the description, whether there is an archive, and if the archive is public or not. If it is public, you can browse through the messages without joining the group. (Click on the word "Public" to view the list of messages.) Clicking on the name of the group from the group listing will show you more detail about the group, including when it was founded, whether membership is open, whether it is moderated, and so forth, plus a calendar showing numbers of messages posted each month (Figure 6.3). The number of members and volume of postings are usually important indicators of the potential usefulness of the group.

Joining a Group

After identifying a group of interest, check first to see that the membership is open. To join, click on Join This Group. You will be asked for your Yahoo! Password, and if you do not have a Yahoo! password, you can get one at this point. After joining, Yahoo! Groups will send you an e-mail message containing a link for you to click that confirms that the e-mail address you used is really your own. Once you have confirmed this and selected a delivery method, you can go to the home page for the group and read and post messages. Also, after you have registered, you can click on My Groups to set your e-mail preferences:

- Individual e-mails – To receive individual e-mail messages
- Daily digest – To receive multiple e-mails in one message
- Special notices – To receive update e-mails from the group's moderator
- No e-mail – The true groups approach, where you go get the messages, rather than receiving them by e-mail

Once you have joined one or more groups, when you sign on, you will be presented with a page providing links to all of the groups to which you belong. You can also use this page to unsubscribe to groups. Look for the Edit My Groups link.

On both the pages that list messages and on the message pages themselves, you have a good variety of navigation and viewing options, such as moving backward and forward in a thread, viewing by thread or by date, viewing the message in brief (simple) form or expanded form, viewing the sender's profile, and searching the archive, among others. The latter is where you have the opportunity to search the actual content of messages. Though most Yahoo! groups don't take advantage of all of the possibilities, each group also is provided with options for the following features and content: Chat, Files, Photos, Polls, Links, Database, Members List, and Calendar. The availability of these features takes Yahoo! Groups far beyond its competitors.

Starting a Group

Yahoo! is definitely one of the easiest—and perhaps actually *the* easiest—place on the Web to set up a group. A group of your own can be great for a course you are teaching, networking and support groups, family, community organizations, and so forth, and you can get one set up in 10 minutes or less.

You choose the category (although Yahoo!'s staff may change the category if they see it and feel the category is inappropriate), name the group, decide if it is to be public, moderated, and so on. Basically, all you have to do is fill in the blanks.

With Yahoo!'s large number of users and members, large number of groups, ease of use, range of options, and accessibility to both those who want to use and those who want to sponsor groups, Yahoo! is an indispensable resource for those who wish to make use of the Internet as a communications channel.

Other Sources of Groups

There are numerous other places where you will find groups, some large and some small, but most have considerably less reach and content than those available through Yahoo! or Google. Nevertheless, the group that may precisely meet your needs may be in one of the smaller collections. Two additional sources, not as large as Yahoo! but having both a large number of groups and members, are Delphi Forums and ezboard.

Delphi Forums

www.delphiforums.com

According to Delphi Forums itself, this site has more than 4 million registered users, 8,000 active forums, 100,000 messages each day, and more than 200 million total messages. As with Yahoo! Groups, with Delphi you can read most messages without registering, but to post messages you must register. Registration is easy and free.

Delphi's lists are browsable using the 22 categories on the home page, and searchable using the search box just above the category list. Terms entered in that box will search both titles of groups and the content of messages. When browsing through categories, you are also given a search option to search just within that category.

You can create a free forum on Delphi, but for fuller capabilities (chat room, blogs, polls, message and forum ratings, etc.), you would need the premium service, which is very inexpensive. If it is really important that you find as many groups out there on your topic as possible, don't ignore a search on Delphi Forums.

ezboard

www.ezboard.com

ezboard has more than a half-million forum "communities" and more than 10 million active users. It is searchable and, if you look carefully, you will find a link that leads to a list of browsable categories. Terms entered in the search box will be searched both in forum titles and in the messages themselves. Registration is free, and there are inexpensive upgrade options. Maintaining a forum of your own here requires one of the upgraded memberships.

Big Boards

www.big-boards.com

Big Boards is a resource guide covering more than 1,700 of the largest message boards and forums (those with more than a half-million posts). You can locate discussions of interest either by using the Big Boards search box or by browsing through the 11 main directory categories (and more than 100 subcategories).

MAILING LISTS

Most of what can be said about the usefulness and nature of groups also applies to mailing lists. As mentioned earlier, the biggest differences with mailing lists are: (1) the message arrives in your e-mail rather than you having to request to see messages, with every message sent to the list coming to you; (2) you have to subscribe, often providing identifying information (and may need to be a member of the sponsoring organization); (3) the content of mailing lists is less likely to be archived and searchable than for groups; and (4) although the e-mail delivery mode makes it easier to access and ensures that you don't miss anything important, mailing lists postings can fill up your mailbox and can be a nuisance to deal with. The comparison is analogous to a company bulletin board compared to the inbox on your desk: Some information is more appropriately accessed by your going to the bulletin board periodically, whereas for some information, you would prefer to get a copy on your own desk. If, on a particular topic, you want to make sure you don't miss anything, a mailing list may better serve you.

One change that has occurred in the last few years is that the concept of mailing lists has, for many users, been obscured somewhat by the "groups" that were discussed earlier in this chapter. Many people read, join, and participate in groups and, as part of that process, somewhere along the line indicate that they would like to receive messages by e-mail (instead of or in addition to seeing messages by going to the group's Web site).

In other cases, users can join many mailing lists from many other types of Web sites just by clicking a link there that says you would like to be put on that Web site's mailing list. Both the groups and Web site-based means of joining a mailing list have indeed made the use of mailing lists easier for many people. Whether a specific mailing list is just one function of a group, is provided by a Web site, or exists by itself in "pure mailing list" form (i.e., just e-mail delivery) probably doesn't and shouldn't make much difference, as long as you get what you need. What is said in the following paragraphs about mailing lists will in some cases be more descriptive of mailing lists that exist mostly on their own, not as a part of a "group" function.

The receipt and distribution of messages on the older "purer" form of mailing lists (those that are not just one function of an online "group" or ones that are joined by just clicking a link on a Web site) are controlled automatically by "listserver" software. Lists are often referred to, inappropriately, as "listservs." LISTSERV is a registered trademark for listserver software produced by the L-Soft company, and the term (legally) should not be applied generically. The other most frequently encountered mailing list managers are Majordomo and Listproc.

For any kind of mailing list, you need to subscribe to participate. (How to find lists will be discussed shortly.) Some sites (for example, lots of association sites and commercial sites) provide a nice Web interface where you just have to fill in the blanks. Other sites provide instructions for sending an e-mail message to the mailing list administrative address and tell you what command you need to put in the header or message in order to join. For example, you might be instructed to send a message to majordomo@alektorophobia.org with the message *subscribe fearofchickens* in the body of the message. The instructions will vary primarily dependent upon the listserver software being used. You will usually receive a reply confirming your membership to the list and referencing an information file explaining how to use the list, ground rules, and so on.

The following are other important points about using mailing lists that are managed by listserver software:

- The e-mail address to which you send administrative messages is different from the one you use for posting messages. It is a great annoyance to list members to see administrative messages in their mailboxes.
- Many lists offer delivery of a "digest" form in which a number of messages are bundled on a regular basis (e.g., daily or weekly).

This is especially useful for lists that have a lot of traffic, and digests can avoid clogging up your e-mail inbox. They may also have an option where you can suspend delivery while you are on vacation.

- Many (probably most) lists will provide an FAQ (Frequently Asked Questions) file or Web page, which is usually worth scanning.
- Some lists provide archives, many of which are searchable.
- Before you sign up, note (from descriptions you find of the list) the level of traffic. If you subscribe to several high-volume mailing lists, you will end up not being able to read them because of the hundreds of messages you receive. For high-volume lists, consider taking advantage of digest versions and "on vacation" options.

Tools and Techniques for Locating Mailing Lists

For many people, their first experience in using mailing lists is through organizations to which they belong. Numerous other lists of interest may be out there and, fortunately, there are some online sites that make them easy to find. Among these are Topica and L-Soft CataList. Yahoo! Groups and Google Groups could also be included among these "finding tools" since, as pointed out earlier, their groups also have an e-mail option.

Topica

lists.topica.com

Topica's thrust is providing mailing list services to companies, associations, and individuals. Many readers who use mailing lists may have noticed that instead of associations managing their own lists, many have taken advantage of this service. Topica (formerly liszt.com) hosts thousands of e-mail newsletters. In addition to association lists and lists created by individuals, many of Topica's lists are commercial, but keep in mind that these are opt-in lists—you only join if you want to. They can be valuable for competitive intelligence purposes, as well as for keeping up-to-date on products and special deals from your favorite suppliers.

You can search by list topic without signing up, but signing up will enable you to have a page that shows all the Topica lists to which you belong and allows you to manage them. To sign up, provide your e-mail address and a password of your choice. You then receive a confirming e-mail to which you need to reply in order to complete the process. Sign up for some lists and, thereafter, when you go to Topica and log in, your page will show your lists. From there you can subscribe, unsubscribe, and set mail preferences. The latter includes options to receive your mail in digest form or receive messages by going to the Topica Web site (more like groups).

Lists of interest can be identified either by using the search box or browsing through the Topica categories. To browse, click on one of the 16 categories at the bottom of Topica's home page, or better, click the More option there. The resulting page will give you a better idea of coverage of the categories.

You can search using the search box on the main page or on the categories pages. Once you are two levels down in the categories or on search results pages, the search box provides an option of searching either Lists (names and descriptions) or the content of messages themselves. Topica allows you to use AND, OR, and NOT (capitalization is not necessary). If you do not use any operator between words, Topica defaults to an OR. You can also use quotation marks to search for phrases. You may want to narrow your search using these techniques, because Topica returns a maximum of 200 matches.

The list descriptions given usually make it easy to determine if this is a list for you (Figure 6.4). The description pages also make it easy to read and

Figure 6.4

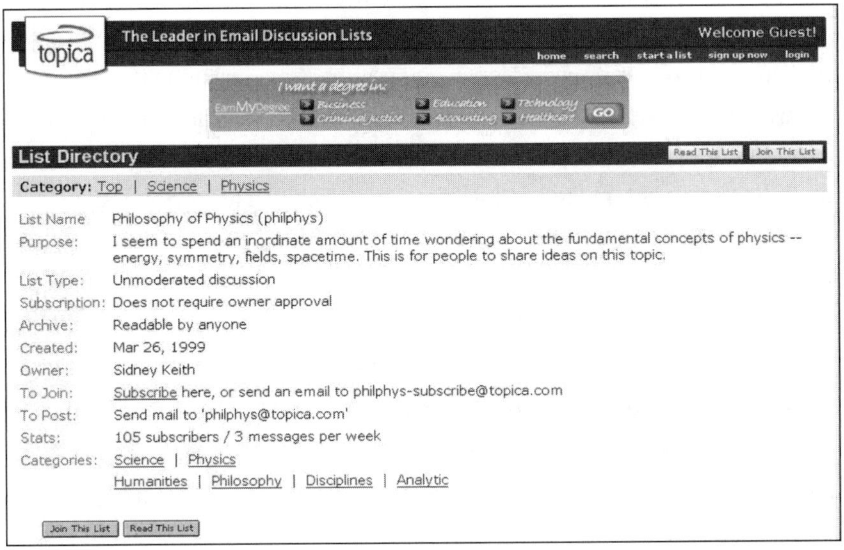

Topica list description

subscribe to (join) the list. On those and other pages you will find how to (very easily) start a list of your own. (First ask yourself, "Does the world really need my list?")

L-Soft CataList, the Official Catalog of LISTSERV Lists
www.lsoft.com/lists/listref.html

As the name says, L-Soft CataList is the official catalog for the 74,000 public lists that use LISTSERV software. In addition to searching list names and descriptions, you can view lists by host country, or view only those with 10,000 subscribers or more, or those with 1,000 subscribers or more.

INSTANT MESSAGING

Instant messaging, pioneered by AOL Instant Messenger with variations by Yahoo! and others, is another incarnation of online interaction for people and is a hybrid of groups and e-mail. Although it was first populated mainly by teenagers—an extension of the historic evolution of hanging out on the street corner or occupying the family phone—instant messaging has now gone beyond the teenage realm. In some corners of the corporate world, IM is beginning to take the place of popping your head into someone's office. It promises to potentially be one more significant productivity enhancer.

If you haven't used or seen it (unlikely at this point), the way it works is that participants create a buddy list of people they want to interact with online on an immediate basis. You send a message to someone on your list, and it will pop up on his or her screen. People who use the same instant messaging service who are not yet a buddy but who want to talk to you can send you a message asking to talk. You also have the option of creating a chat room in which multiple people are invited to join the conversation. This technology is well developed but not yet in the forefront of professional communications. It is, however, moving in that direction. Ask a local kid to show you how it works.

NETIQUETTE POINTS RELATING TO GROUPS AND MAILING LISTS

Readers of this book most likely already have a good sense of Netiquette (Internet etiquette), but some may profit by these selected points relating to groups and mailing lists:

1. Lurk before you leap. Lurking or hanging around just observing a discussion without participating is definitely a good idea. It may involve just reading a few messages or a few threads, and you may find yourself ready to leap in and join the conversation in a matter of minutes. Read enough messages (and preferably the FAQ or similar documentation) to be sure that the conversation is at the level appropriate to your needs and knowledge. If a group is very technical, the members get annoyed at beginners asking extremely simple questions. If there is a searchable archive, check it out. Don't get caught trying to start a discussion about a topic that has already been beaten to death.

2. Don't use newsgroups or e-mail lists for advertising. Depending on the group or list, there might be times when it would be acceptable to respond to a posting that may have requested a service you provide, but be careful. You can easily irritate many people. In such a case, you can play it safe by responding directly to the poster by e-mail, rather than responding to the group or list as a whole.

3. Don't get sucked into a flame war (an angry or unnecessarily strongly worded series of messages, aka flaming). Remember the sad truth that there are people out there who have nothing better to do than waste their time being nitpicky, rude, and generally obnoxious. The advent of groups and lists has become a wonderful channel for their frustrations and repressed feelings.

4. Only forward messages if allowed. Some associations, particularly, have rules regarding privacy of messages, often relating to such things as client privilege and competitive intelligence. Follow those rules very carefully. This mistake can cause you to be banned from a group—and worse.

5. Use crossposting (posting the same message to multiple groups or lists) advisedly. It clutters up people's mail and time.

CHAPTER 7

AN INTERNET REFERENCE SHELF

All serious searchers have a collection of tools they use for quick answers—the Web equivalent of a personal reference shelf. The challenge is to make sure that you have the right sites on your shelf. This chapter provides a selective collection of sites that should be on most researchers' shelves. Different researchers have different quick-reference needs requiring different tools. For many of us, we may have found out about most sites through a friend or by simply stumbling across them. Here we highlight reference tools that provide quick answers to some of the most frequently asked questions, from the mundane to the esoteric.

This chapter goes hand-in-hand with Chapter 3. For subject areas of interest to you, many of the resource guides of the types covered in Chapter 3 should be in your reference collection, in the same way that the reference section of a library usually contains a good collection of resource guides. In addition to quick-answer sites, a number of resource guides for reference tools in particular areas, such as statistics, government information, and companies, are also included here.

Going from general to specific, we look first at some prime general tools, such as encyclopedias, and then move in the direction of tools that can provide specific bits of information. For many of the categories, as well as listing specific sites, some suggestions will be provided about using the resources effectively.

Remember that all of the links presented here, as well as links for all sites covered throughout this book, are available at www.extremesearcher.com.

THINKING OF THE INTERNET AS A REFERENCE COLLECTION

Especially for people with broadband connections, going to the Internet rather than to printed resources for frequently sought information has become more and more common. With practice, it becomes quicker and easier (and in some cases, such as telephone directory assistance, much cheaper). The biggest tricks are, first, simply understanding the range of quick-reference tools that are out there, and, second, getting in the habit of using them— remembering to use them and bookmarking them. Another trick is not to fall into the trap of always going to the Internet first. (I have an encyclopedia right behind me that I often grab rather than reaching for the keyboard.)

The tools listed in this chapter provide a start in making sure the reader has a sense of the breadth and variety of quick-answer sites. The next step in understanding the range of these tools is to spend some time browsing one of the several reference resource guides listed at the end of this chapter. Plan to spend at least 20 minutes poking around these sites. Almost anyone can find something new and interesting in them.

CRITERIA USED FOR SELECTING THE TOOLS COVERED

Selection of the tools covered here was based on several factors. The first factor is my experience as a long-time Internet user and former reference librarian as well as experience in observing and talking with thousands (literally) of Internet users from a variety of organizations and countries. The second factor is the measure of a site's utility for a wide range of users. Some sites were chosen because they provide good examples of the range of these tools, and others were chosen because they provide examples of particular features to look for when examining and using reference sites. In several instances, multiple sites serve basically the same function (such as the travel reservation sites). More than one of such types is included in order to point out the differences and the utility of using more than one, rather than choosing a favorite and always going there.

TRADITIONAL TOOLS ONLINE

A number of online tools are electronic versions of common printed tools, including encyclopedias, dictionaries, almanacs, and the like. These are excellent for quick answers and for background relating to more specific research. In these (and many other tools), a number of factors contribute to their usefulness. These factors are important to know in some circumstances, irrelevant in other circumstances, and often are the same ones to be considered when using printed reference tools:

- Does the tool contain everything that the printed version contains? HighBeam Encyclopedia (www.encyclopedia.com) contains everything the printed equivalent does (and more), whereas the free online version of Encyclopedia Britannica contains only a small portion of the printed content.
- Does it contain things the printed version does not? Many of these tools provide collections of links and often news headlines that the hardcopy version does not provide.
- How current is it? Bartlett's Familiar Quotations (available as part of Bartleby.com) is the 1919 edition.
- Is the entire site free? Or is there a fee required to access part of the content? For many of the tools that require a subscription, the fee is not too costly, and you may find the expenditure worthwhile.

The annotations for the sites discussed here, which are purposely brief and not intended to be reviews of the sites, include the major points that researchers should consider when determining whether to use the tool ("… too great brevity of discourse tends to obscurity; too much truth is paralyzing," according to Blaise Pascal in a quote located by using Bartleby.com).

ENCYCLOPEDIAS

HighBeam Encyclopedia
www.encyclopedia.com

HighBeam Encyclopedia includes 57,000 frequently updated articles from the Sixth Edition of the *Columbia Encyclopedia* (Figure 7.1). Unlike Encarta and Encyclopedia Britannica Online, all articles are free. Articles can be located by browsing alphabetically or by searching (using the search box). When searching, terms are automatically ANDed, but you can specify an OR between words or use quotation marks for phrases. For articles on people, search as a phrase (using quotation marks) with the last name first. HighBeam Encyclopedia also provides links to news and magazine articles through eLibrary, but these require a fee.

Figure 7.1

Article from HighBeam Encyclopedia

Encarta

encarta.msn.com

The more than 4,500 detailed articles here are usually lengthier than the articles found at HighBeam Encyclopedia. Some are free, but access to many articles requires a subscription. When searching, terms are automatically ANDed; you cannot use Boolean operators or quotation marks.

Encyclopedia Britannica Online

britannica.com

As the online version of the renowned *Encyclopedia Britannica*, this site provides *very* brief articles for free, but the vast majority of the content requires a subscription. Considering the quality of this encyclopedia, you may find that buying a subscription (with access to more than 120,000 articles) is well worth the price. You can either browse or search, and results include the encyclopedia articles and carefully selected Web sites. Take advantage of the interactive timelines available on the free portion of the site.

Wikipedia

wikipedia.org

Wikipedia, which is an Internet-only encyclopedia, is by far the largest encyclopedia in existence. It is also an example of a WikiWiki site, a collaborative project by Internet users that allows easy input and online editing by any user. Because of this, intense debates have ensued about issues of quality, reliability, and accuracy. But remember that no other encyclopedia has ever had as many editorial eyes examining the content, and in contrast to printed encyclopedias, Wikipedia provides an extremely high level of currentness.

Wikipedia contains well over 2 million articles in its English version and also has versions in more than 40 languages with more than 10,000 articles each (plus smaller versions for many other languages). It is both browsable and searchable.

HowStuffWorks

www.howstuffworks.com

HowStuffWorks is an example of a specialized but broad-reaching encyclopedia with articles on, indeed, how stuff works. Content is organized into channels for autos, science, health, entertainment, computers, electronics, home, money, and people, each with numerous subcategories. Find what you are looking for by browsing the channels or by using the search box and exploring subjects ranging from how solar cells work to how brainwashing works to how pop-up turkey timers work.

DICTIONARIES

yourDictionary.com

www.yourdictionary.com

yourDictionary.com is a resource guide that provides links to more than 2,500 dictionaries and grammar for more than 300 languages, as well as a variety of other language-related resources. It includes multilingual dictionaries and specialized subject dictionaries, including technical and scientific dictionaries. The quality and extensiveness of the dictionaries varies, but for most languages you will have a choice among a number of dictionaries. When you consider that few libraries in the world have as many language dictionaries on their shelves as this site brings to your fingertips, you can better understand the potential of the Web as a reference resource.

Dictionaries—Selected Examples

In addition to taking advantage of yourDictionary.com, it may be worth-while to bookmark one dictionary for each language that you are most likely to use. Following are some recommendations.

Merriam-Webster Online

www.m-w.com

This is a full-featured English dictionary with pronunciation (with audio), part of speech, etymology, and a thesaurus (Figure 7.2). Give the word games a try as well. An unabridged version with an atlas and other tools is available for a subscription fee.

Figure 7.2

Definition from Merriam-Webster Online

Diccionarios.com

www.diccionarios.com

This general Spanish dictionary includes translations between Spanish and Catalan, English, French, German, Italian, and Portuguese. It contains 95,000 entries and provides audio for pronunciations. Without a subscription, you are limited to 25 lookups.

LEO (Link Everything Online)

dict.leo.org

LEO contains more than 425,000 entries. Although it does not provide a complete dictionary entry for a term, it does provide a quick English/German and German/English lookup. You will also find audio pronunciations and a display of usage and idiomatic expression examples, with links to such things as declension tables.

COMBINED REFERENCE TOOLS AND ALMANACS

Answers.com

answers.com

Go to Answers.com to get very quickly and simply on one page: dictionary definitions, encyclopedia articles, maps, local time, a currency converter, statistics, etc. These come from more than 60 reference tools, including multiple general encyclopedias, specialized encyclopedias, dictionaries, a thesaurus, glossaries, study guides, a company directory, a recipe collection, a cartoon collection, news sources, and an extensive collection of Answers.com proprietary information. The downloadable 1-Click Answers program lets you do an ALT-Click on any word on your screen (for Windows or Mac OS-X) and go directly to the Answers.com page for that word.

InfoPlease

www.infoplease.com

No brief description can substitute spending time exploring this site, which is much more than just an almanac. Explore each of the main sections: Daily Almanac, World & News, United States, History & Government, Biography, Sports, Arts & Entertainment, Business, Society & Culture, and Health & Science, and Homework Center. The site contains the Information Please almanacs, an encyclopedia (*Columbia Encyclopedia*, sixth edition), InfoPlease Dictionary (125,000 entries), InfoPlease Atlas, biographies (30,000 of them), and more. Lots of little gems can be found, such as the (greatly abridged) extracts from the Encyclopedia of Associations, chronologies, statistics, calendars, country profiles, and so on. For non-U.S. users, the

World link will move you away from the U.S. orientation of the home page. One of the many interesting features is the Cite link, which shows you how to cite the item being viewed. When using the main search box, the search is performed automatically on all of the almanacs, the encyclopedia, and the dictionary. Terms you enter are ORed, but items with all of your terms (AND) will be listed first. Quotation marks can be used to search phrases. By using the pull-down window near the search box, you can limit your search to specific almanacs, biographies, the dictionary, or the encyclopedia.

A9.com

a9.com

A9.com, a partnership between Amazon and a variety of other information sources, provides a site where you can search a number of sources at one time and have the results appear side by side (in very skinny windows if you selected several sources). You can select as many sources (databases) as you wish using checkboxes from a list that includes: Windows Live (Web search), Books (Amazon, of course), IceRocket Blog Search, People (from ZoomInfo Search), News (from MSN News Search), Wikipedia, Yellow Pages (from multiple sources), Reference (from Answers.com), Movies (from the Internet Movie Database), and many others (from a list of more than 300 sources). You can search in one or more of the databases to begin with, then check additional boxes and those will be added. A Near box lets you specify a location for those searches where locality is relevant. If you sign in, you also have a record of your search history, a diary to store notes, and a bookmarks option.

ADDRESSES AND PHONE NUMBERS

There are many places to go on the Web for phone numbers and addresses worldwide. For a specific country, start by identifying the available directories by using a resource guide such as Wayp International White and Yellow Pages, but don't expect 100 percent success (or even 70 percent) in any of the directories. Some of the directories may be incomplete or a bit dated; depending on the country and the Web site, some of the yellow pages are Internet-only (without an equivalent printed version) and may be fairly limited. However, some are quite extensive. Searchability and extensiveness of the white pages listed here also vary considerably. But if you ordinarily use telephone directory assistance, these sites will allow you to find many people a lot easier and a lot less expensively. For U.S. phone numbers, Google (google.com) may be your best bet. When searching, remember that names may be listed in a variety of ways, such as with first initial, instead of the full first name.

Infobel

www.infobel.com

Infobel provides access to phone directories for about 200 countries and contains links to white pages, yellow pages, business directories, and e-mail directories. Which of these are available depends upon the country.

Wayp International White and Yellow Pages

www.wayp.com

Wayp is a resource guide for white and yellow pages directories, arranged by continent and country. Click on the name of a continent to see which directories are available for each country.

Yahoo! People Search

people.yahoo.com

For finding addresses, phone numbers, e-mail addresses, and more, Yahoo!'s People Search covers U.S. numbers and addresses as well as provides a reverse phone number search and an e-mail address search that works reasonably well. For non-U.S. numbers and addresses, use the relevant country-specific Yahoo! site and look on the main page there for links to phone directories.

AnyWho

www.anywho.com

AnyWho has U.S. yellow pages and white pages from AT&T, plus a few links to international directories (under the International link). Links are provided for maps, area codes, and toll-free numbers. AnyWho also offers a reverse phone lookup. If you have a phone number and don't know the name of the person, click the Reverse Lookup link, enter the number, and you will probably get the owner's name.

Superpages.com

superpages.com

Though it covers just the U.S., Superpages.com provides not only a lookup of people and businesses, but links to maps and driving directions, and both a reverse phone lookup and a reverse address lookup. It also offers a ZIP code and area code search and a My Directory option where you can save phone numbers and addresses you have located.

QUOTATIONS

The Quotations Page

www.quotationspage.com

This is a resource guide with a searchable database of more than 24,000 quotations from more than 2,700 authors. You can either search or use the subject directory, and you will also find links to other sites for various kinds of quotes: famous, humorous, scientific, and others. The Quotations Page is a good source if you are preparing a talk, an article, or a paper. Quote something from Lucius Accius, and people may think you have actually read his works.

Bartleby.com

www.bartleby.com

Bartleby.com also belongs in the category of "just plain amazing" sites (Figure 7.3). Chief among its quotation sources are *Bartlett's Familiar Quotations* (1919 edition), *Columbia Quotations*, and *Simpson's Quotations*, but it also contains a wonderful collection of other quote sources, handbooks, anthologies, collected works of famous authors (including Shakespeare), and other reference tools. The content is primarily humanities, but Bartleby even throws in some science. The contents of all of these resources can be searched together, or you can use the pull-down windows from the main page or on the Reference, Verse, Fiction, or Nonfiction tabs to individually search more than 200 full-text works. The following list is just a selection of what is available at Bartleby.com:

> *Columbia World of Quotations*, 1996
> *Simpson's Contemporary Quotations*, 1988
> *Oxford Book of English Verse*, 1919
> *Yale Book of English Verse*, 1919
> *Columbia Encyclopedia*, sixth edition, 2001
> *Columbia Gazetteer of North America*, 2000
> *The World Factbook*, 2003

Figure 7.3

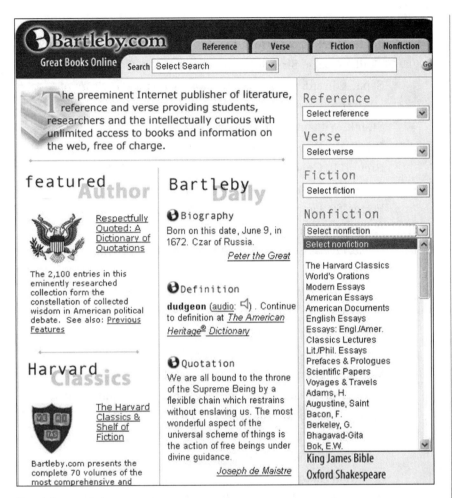

Bartleby.com's home page

American Heritage Dictionary of the English Language, fourth edition, 2000

Roget's II: The New Thesaurus, third edition, 1995

Roget's International Thesaurus of English Words and Phrases, 1922

Bartlett, John, Familiar Quotations, 10th edition, 1919

The Columbia World of Quotations, 1996

Simpson's Contemporary Quotations, 1988 ("The most notable quotations since 1950")

American Heritage® Book of English Usage, 1996

The Columbia Guide to Standard American English, 1993

Fowler, H. W., *The King's English*, second edition, 1908

Quiller-Couch, Sir Arthur, *On the Art of Writing*, 1916 and 1920

Quiller-Couch, Sir Arthur, *On the Art of Reading*, 1920

Sapir, Edward, *Language: An Introduction to the Study of Speech*, 1921

Strunk, William, Jr., *The Elements of Style*, 1918

The Bible, King James Version, 1999

Brewer, E. Cobham, *Dictionary of Phrase and Fable*, 1898

Bulfinch, Thomas, *The Age of Fable*, 1913

Frazer, Sir James George, *The Golden Bough: A Study in Magic and Religion*, abridged edition, 1922

Cambridge History of English & American Literature (18 vols.), 1907–1921

Eliot, Charles W., ed., *The Harvard Classics and Harvard Classics Shelf of Fiction* (70 volumes), 1909–1917

Eliot, T. S., *The Sacred Wood*, 1920

Shakespeare, William, *The Oxford Shakespeare*, 1914

Van Doren, Carl, *The American Novel*, 1921

Gray, Henry, *Anatomy of the Human Body*, 20th edition, 1918

Farmer, Fannie Merritt, *The Boston Cooking-School Cook Book*, 1918

Post, Emily, *Etiquette*, 1922

Inaugural Addresses of the Presidents of the United States, 1989

Robert, Henry M., *Robert's Rules of Order Revised*, 1915

FOREIGN EXCHANGE RATES/CURRENCY CONVERTERS

If you travel internationally, have family or friends living in other countries, or purchase items outside the U.S., you may frequently need to know the U.S. dollar equivalent of a certain foreign currency. There are many sites on the Web that do these calculations. Yahoo! has one of the best.

Yahoo! Finance—Currency Converter

finance.yahoo.com/currency

You have to look fairly closely on Yahoo!'s Finance page to find the link to the currency converter, but if you bookmark this site, you will discover that

TIP:

If a quotation sounds like a famous quotation, try Bartleby.com first. If you don't find it there, try a search engine and search for the quote as a phrase. Bartleby.com has the advantage of greater authority, while the search engines have wider reach and more current material.

it provides a convenient table for some major currencies and a conversion calculator that handles more than 150 currencies. In the chart, if you click on the name of the currency, you will get a graph showing fluctuations.

WEATHER

Both for local weather and for travel planning, a good weather site is essential. A good option is your own personalized portal, such as My Yahoo! or My Netscape, that automatically supplies the weather forecast for the cities you specify. If you use a news site as your start page, look there to see if you can select weather for specific cities. If you want a weather-only site, try Weather Underground.

Weather Underground
wunderground.com

Click on the appropriate region of the U.S. map or the world map to get weather for a particular location. You can also choose temperature to appear in either Fahrenheit or Celsius (or both), and the site provides links for what seems like an endless collection of weather-related data and maps. One of the advantages of this site over other weather sites is that you can personalize it by choosing which map (U.S., Europe, etc.) will be shown automatically, and you can also choose which cities to be shown (worldwide).

MAPS

Perry-Castañeda Library Map Collection
www.lib.utexas.edu/maps

The Perry-Castañeda Library Map Collection is a tremendous collection of maps plus links to gazetteers and so forth (Figure 7.4). Most of the more than 5,000 maps on this site are public domain, and no permission is required to copy or distribute them. The CIA actually produces a large portion of the maps. The site also has a fascinating collection of historical maps. Beyond the maps on the site, there are links that lead to thousands and thousands of maps found on other sites. Take time to read the FAQ, especially for the useful tips on printing the maps. The General Libraries at the University of Texas should be thanked profusely for providing this resource.

Figure 7.4

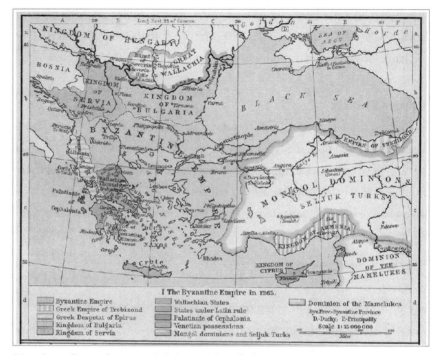

Map from Perry Castañeda Library Map Collection

David Rumsey Historical Map Collection

www.davidrumsey.com

This collection contains more than 13,000 high-resolution maps online. It focuses on rare 18th- and 19th-century North and South America maps, but it also includes historical maps of other continents. The various viewers provided on the site make it easy to navigate and examine the map detail.

GAZETTEERS

Global Gazetteer

www.fallingrain.com/world/

This gazetteer provides a directory of more than 2.8 million cities and towns in more than 180 countries. Locate the place of interest by first browsing by country, then by region (state, provinces, etc.), and then alphabetically. Each place has a satellite or topographic image, latitude and longitude, elevation, population, weather data, nearby cities and towns, nearby airports, and more. Data comes from the U.S. government's National Geospatial-Intelligence Agency and other sources. (Global Gazetteer's population estimates are questionable, however. My hometown's real population of about 300 is listed as almost 3,000.)

World Gazetteer

www.world-gazetteer.com

Latitude, longitude, current population, size rankings, and other statistics are available at the World Gazetteer site for countries, administrative divisions, cities, and towns. The pronunciation table it provides for dozens of languages will be useful not just here but for other applications.

ZIP CODES

U.S. Postal Service ZIP Code Lookup

www.usps.com/zip4

If you have the street address, the U.S. Postal Service site can provide the nine-digit ZIP code, while the Search by City tab provides a list of ZIP Codes associated with a particular city. You can also find the ZIP code for a company and all places in a particular ZIP code.

STOCK QUOTES

As with many other frequently asked reference questions, numerous places on the Web can help you find stock quotes. For the searcher who needs stock quotes frequently, it will be worthwhile to investigate several sites and determine which one is the best for you by looking at ease of use, clarity of presentation, detail provided, personalized portfolio features, types of charts and graphs available, and presence of associated news stories. As with weather information, consider using a personalized portal, such as My Yahoo! or My MSN, that can integrate selected stock information and a personalized portfolio into your start page. Remember that these free quotes are typically delayed by 20 minutes. If you use a major brokerage house or an online trading service, look at their sites. You may qualify to sign in as a client and receive real-time data and order capabilities. CNN is one example of the many places for free stock information online.

CNNMoney

money.cnn.com

CNN's site is very rich, packed with detailed stock quotes, financial news, company backgrounds, a currency converter, e-mail newsletters, financial tools, and other kinds of market-related information. You can set up and track your own portfolios for free. Streaming real-time data is available for a subscription fee.

STATISTICS

Although not every statistic you might want will be available on the Internet, finding statistics via the Web makes locating a needed statistic amazingly easier than just a few years ago. The expanse of statistical information is immense, as is the amount that can be said about finding statistics on the Internet. A few very basic hints and resources are provided here. For more detail, there are excellent books on the topic. For help in finding business statistics, refer to Paula Berinstein's book, *Business Statistics on the Web: Find Them Fast—At Little or No Cost* (CyberAge Books, 2003).

Because the topic of statistics is so broad, you are often best off starting with one of the numerous resource guides. Other than resource guides, only a handful of specific sources for the most commonly sought statistics are given here.

Keep the following hints in mind:

- There are three main ways of finding statistics on the Internet:
  1. Go to a site you think may contain the statistic and search or browse. For example, try the relevant governmental department (e.g., Department of Agriculture for agricultural statistics). Think about what agency or other organization would have an interest in collecting the data you are trying to find.
  2. Go to a collection of links to statistics sites (such as those listed later).
  3. Use a general Web search engine such as Yahoo! or Google. Far more statistical material is indexed by search engines now than was the case a few years ago, especially because of the indexing of PDF files, Excel spreadsheets, and other document types. A search strategy can often be very straightforward. For

collections of statistics in a particular area, try a search such as health statistics. For more specific statistics, try a combination of one or two subject terms plus the place and perhaps the year (for example, *avalanche fatalities norway 2002*).

- Good news: There is plenty of redundancy of identification and access; in other words, there are many routes online to the same statistic.

- When you find a statistics site you might use again, *bookmark it*. To make it easier to use bookmarks, create folders to organize similar types of sites.

- On statistics sites, take advantage of site search boxes and site maps.

- Watch for terminology. Unless you are familiar with the topic, the terminology may not be obvious. The term "housing starts" may not be what you think to look for immediately when searching for statistics on the number of new homes being built.

Statistical Resources on the Web—Comprehensive Subjects
www.lib.umich.edu/govdocs/stcomp.html

This is one of many excellent specialized directories maintained by the University of Michigan Documents Center, and is one of the best starting places for finding statistics collections.

SOSIG—Statistics and Data
www.sosig.ac.uk/statistics

Though the main theme of the SOSIG (Social Science Information Gateway) site is social sciences, the collection of links in its Statistics and Data section covers more diverse areas, such as health and finance.

U.S. Statistics

USA Statistics in Brief
www.census.gov/compendia/statab/brief.html

This site contains selected tables from the venerable *Statistical Abstract of the United States*, including summary tables for a broad range of subjects plus basic state population data (Figure 7.5). The full *Statistical Abstract of*

Figure 7.5

U.S. Census Bureau

USA Statistics in Brief--Population by Sex, Age, and Region

POPULATION	2000	2001	2002	2003	2004
Resident population (1,000)	281,425	285,102	287,941	290,789	293,655
Male (1,000)	138,056	140,013	141,519	143,024	144,537
Female (1,000)	143,368	145,089	146,422	147,765	149,118
Under 5 years old (1,000)	19,185	19,361	19,548	19,791	20,071
5 to 17 years old (1,000)	53,122	53,250	53,316	53,259	53,207
18 to 44 years old (1,000)	112,183	112,755	112,941	113,161	113,386
45 to 64 years old (1,000)	61,947	64,408	66,551	68,635	70,698
65 years old and over (1,000)	34,986	35,328	35,585	35,943	36,294
Northeast (1,000)	53,595	53,937	54,187	54,426	54,571
Midwest (1,000)	64,395	64,819	65,110	65,429	65,730
South (1,000)	100,236	101,838	103,157	104,491	105,945
West (1,000)	63,199	64,508	65,487	66,442	67,409
Percent of population--	**2000**	**2001**	**2002**	**2003**	**2004**
Male (percent)	49.1	49.1	49.1	49.2	49.2
Female (percent)	50.9	50.9	50.9	50.8	50.8
Under 5 years old (percent)	6.8	6.8	6.8	6.8	6.8
5 to 17 years old (percent)	18.9	18.7	18.5	18.3	18.1
18 to 44 years old (percent)	39.9	39.5	39.2	38.9	38.6
45 to 64 years old (percent)	22.0	22.6	23.1	23.6	24.1

USA Statistics in Brief

the United States is available at www.census.gov/prod/www/statistical-abstract.html.

FedStats

www.fedstats.gov

FedStats contains links to statistics produced by more than 100 U.S. Federal agencies. You can browse or use the search feature to search across agencies.

BOOKS

Most book searches on the Internet fall into one of two categories: (1) finding information *about* books—in other words, what books are available on a particular topic or by a particular author—and verifying bibliographic information, or (2) trying to locate the entire book online. Unless the book was published close to a century ago, you shouldn't expect to get the complete book in full text online. Nevertheless, thousands of books are available in full text and the number is growing rapidly. If the book is in English and is by a famous pre-20th-century author, you have a pretty good chance of finding the full text online.

Finding Information *About* Books— Bookstores

Keep in mind that the large online book vendors' sites are not just good for buying books, but also for identifying books currently in print on any topic, or out of print but still available for sale by used- or rare-book dealers.

Amazon
www.amazon.com

Amazon lists millions of book titles for sale with good discounts. The site is searchable by author, title, subject, ISBN, or publication date, and it is browsable by subject. Click on Books, then on Advanced Search, for these search options. Amazon now includes millions of used, rare, and out-of-print books from hundreds of booksellers that were previously available at bibliofind.com. Take advantage of the book categories on the left of the book search page. As you are browsing, look for books labeled with Amazon's Search Inside the Book feature, which provides images of selected parts of the book, including the covers, the table of contents, sample pages, the index, and more.

Barnes & Noble
www.barnesandnoble.com

Competing nose-to-nose with Amazon, Barnes & Noble also provides access to millions of books (and other merchandise). The search box on its home page lets you search by author, title, or subject. Click the Search button and then More Search Options for a larger selection of searchable fields. It also has a collection of millions of out-of-print, used, and rare books from dealers around the world (click on the Used & Out-of-Print tab).

Finding Information *About* Books— Bibliographic Databases

To find what books have been published at any time on any topic, go to the online catalog of one of the major national libraries. For English materials (although, of course, they are not limited to English materials), you might start with either The British Library or the U.S. Library of Congress.

Library of Congress Online Catalog
catalog.loc.gov

The Library of Congress online catalog includes 12 million records for books, serials, computer files, manuscripts, maps, music, and audio/visual materials (Figure 7.6). The Basic Search option searches by title, author, subject, call number, and keywords, and by LCCN, ISSN, or ISBN. Guided Search limits searches to date of publication, language, type of material (e.g., book, serial, music), location of the collection within the Library of Congress, place of publication, and 17 other fields. The OR, AND, and NOT options can be used by means of the pull-down windows and radio buttons. You can also truncate by using a question mark at the end of the word.

Figure 7.6

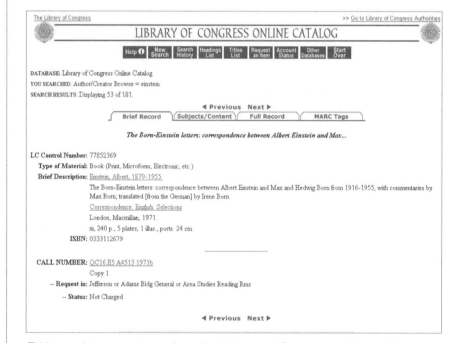

Bibliographic record page from the Library of Congress online catalog

The British Library Integrated Catalogue
blpc.bl.uk

This site provides not just a search of 12 million items in the British Library Public Catalogue, but also lets you order photocopies or a fax, or request loans. The main search (Integrated Catalogue) covers books, cartographic materials, newspapers, printed music, etc., and links are provided to the online catalogs for other materials—British Library Direct (to order),

Manuscripts, Sound Archive, Images Online (to find and purchase), and Collect Britain (maps, prints, and photographs on British history). The main search allows searching by words or phrases (using AND, OR, NOT), or by author, title, publication year, publisher, and subject. An advanced search provides even additional options.

Google Book Search
books.google.com

Google Book Search is a search of a collection of both new and old books, made possible due to Google's arrangements with publishers and several major libraries. For books under copyright, you can see actual pages of the book if the publisher has given permission, although you will need to log in to your Google account in some cases. For books that are out of copyright, you can see the Full Book View with all pages of the book. You can search using the same Boolean expressions as with regular Google (AND is implied, and you can use OR, and a minus sign for NOT). You can also use the following prefixes: "inauthor:", "intitle:", "inpublisher:", "date:" (e.g., *date:1960–2006*), and "isbn:". On the advanced search page, menus and boxes let you search for All books or Full View books and by title, author, publisher, publication date, and ISBN.

Your Local Library's Online Catalog

For something more local, check the online catalog of your local library. If it has a Web accessible catalog, you'll find the site for the catalog easily through a search engine, or you may find it by going to the Library of Congress Gateway to Library Catalogs (lcweb.loc.gov/z3950/gateway.html).

Full-Text Books Online

If you are trying to find a specific work online, a search engine usually works quite well. However, it may be easier to use a site that compiles a large number of such works and that will usually enable you to browse by title or author. Bartleby.com provides more than 200 full-text books including a number of useful reference works. But for more than 20,000 available books, consult Project Gutenberg, and for more than 30,000 titles, look at The Online Books Page. The vast majority of the works in these collections are no longer under copyright; with a few exceptions, they are all from before the

1920s. (Unfortunately, the increased availability of 20th-century texts threatens to be slowed by attempts by both the EU and the U.S. Congress to extend copyright virtually into perpetuity.) The sites discussed here are definitely sites to which the word "amazing" must be applied. Whether you want to find Cicero or the Bobbsey Twins, these are good places to start.

The Online Books Page

digital.library.upenn.edu/books

This resource guide contains links to more than 30,000 books in English. The creator and editor of the site, John Mark Ockerbloom, founded it in 1993, and he has been adding to it ever since. To be included, books must be in English and in full text, and must qualify as significant by being listed in the online catalog of a major library or be otherwise recognized. The site, which is easily searchable by title, is also browsable by author, title, subject, and serial title.

Project Gutenberg

www.gutenberg.org

Project Gutenberg, established in 1971, is designed to place online, in easily accessible format, as many public domain electronic texts (eTexts) as possible. So far, it has provided more than 20,000 texts. Although the majority of books are in English, Project Gutenberg contains (a few) books from 14 other languages. The breadth of texts available makes this an excellent research site, but also consider it a source of eTexts to read on your laptop. Because most of the books are stored in ASCII text, all are small enough to be loaded on a flash drive. You will also now find a number of books in (computer-generated) audio format.

Bartleby.com

www.bartleby.com

For a list of the books covered by Bartleby.com, see the previous section on quotations.

HISTORICAL DOCUMENTS

EuroDocs: Primary Historical Documents from Western Europe

eudocs.lib.byu.edu

A resource guide, the EuroDocs site provides links to Western European documents that are online in transcribed, facsimile, or translated form. They are first arranged by country and then chronologically. The site is now in a wiki format.

A Chronology of U.S. Historical Documents
www.law.ou.edu/hist

The Chronology of U.S. Historical Documents site contains links to more than 150 full-text documents from the pre-Colonial period to the present.

University of Virginia Hypertext Collection
xroads.virginia.edu/~HYPER/hypertex.html

The University of Virginia offers a collection on its site of classic and other texts in the area of American Studies, including books and journals.

GOVERNMENTS AND COUNTRY GUIDES

In lots of situations, information about specific countries is needed—basics such as population, names of leaders, flags, or maps, or more detailed information on economics, geography, and politics. Numerous resources provide this information, and those resources differ primarily in terms of amount of detail and categories of data covered.

Governments on the WWW
www.gksoft.com/govt

Governments on the WWW is an excellent resource guide. Arranged by continent and country, the links on this site connect you to official government sites (including individual sites for parliaments, offices, courts, and embassies), banks, multinational organizations, and political parties. Though the site is slow in updating information, most links are valid.

Foreign Government Resources on the Web
www.lib.umich.edu/govdocs/foreign.html

This resource guide provides links to government sites by country and by topic, such as constitutions, embassies, and flags. (The "Foreign" in the title of this site means "non-U.S.")

CIA World Factbook
www.odci.gov/cia/publications/factbook

This annually revised work provides easily usable and quite detailed country guides. Each country's data is arranged in the following sections: Geography, Communications, People, Transportation, Government, Military, Economy, and Transnational Issues. Also notice the Chiefs of State link on the main page. This is an extremely rich site, and even if you do not think you will use it frequently, you will find the time spent exploring it worthwhile. As an indication of how widespread the respect for this site is, the Basic Facts on Iraq section of the official site of the former Permanent Mission of Iraq to the U.N. (under Saddam Hussein) was mostly taken word-for-word from the CIA World Factbook!

U.K. Foreign & Commonwealth Office—Country Profiles
www.fco.gov.uk

To get to this section of the U.K. Foreign and Commonwealth Office site, click on the Countries & Regions link on the main page of the site. The profiles here, prepared by FCO desk officers, provide general facts and background about the country, recent history and political developments, international relations, and bilateral relations with the U.K.

U.S. Government

FirstGov.gov
firstgov.gov

FirstGov.gov is the official Internet gateway (portal) to U.S. government resources and is a good starting place for locating information from or about government agencies. The site has four main divisions: Citizens, Businesses and Nonprofits, Federal Employees, and Government-to-Government. Take advantage of the menu on the left for an alphabetic list of federal government agencies and links to state, local, and tribal government information.

GPO Access
www.gpoaccess.gov

Use this site to search the Federal Register, Code of Federal Regulations, Commerce Business Daily, Congressional Record, Government Manual, and other U.S. Government databases, either singly or together.

THOMAS: Legislative Information on the Internet
thomas.loc.gov

THOMAS has a variety of detailed and easily searchable databases with information on and related to federal legislation, including bills and resolutions, activities in Congress, the Congressional Record, schedules, calendars, committees, presidential nominations, treaties, and more. It also contains links to the Senate and House Web sites and to other government information. This is an excellent place to start a search on legislation currently in process or on a specific topic, or for tracking a particular current bill.

Open CRS

www.opencrs.com

On an ongoing basis, the Congressional Research Service (CRS) of the Library of Congress produces a collection of highly respected, nonpartisan reports on a wide variety of subjects relating to current political events and situations. Unfortunately, Congress (which, perhaps obviously from the name, controls the Library of Congress) pointedly prevents CRS from distributing the reports directly (though some members have fought hard to change this situation). To "democratize" the availability of non-confidential CRS reports, the Center for Democracy & Technology has created this Web site, which collects reports that have been released. The reports included here are only a small portion of the reports produced by CRS, but this site is a good starting place to find out, as far as currently possible, what reports have been made publicly available and to access those reports online.

U.S. State Information

Library of Congress—State and Local Government Information

www.loc.gov/rr/news/stategov/stategov.html

The Library of Congress State and Local Government directory is a resource guide with a convenient collection of links to state, county, and local government information.

U.K. Government Information

Directgov—Web Site of the U.K. Government

www.direct.gov.uk

Directgov is a searchable and browsable collection of information, news, and links to U.K. public sector information, including both central and local

TIP:

For official state sites, use the following URL "recipe":

www.state.pc.us
(pc = postal code)
Example:
www.state.md.us

government information and links. The Directories section leads to contact information for not just governmental agencies, but also charity and voluntary organizations in the U.K. For those who want to find out how all levels of government in the U.K. work and are organized, use the Guide to Government section. The Do It Online section provides easy access to how to get things done, both online and offline.

COMPANY INFORMATION

Entire books have been written on finding company information on the Internet. Anyone who searches for company information frequently will want to spend time with one of those books, and may already be familiar with the quick-reference company sites included here. For those who have only occasional need for company information or who are just getting into the area, the following sites will provide a start.

First, we should cover a few basic pointers about tools for finding company information. For company information, it helps to start by thinking about what kinds of company information you might reasonably expect to find on the Internet. You might think of three categories:

1. Information that a company *wants* you to know, such as its stature, its products or services, and any good news about the company

2. Information that a company *must* let you know, such as information required by government laws and regulations (e.g., Securities and Exchange Commission filings in the U.S. and Companies House filings in the U.K.)

3. *What others are saying* about the company

To find out what a company *wants* you to know, start with the company's home page. Depending on the company, you will probably find detailed background, products and services, company structure, press releases, and so on. To find a company's home page, you can just enter the name in any of the largest search engines. The company home page will usually be among the first few items retrieved.

To find out what a company *must* let you know, first keep in mind that this applies only to publicly held companies. Others typically do not *have* to divulge very much information publicly. For U.S. publicly held companies, SEC filings are available through several sites, but Hoover's, a major company directory that will be discussed later, makes these filings available conveniently along with other useful data about a company. For public companies in other countries, the amount of mandated information is usually much less than that required of U.S. companies, but start by looking at the CorporateInformation Web site.

For the third category of company information—*what others are saying about a company*—some items to keep on your Internet reference shelf are newsgroup resources (especially Usenet groups as available through Google Groups and other groups sources discussed in Chapter 6) and news stories (through MSNBC, CNN, and BBC). For some key news sites, see Chapter 9.

These resources, however, are basically useful for finding information about a specific company you already have in mind. Many company questions focus on "What companies are out there that match a particular set of criteria?" For example, who are some of the largest seafood packers in Maryland? What is the name of a plumber who serves my neighborhood? These questions are often answered by using directories or online yellow pages of the types listed earlier in this chapter.

Company Directories

Company directories on the Web differ in terms of:

- Number and type (public, private, U.S., non-U.S.) of companies included
- Free, paid subscription, or pay-per-view
- Searchability (name, industry location, ticker symbol, size, etc.)
- Amount of information provided about each company (usually the more companies included, the less information about each)

CorporateInformation

www.corporateinformation.com

This site, from Wright Investors' Service, provides tens of thousands of company research reports, profiles, and analyses for companies in 59 countries. For many users, the most useful and unique part may be the links to company directories and other resources arranged by country. Use the Advanced Search link and choose the country. Full company reports from Wright Investors' Service require a fee, but free snapshot reports are provided for 31,000 companies.

Hoover's

www.hoovers.com

Hoover's provides information on 43,000 U.S. and non-U.S., public and non-public companies, and more than 600 industries, including company profiles, news, lists, filings, and other data (Figure 7.7). Much of the information is free, but other information and features (building and downloading lists, etc.) are available by subscription only. The free portion is searchable by company name, ticker symbol, keyword, and executive name, and includes both U.S. and non-U.S. companies. Spend some time exploring this site to get a feel for how much information is there.

Figure 7.7

Company profile on Hoover's

ThomasNet

www.thomasnet.com

If you need to buy a manufactured product and want to find out who makes it or who can get it for you, this Web site is the place to go. This online version of the well-known print version of *Thomas Register* allows you to browse or to search by company name, product/service, or brand name. It covers 650,000 U.S. and Canadian suppliers, manufacturers, distributors, and service companies, arranged under 67,000 headings. Searches can be narrowed by location, company type, ownership, and certification. The information you find contains company profiles, contact information, and links to Web sites.

Also see the following two product directories that are discussed in Chapter 10:

Kompass

www.kompass.com

Kellysearch

www.kellysearch.com

Company Phone Numbers and Addresses

Don't forget that the company's home page will usually provide phone numbers. Also be sure to check the phone directories listed earlier in this chapter.

Associations

If you know the name of an association and need further information, usually the best place to start is with the association's home page. From the other direction, if you need to find the names of associations that relate to a particular topic, there are a couple places to consider as starting points:

1. Use a search engine and search for the subject and terms such as association society, organization:

    Example: *"solar energy" (association OR society OR organization)*
    or,
    solar (energy OR power) (association OR society OR organization)
    or, just

> *solar (association OR society OR organization)*

2. Use the directory provided by the American Society of Association Executives.

American Society of Association Executives Gateway to Associations
www.asaecenter.org/Directories/AssociationSearch.cfm

This ASAE Gateway provides links to thousands of association sites, which you can search by name, location, geographic scope, and organization type.

PROFESSIONAL DIRECTORIES

To find directories for a specific profession, try a search on the name of the profession and the word "directory." It works sometimes; sometimes it doesn't. Two of the most widely useful directories, for physicians and lawyers, are listed here.

AMA DoctorFinder
webapps.ama-assn.org/doctorfinder

This AMA (American Medical Association) site offers "information on virtually every licensed physician in the United States and its possessions including more than 690,000 doctors of medicine (MD) and doctors of osteopathy or osteopathic medicine (DO). All physician credential data have been verified for accuracy and authenticated. ..." The broader AMA site (www.ama-assn.org) also contains substantial additional resources such as patient education information, advice on dealing with doctor-patient issues, etc.

Lawyers.com
lawyers.com

Lawyers.com allows a search of law firms or attorneys in more than 170 countries by practice area, name, location, and language spoken by the attorney or firm. For maximum search power, click on the Advanced Search link. Searches on Lawyers.com use the Martindale-Hubbell database that will be familiar to any legal researcher.

LITERATURE DATABASES

As great as Internet resources are, they still cover only a tiny portion of what we think of as the world's literature. In addition to only a tiny part of

1 percent of the world's books having their full text available through the Web, the vast majority of journal articles (especially those more than a few years old) are not available on the Web in full text. But, just as even a very large library owns only a small portion of extant literature, both a library and the Internet at least provide pointers to the broader corpus.

You will find a number of bibliographic databases on the Web that let you identify at least portions of what has been published on a particular topic, by a particular author, and so on. Many of these databases are available only through subscription, but many are available free, particularly on some large government-sponsored databases. For books, you can go to major national libraries' catalogs, and for journal literature, go to databases such as MEDLINE, ERIC, and others. Depending upon the subject area and other factors, for much "scholarly research," sites such as IngentaConnect, FindArticles, and Google Scholar are not a substitute for searching the proprietary, subscription literature databases in libraries. Those databases may provide more comprehensive coverage, provide greater clarity about the extent of coverage, and are more definitively "scholarly" and more "searchable" because of better commands, structure, and indexing.

To identify bibliographic databases on the Web for a particular subject, use the resource guides (discussed in Chapter 3) for that area. A good resource guide for any subject will clearly identify important literature databases in that area. Though the site may not have been updated recently, take a look at the list of bibliographic databases found at Free Bibliographies and Bibliographic Databases on the Web. For single-site access to a broad range of scholarly journal literature, try IngentaConnect, Google Scholar, and FindArticles. Others databases, such as Scirus (www.scirus.com), CiteSeer (citeseer.ist.psu.edu), PubMed (www.ncbi.nlm.nih.gov/entrez), SMEAL search (smealsearch1.psu.edu), Infotrieve ArticleFinder (www4.infotrieve.com), and others provide such access, but to a smaller range of topics, such as science or business.

Free Bibliographies and Bibliographic Databases on the Web
www.leidenuniv.nl/ub/biv/freebase.htm

From the Universiteitsbibliotheek at the University of Leiden, this site contains links to more than 2,000 bibliographic databases and specific bibliographies.

IngentaConnect

www.ingentaconnect.com

When you search the IngentaConnect site, you have access to 30,000 publications, mainly journals (from all fields) and more than 20 million articles. These publications include trade, scientific, and technical journals with coverage going back to 1988. IngentaConnect is searchable by keyword, author, or journal title. When searching, remember that you are searching titles and article summaries, not the full text, so you may need to be a bit more imaginative in your choice of terms.

FindArticles

www.findarticles.com

With FindArticles, you have access to bibliographic records for—and a mechanism to purchase—more than 10 million articles from more than 2,000 general, academic, industry magazines and journals, some dating back to 1984. The good news is that a large portion of the collection is free. Those that are not free ("premium" publications) are available through a partnership with HighBeam Research (highbeam.com), a subscription-based journal article service. In FindArticles, you can browse by subject area, by journal titles, and by content of issues of specific journals. You can search on the main page by keyword and limit your search to only free articles or to any of the nine main categories. Search terms are automatically ANDed, and the main search covers titles, authors, and text. Using the advanced search page, you can narrow your search specifically by author, title, or body, specific publications, or date ranges, and cover all articles or only the free ones.

Google Scholar

scholar.google.com

Google Scholar is a collection of "peer-reviewed papers, theses, books, preprints, abstracts and technical reports," made available by agreements with publishers, associations, universities, and others. For searching, you can take advantage of Google's "OR" capability, plus the "intitle:", "allintitle:", "site:", and "author:" prefixes. An advanced search page lets you use simple Boolean and search by author, publication (i.e., journal), or date (or date range), and also narrow your search to one or more of seven broad subject areas. Clicking on the title will take you to an abstract of the article, and in some cases, the full article. In addition to basic bibliographic information, you may find a link to the library (or other database) from which Google indexed the item, and a link (for some books) that lets you find the book in a local library. Other links may lead you to articles that cite the article you retrieved and to sites where you may purchase the articles

Yahoo! Subscriptions Search

search.yahoo.com/search/options

Yahoo!'s Subscriptions Search, available on Yahoo!'s advanced search page, provides a search of several commercial databases that cover journal articles. See Chapter 5 for more details.

COLLEGES AND UNIVERSITIES

Peterson's

petersons.com

The Peterson's site offers a broad range of information for those looking for a school. From the main page, choose the level of education in which you are interested, and from there, you can find categories such as Find a School, Pay for School, etc. In the Find a School section, you can successively narrow your search for schools by a broad range of criteria, such as location, major, tuition, size, GPA, type of college (e.g., four-year institution), religion, and dozens of other, more specific, criteria. If you have a specific school in mind, you can also search by the name of the school. You can sort results, create lists of schools in which you are interested, export results to a spreadsheet, and much more.

College Board

www.collegeboard.com

The College Board site provides a variety of resources relating to the Scholastic Aptitude Tests (SATs) and other tests, finding a college, and financing an education. A tremendous amount of practical advice is included, on such things as writing essays for college applications, transitioning to college, etc. It contains information on 3,600 schools and presents a useful side-by-side comparison option. With the College MatchMaker section, you can narrow your search by dozens of criteria, create a list of your selections, and easily sort out your options.

TRAVEL

Travel is one area where you definitely need to know and use more than one Web site. Especially for travel reservation sites, don't count on any one always providing either the lowest cost flight or the itinerary that best suits your needs. On the other hand, loyalty to one site, and consequent heavier usage of that site, may get you special deals and discounts. Even if you don't book your own flights, these sites can be useful before you call your travel agent. If you use these sites to select your flight first, you have more time to consider your itinerary than you would on the phone with the travel agent.

When using the Web for travel planning, don't think only of reservation sites. Take advantage of travel guides, discussion groups, and thousands of other sites that provide information on your destination, how to get there, and what to do and how to get around while you are there. (For a broader sampling of what is available, look at the companion site for the author's book on using the Internet for travel, *The Traveler's Web*, at www.extremesearcher.com/travel).

Destination Guides

Fodor's
www.fodors.com

Fodor's, the print publisher, has a reputation for publishing what many travelers consider to be the best travel guides out there. Its Web site is an extremely rich resource with a useful collection of travel information, from what to see in a particular city to tipping practices worldwide.

Lonely Planet
www.lonelyplanet.com

The Lonely Planet site is a down-to-earth online guide to world travel from another well-known publisher of travel guides. For an excellent travelers' discussion group, try the Thorn Tree Forum on this site.

Reservation Sites

Travelocity
travelocity.com

As with most other travel reservation sites, Travelocity provides not just airfare, but rail fares, car rentals, hotel reservations, cruises, and more. It also provides travel guides and advice. On Travelocity, read the tips for identifying lowest fares.

Expedia

expedia.com

Expedia sometimes has lower prices than Travelocity (and vice versa). Some users will prefer the way in which Expedia lets them search for fares and itineraries, and the way in which the results are presented.

Orbitz

orbitz.com

The third of the "big three" reservation sites, Orbitz provides differences in navigation and display of results. Compare the three to see which best suits your needs, but if you want the lowest price and best itinerary, check all three. On this and other travel reservation sites, check out the deals and the savings available by booking combinations of travel, hotels, and car rentals.

FILM

Internet Movie Database (IMDb)

www.imdb.com

Whether you are looking for current show times or a list of all of the movies in which Kevin McCarthy appeared, IMDb is the place to go. It is not just a database of movies, but a movie portal with many resources, including commentary, movie and TV news, new releases, etc.

REFERENCE RESOURCE GUIDES

The sites discussed in this chapter only scratch the surface in terms of what is available. For other reference-shelf sites, consult the general reference directories (resource guides) discussed in Chapter 3. For a good printed reference tool covering the kinds of sites mentioned in this chapter, see *The Web Library: Building a World Class Personal Library with Free Web Resources* by Nicholas G. Tomaiuolo (CyberAge Books, 2004).

TIP:

To find time-tables, use a search engine and search for something such as *timetable prague vienna rail.*

CHAPTER 8

SIGHT AND SOUNDS:
FINDING IMAGES, AUDIO, AND VIDEO

"Amazing" is about the only word that adequately describes the collection of multimedia (images, audio, and video) resources on the Web. Images are not only available, but they are searchable—not as searchable as we would like, but still searchable. Whether you need a photo of the person you are about to meet, or of the streets of a specific town in a remote country, or of an obscure microorganism, you have a pretty good chance of finding it on the Web. Audio and video files can be tremendously useful, whether you are using open sources for military intelligence purposes or for a discussion of Winston Churchill's "Finest Hour" speech in a history classroom. This chapter summarizes what is available, provides some basic background and terminology for understanding and using these resources, points to the tools for finding what you need, and offers some techniques to do so most effectively.

THE COPYRIGHT ISSUE

Prior to using—or discussing—any of the resources here, the overarching issue of copyright must be considered. Although most people using the Internet for research, teaching, and other professional applications already know the issue and its implications, the importance of the copyright issue should be emphasized. The good news is that hundreds of millions of images, audio, and video files can be found easily on the Web. The bad news is that you may not be able to use those images as you might like. Whenever using images (and any other original works) in any way, remember first of all that the vast majority of images on the Web belong to someone: They are copyrighted. Some people (even some who should know better) still have the attitude that "I found it on the Internet, so I can use it any way I want." As most readers of this book know, that's simply not so. This does not mean that you

189

cannot use these types of files in a variety of ways, but it does mean that you must use them within "Fair Use" and other provisions of copyright law.

If you have found an image of interest and want to use it in a report, on your own Web page, or for other purposes, you cannot legitimately do so without getting the permission of the copyright owner in most cases. First, look on the site where you found the image. You may be lucky and find a copyright statement that specifies when, where, and how you may use images from that site. (For a good example of such a statement, look at the NASA statement at www.nasa.gov/audience/formedia/features/MP_Photo_Guide lines.html, but don't expect most sites to have such a clear statement with such minimal conditions.) For people in companies, universities, school systems, and other organizations, your organization may have published copyright guidelines for your use. For the layperson who is trying to understand and interpret the actual laws, it will probably be more of a challenge than your time allows. For a very basic understanding of copyright issues, look at the article on copyright in the Patents, Copyright & Art section of Nolo (www.nolo.com).

IMAGES
Some Technical Background

To view images on your screen, no technical knowledge is required. If, however, you plan to save images and use them ("remember copyright") on a Web page, or print the image you save, a few tips are in order.

Digital Image File Types

Web browsers can typically display only three image file formats: Joint Photographic Experts Group format (JPEG or JPG file extensions), Graphics Interchange Format (GIF file extension), or Portable Network Graphics format (PNG). The latter format is now relatively rare. Some search engines will allow you to narrow down your image search by these file types, but it is unlikely that you will to need to do so.

Image Size

You will usually see image size referred to in pixels ("picture elements"), which are the space-related elements that make up a digital image. You can think of them as the "atomic" level of an image—the smallest unit of a digital image. An Internet user can think of a typical monitor (with typical settings) as displaying about 72 or 96 pixels per inch (ppi). Depending on a number of factors, you can expect an image that has dimensions of 140 pixels by 140 pixels to take up about a 2-inch-square on a typical screen.

Capturing Images

An image file can be saved to your disk by doing the following:

1. Hold your cursor over the image you wish to capture.
2. Click the right mouse button.
3. From the menu that pops up, choose Save Image As (in Firefox) or Save Picture As (in Internet Explorer).
4. Select the folder where you want to save the image and rename the file if you want. Do not assign or change a file extension. It is important that the original file extension (.gif, .jpg, .jpeg, or .png) be retained.

Editing Images

A discussion of image editing is beyond the scope of this book. However, since the object of an image search is often to get a print copy of the image, searchers may need to do some minor editing of what they find. Operations such as cropping (trimming) and resizing are fairly common and easy to do. Anyone who has purchased a scanner or digital camera probably received software that offers these functions. Image-editing programs are often packaged with scanners and digital cameras, and almost any photo-editing software will provide the basics. Windows operating systems also often include an image-editing program such as Imaging for Windows or Paint. But some of these, surprisingly or not, may not offer some of the basic operations you might want to use. For the Internet user who wants more high-powered image editing, two of the better-known choices are PaintShop Pro and PhotoShop. (PhotoShop Elements, a reasonably priced option, comes close to offering a surprising number of options similar to PhotoShop.) Some substantial programs can be downloaded for free. The main problem with photo editing is that it quickly becomes addictive. When you have decided on a program to use, do a quick search in one of the search engines for the program "AND" the term "tutorial." There are dozens of good photo-editing tutorials out there.

Types of Image Collections on the Web

The Web offers many image collections. Some are collections of images found on various pages throughout the Web, such as the image collections found on Google and Yahoo!. Some are specialized by topic and represent the collections of specific organizations, such as the Australian National Botanic Gardens' National Plant Photographic Index (www.anbg.gov.au/anbg/photo-collection). Others are specialized by topic and represent the holdings of multiple institutions or sites, such as The Digital Scriptorium of … Medieval and Renaissance Manuscripts (sunsite.berkeley.edu/Scriptorium). Some collections are arranged by format or application, such as the numerous clip art collections. Another category, especially important for those who need good images that they can safely (legally) re-use in publications or elsewhere, is the commercial collection, such as Corbis (corbis.com).

Searchability of Images

Though there are now more than a billion images that can be searched on the Web, the search capabilities are fairly limited and rather approximate. This is primarily because the amount and quality of indexing that can currently be done by search programs is quite limited. Technologies are in development that will be able to see a picture of a tree, and without any text already attached to the image, be able to tell that the tree is a tree, maybe even to identify it as a spruce and maybe as a blue spruce. Implementation of this on a large scale for Web applications may take a while. Except for relatively small collections, Web search engines currently do not have much to work with when identifying and indexing what a picture is showing. In most cases, the most that can be used for indexing is the name of the image file (e.g., sprucetree.jpg), the ALT tag that may be included, a caption if the image is in a table, and text that is near the photo. Indexing based on text near a photo becomes somewhat of a gamble and can account for many of the false hits that may occur in image search results. In some cases, image collections may provide an opportunity for users to add "tags" to images that become part of the indexing, but that approach also carries with it a number of problems. That said, with a little imagination and a little patience and tolerance, the searcher can usually find a useful image quickly and easily using the collections and search techniques now available.

TIP:

When searching for images, start by limiting your query to one or two words. Most images only have very few words of indexing associated with them. If you search for *Boeing 747*, you will get substantially fewer good pictures of the plane than if you searched for just *747*.

Directories of Image Resources on the Internet

As with almost any other type of Internet content, there are specialized directories (resource guides) that offer easy identification of image collections. The three that follow are well-known and useful examples that can direct you to sites that contain collections of images. For all three of these sites, the directory is on one long page, so if you want to find a specific topic quickly, you may want to take advantage of your browser's Find in This Page option under the Edit menu.

Finding Images Online—Directory of Web Image Sites

www.berinsteinresearch.com/fiolinks.htm

This site is created by Paula Berinstein, author of *Finding Images Online* (CyberAge Books, 1996). The site contains more than 1,000 links to collections of images, arranged alphabetically by category.

Digital Librarian: A Librarian's Choice of the Best of the Web—Images

www.digital-librarian.com/images.html

Here you will find more than 800 well-annotated links to image collections. For maps, check the companion Maps and Geography collection (www.digital-librarian.com/maps.html). Be aware that the search box on the page is not a search of the page, but a search of Amazon.

BUBL LINK—Image Collections

bubl.ac.uk/link/types/images.htm

BUBL LINK has links to about 160 image collections, with good and often very extensive descriptions of each site. In addition to the obvious usefulness of these annotations, this means that using your browser's Find In This Page option can help you search effectively on the page by topic.

Search Engine Image Collections

Image collections from the major general search engines (Google, Yahoo!, Ask.com, and Windows Live) are the largest on the Web. With images from billions of Web pages covered in their Web databases, these search engines provide not only access to hundreds of millions of images but also easy searchability (given the limitations on image searching previously discussed). As with a regular Web search, use more than one engine. For any particular search, which images they retrieve will vary considerably as well as how many. Of these four engines, Yahoo! and Google typically retrieve more images than Windows Live and Ask.com. Keep in mind that the number of images retrieved does not necessarily reflect the relevance of the images to your specific search. Searchability and display of image results will also differ among these engines.

Yahoo!'s Image Search (search.yahoo.com/images)

Though Google claims its image search is the most comprehensive, benchmarking shows that Yahoo!'s image search more often than not retrieves more images. Yahoo! claims more than 1.6 billion images in its database, which contains images identified from Web pages covered in Yahoo!'s Web database and also images from Yahoo! News and Yahoo! Movies. To search, either click on the Images tab on the main Yahoo! Search page and then enter your search, or click on the Images tab after doing a Web or other search. The latter will automatically search your terms in the Images database. You can also go directly to search.yahoo.com/images. For a bit more searchability, take advantage of the Advanced Image Search link.

Image Searchability—Main Image Search Page

In the search box, you can enter one or more terms and use quotation marks for phrases. Terms are automatically ANDed. You can use the "site:" prefix to limit your results either to a specific Web site or to a top-level domain, such as gov.

> Example: *"space shuttle" site:gov*

You cannot use the minus sign to exclude a term or use an OR. To use NOT or OR, use Yahoo!'s advanced image search.

Advanced Image Search Page

Yahoo!'s advanced image search page (Figure 8.1) lets you:

- Apply simple Boolean by checking "all of these words," "any of these words," or "none of these words"
- Search for an exact phrase
- Specify image size: any size, wallpaper, large, medium, or small
- Choose coloration (any color, color only, or black and white only)

Figure 8.1

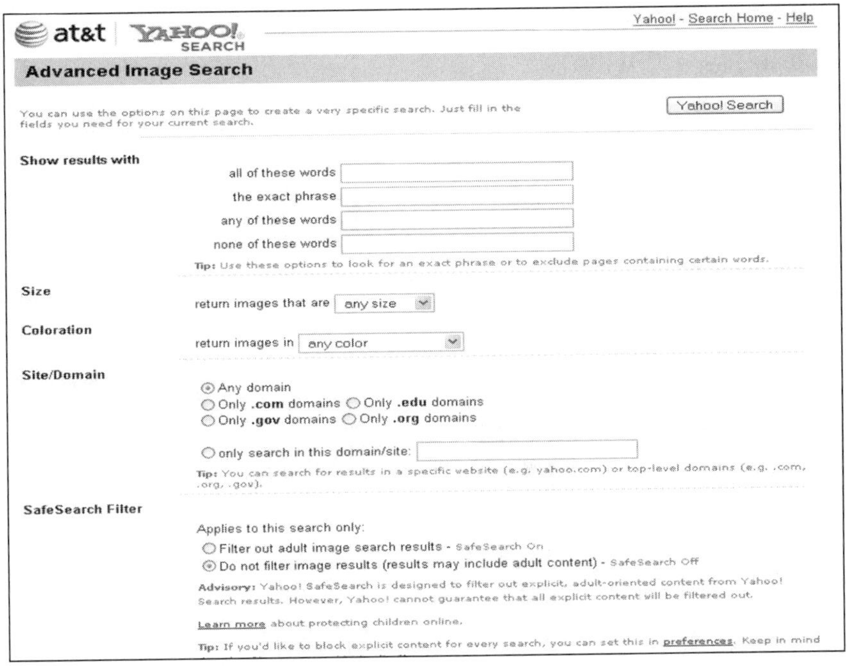

Yahoo!'s advanced image search page

- Choose site/domain (use radio buttons for .com, .edu, .gov, .org, or a specific domain you enter in a text box)
- Use a SafeSearch filter to filter out adult image results

Image Results Pages

Yahoo!'s image results pages show the number of images found and thumbnails of the first 20 images, file names, dimensions in pixels, file sizes, and the addresses of the Web pages on which they were found (Figure 8.2). Links near the top of the page let you narrow the results by size or color. To go beyond the first 20, use the links at the bottom of the results pages.

Click on one of the thumbnails to go to a split screen with the thumbnail in the top frame and the page on which the image was found in the bottom frame. In the top frame, you will also find links to view the image alone, mail it to a friend, save to My Web (if you use Yahoo!'s My Web feature), and go to the Web site. Click on the Close Yahoo! Frame link to remove the top window.

Figure 8.2

Yahoo!'s image search results page

Google's Image Search (images.google.com)

Google says that it has the Web's "most comprehensive image search," claiming more than 1.8 billion images. To get to it, either click on the Images tab on Google's main page or go directly to images.google.com. Once in Google Image Search, you can simply enter your terms in the search box, or you can click on Advanced Image Search to go to the advanced version.

Image Searchability—Main Image Search Page

On Google's main image search page, all terms are automatically ANDed. If you enter *temple esna,* you will get only those images indexed under both terms. Quotation marks can be used for phrases, and a minus sign in front of a term can be used to eliminate items indexed under that term. You can also use the OR as with a regular Google Web search. To retrieve all images indexed under the term "temple" and also under either "esna" or "khnum," search for:

> *temple esna OR khnum*

You can also use any of the prefixes used in Google's Web search. For images, the "site:" prefix will limit image retrieval to a particular Web site.

This can be used in combination with other operations such as the OR. For example, images of either a corn or maize kernel from the U.S. Department of Agriculture site are available by searching for:

corn OR maize kernel site:usda.gov

Advanced Image Search Page

Using the advanced image search page (Figure 8.3), you can:

- Use the Find Results boxes for simple Boolean ("all the words," "any of the words," or "not related to the words")
- Specify a phrase search by using "related to the exact phrase" (using quotation marks around the phrase in any of the boxes works just as well)
- Use the Size box to specify images of the following sizes: "any size," "icon sized," "small," "medium," "large," "very large," or "wallpaper sized"
- Specify either JPG or GIF formats using the Filetypes box (default is "any filetype")
- Specify "any colors," "black and white," "grayscale," or "full color" images
- Retrieve things only from a specific domain (such as gov or fda.gov)
- Use the SafeSearch option to set adult content filtering at "No Filtering," "Use Moderate Filtering" (the default), or "Use Strict Filtering" (available only in the English version of Google)

Image Results Pages

As the result of a search, Google will return a page containing thumbnail images for the first 20 images retrieved (with links at the bottom of the page for additional results). Included with each thumbnail is a snippet of the text around the word that retrieved the image, the dimensions in pixels, the size of the file (e.g., 16k), the file type (e.g., JPG), and the URL for the page on which it was found. As with Web results, image results are clustered, and only the first image (ranked by relevance) from a particular site will be displayed. If there are more matching images from that site, a "More results from ..." link will be shown.

Figure 8.3

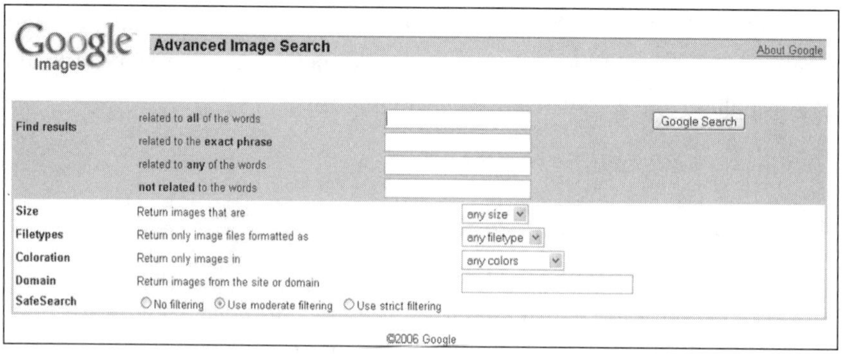

Google's advanced image search page

When you click on the image on a results page, it will take you to a split screen: in the top frame, a thumbnail with links to See Full-Size Image (to remove that frame) and go to the Web site; and in the bottom frame, the Web page where the image was found.

Other Searchable Collections

There are a number of other searchable collections that contain images from Web pages. The general Web search engines just discussed contain the largest collections by far, but you may want to examine the three directories of image resources listed earlier to identify searchable collections in specific subject areas. The following description of Picsearch highlights one of the best-known alternate Web-image search engines.

Picsearch

www.picsearch.com

Picsearch provides the image databases and search technology behind the image searches on both Ask.com and Windows Live. The terms you enter in the main search box are automatically ANDed, and you can use a minus sign to eliminate a term. But Picsearch does not allow for either phrase searching or the use of an OR. The Picsearch advanced search page lets you limit by Only Images, Only Animations, Images and Animations, Only Color, Only Black&White, Color and Black&White, and by size.

Getting Images You Can Use

If you are looking for a high-quality image for use in a publication or on a Web site and you don't want to worry about possibly violating copyright or tracking down an owner to ask permission, consider going to a commercial collection of images (stock image library) where you can buy the right to use an image. Corbis and Fotosearch are two examples of sites where you can do this. Other Web sites, such as Stock.XCHNG, provide a place where photographers display their works so others can use the images without charge. Another free option is the image collection searchable through the Creative Commons Web site.

Corbis
corbis.com

Drawing upon a range of collections—the Bettmann Collection, the Hermitage Museum, UPI, and 3,000 other collections—Corbis collects and sells a variety of photography, fine art, illustrations, etc.

Fotosearch
www.fotosearch.com

Fotosearch lets you browse, search, and view images (for free), and then purchase usage rights for more than 1.3 million images from more than 50 image publishers.

Creative Commons
creativecommons.org

Creative Commons is a nonprofit organization that provides a registry of "some rights reserved" materials, including images, audio, video, text, and teaching materials. On the Creative Commons home page, click on the Images section and then enter your term or terms in the search box, and click the box indicating the purpose for which you wish to use the images.

Stock.XCHNG
www.sxc.hu

With the SXC site, you can browse or search more than 200,000 stock photos from more than 15,000 photographers. You must be signed up to download the full-size image, but if you want to use high-quality photos for free, signing up will be worth the couple minutes it takes.

Exemplary Individual Collections

By browsing through the directories of image resources discussed earlier, users can view hundreds or perhaps thousands of sites that contain useful collections of images. The following are just two examples of specific collections that demonstrate the possibilities.

American Memory Project

memory.loc.gov

From the Library of Congress, this collection contains more than 7 million digital items from more than 100 historical collections at the Library of Congress. It contains Maps, Motion Pictures, Photos & Prints, Sound Recordings, and Written Materials (Books & Other Printed Texts, Manuscripts, Sheet Music). Even though this is a government site, most of the material on this site is protected by copyright. Use the Collection Finder section to browse by collection or topic, or use the Search page to search across collections.

WebMuseum (Paris)

www.ibiblio.org/wm (or more specifically, www.ibiblio.org/wm/paint)

This impressive collection of artwork is a collaborative project headed by Nicolas Pioch. It is searchable by artist (about 200 of them) and by theme/period (from Gothic to the 20th century, plus Japanese art from all periods).

Web Sites for Storing and Sharing Your Own Photos

A number of Web sites let you store your own photos online for free and share them with friends, or you can use the site as a place to keep your photo files. Flickr is the best known among these sites.

Flickr

flickr.com

Flickr (now owned by Yahoo!) is one of many photo-sharing (and storing) sites on the Web. It is among the biggest (with tens of millions of photos), best known, and most fully featured. With it, you can upload and save your own photos, as well as arrange them in albums, organize them, tag them and describe them as you wish, share them online, and have them printed. You can browse, search, and view your own photos, and those of others who have made their photos public. To find photos of interest, you can browse by category or a number of other approaches. Using search boxes, you can use AND, OR, or NOT to search everyone's photos, just your own, or those of your contacts. There are at least a dozen other significant features to use for either finding pictures or managing your own photo collections on Flickr. Without a paid subscription, the number of photos you can load in any month and the total number of photos you can store is substantial, but there is a limit. Flickr is another place where you can find yourself happily spending much more time than you imagined.

Clip Art

While still in the category of images, clip art addresses a somewhat different function and requires different sources. In the Web context, it usually refers to artwork on the Web, usually but not always free, for use on Web sites or printed documents. Numerous collections and directories exist for these resources, two of which are listed here. Users should read the fine print carefully. Most of the artwork is free, but you may be required to give a specific acknowledgment of the source.

Free Graphics

www.freegraphics.com

Free Graphics is a resource guide with links to collections of free clip art, graphics, photos, Web page templates, and more. The site is searchable and browsable by over a dozen categories.

Barry's Clipart

barrysclipart.com

This collection is both searchable and browsable by topic. The tabs at the top of the page lead to other large clip art collections.

Yahoo! Directory > Graphics > Clip Art

dir.yahoo.com/Computers_and_Internet/Graphics/Clip_Art

This section of Yahoo!'s directory provides links to more than 100 collections of clip art, arranged alphabetically and by category.

AUDIO AND VIDEO

Although less frequently used by researchers than the image resources on the Internet, audio and video files have a variety of applications beyond just entertainment (though all work and no play makes the extreme searcher a dull person). Accessing these resources is much easier than it was a few years ago, since most computers come with the necessary players, or they at least make it easy to identify and download the necessary player. For most types of files, the same players can be used for both audio and video. One of the greatest advances that has made these files easy to use was the advent of "streaming" audio and video players that allow you to begin hearing or seeing the file without having to wait until the file downloads completely, and consequently, to make use of files of almost any length. The current remaining drawback in using larger files is for those users who still do not have a broadband connection. For them, the slow loading time may make many files, especially video, virtually inaccessible.

As with viewing images, hearing and viewing sound and video files is easy. Searching them is the challenging part, mainly because of lack of indexing. Most audio and video files are indexed only under a very few words. However, software is now available that allows, on a large scale, detailed indexing (and searching) of these kinds of files, and it is beginning to be used.

Players

For virtually all of the older sound and video file types you are likely to encounter (wav, au, avi, midi, etc.), your computer probably came equipped with the software necessary to play them. The same holds true for many of the more recent file types, especially the currently dominant, highly compressed, but high-quality sound and video file format MPEG (Moving Pictures Expert Group format, with mpeg, mpg, mp2, mp3 file extensions). If you encounter a file type not currently supported, there is a good chance that there will be a link on the page that leads you to an easy free download of the necessary player. Among the players that many users are likely to encounter are Windows Media Player (pre-installed with all recent Windows operating systems), RealPlayer (a free download for the basic version and upgrades for a fee), Winamp, Musicmatch, QuickTime (essential for Apple users, but also available in a Windows version), and DivX—"The Playa" (for DVD), among others.

Audio

Music, historic speeches, online radio stations, and other sound resources can be valuable for many reasons, but in terms of frequency of use, the most frequently accessed audio content type on the Internet is music. Unfortunately, much of the accessing that is done is illegal due to the violation of copyright. However, there is ample opportunity for legal access to music and also access to other types of useful audio content.

Since unaware serious searchers (and their employers) could easily become the target of copyright infringement suits, the copyright issue should be foremost in the minds of those who download audio and video from the Internet. The popularity of file sharing (peer-to-peer or P2P) among computer users on the Internet became very popular very quickly with the advent of the Napster program. (Napster's first life was short, 1999–ca. 2000, but it has now been rehabilitated and legally reincarnated.). The Napster file-sharing concept, though, begat a number of other P2P programs such as Kazaa, Grokster, Morpheus, and Gnutella that allowed listeners to continue avoid paying for music. The intent of this book is neither to sermonize nor editorialize, but the serious searcher must be aware of the copyright issue.

The next several pages list directories of audio resources, sites that help you find the audio you are looking for, and sites that focus on specific types of audio resources (music, podcasts, radio, speeches, and movie sound clips).

World Wide Web Virtual Library—Audio

archive.museophile.sbu.ac.uk/audio

This directory has more than 150 links to audio resources on the Internet, including general repositories, newsgroups, radio, software, and other sites.

Digital Librarian: A Librarian's Choice of the Best of the Web—Audio

www.digital-librarian.com/audio.html

The Audio section of the Digital Librarian site features more than 500 links—annotated and arranged alphabetically—mostly to sites containing collections of various kinds of audio.

Audio Search Engines

For several years, AltaVista and AlltheWeb were the primary search engines for finding audio files. Although they still have audio search options, their capabilities have been diminished and leadership in audio search has passed to others. The following search engines vary significantly in the content they cover, their searchability, and the added services they provide (such as music sales). Some cover audio as well as video.

AltaVista—Audio Search

www.altavista.com/audio

AlltheWeb—Audio Search

multimedia.alltheweb.com

Both of these sites, which used to be the prime audio search sites, are now owned by Yahoo!. They both are static, use the same audio databases, and identify the same sites. Search functionality is now minimal, with each automatically ANDing terms and providing a NOT capability if you use the minus sign in front of the term, but neither providing OR capability. AltaVista has a bit more searchability. On results pages, you can narrow the results to certain formats (MP3, WAV, Windows Media, Real, AIFF, or other), and specify files with all durations, durations of less than a minute, or more than a minute. AltaVista also features more information about the files (name, type, duration, URL, file size, etc.).

Yahoo!'s Audio Search

audio.search.yahoo.com

Yahoo!'s audio search provides searching options and access to more than 50 million audio files. These include music, newscasts, interviews, speeches, podcasts, sound effects, e-books, and other audio. It also serves as a music comparison-shopping site that lets you choose from numerous music providers.

To search, just enter some terms (subject, artist, album, etc.) in the search box. There is no advanced search page, but once you've done a search, you will find options on the results pages for narrowing results by Music, Podcasts, or Other Audio. For songs, you can refine your search by using the links for Song, Artist, or Album. A More Options link provides narrowing by a specific format, duration, source (Web & Audio Services or Audio Services Only), and Releases ("Include alternates, imports, EPs, etc" or Major).

For music, search results show the artist, title, duration, link to a sample (if available), number of download locations, and links to reviews and to a record for the entire album. Clicking on a title will take you to a "music shopping" page that lists the services from which you can purchase the piece (e.g., Audio Lunchbox, eMusic, iTunes, MusicMatch, Napster, Rhapsody, and Yahoo! Music). For each service, that page also lists the format (MP3, etc.), platform (Win or Mac), whether burning to a CD is allowed (yes or no), whether copying is allowed (yes or no), track price, subscription price, and delivery method (e.g., download). The Download button leads you to the page on the audio provider's site where you can purchase (and download) the item. For those buying music, a link on the results page to select your Preferred Audio Service lets you select your favorite audio provider service. If your service provides that song when you search, a direct link will be provided next to the item on the results page that takes you to the appropriate page on the provider's site.

For podcasts, results will show the podcasts series and episode, the URL, publication (broadcast) date, a snippet of text describing the podcast, buttons for an RSS feed, and instructions on how to add the feed to your My Yahoo! page.

The Yahoo! Audio Search site exemplifies the next step that audio and video search engines and providers are taking to enhance the indexing (and consequently, the searchability) of audio and video content. For Yahoo! Audio Search, information for indexing is gathered not just from the usual information gathered by crawling sites and from data provided at the music supplier sites, but from metadata provided directly by suppliers using Yahoo!'s Media RSS Feed technology. The latter allows for transcripts and a variety of metadata by means of XML "enclosures" that can be provided along with the actual audio or video content of the file.

Singingfish

singingfish.com

Singingfish searches both video and audio. On the main page, you can simply enter terms in the main search box, or you can use the menus on the left of the screen to do the following: search for audio, video, or both; specify duration (any, less than one minute, more than three minutes); specify format (mp3, Real, avi, mpeg, Windows, QuickTime, Flash); and narrow content by category (all, music, news, movies, sports, TV, radio, and finance). Singingfish is what AOL uses for its audio/video search.

FindSounds

www.findsounds.com

This site is included here as an example of a more specialized audio site. FindSounds specializes in sound effects (and similar sounds such as musical instrument samples). The main page lets you search by topic, file formats, number of channels, minimum resolution, minimum sample rate, and maximum file size. Click on the Types of Sounds You Can Find link for a directory of sounds (categories for animals, birds, holidays, etc.). The results pages show a waveform display, indicating not only loudness (amplitude), but, by use of color, frequency content. Here you can hear a hippo and the sounds of a siren, a sapsucker, shotgun, storm, snare drum, and even a snore.

Internet Archive—Audio Archive
www.archive.org

The Internet Archive has stored more than 80,000 recordings, including 35,000 recordings from concerts (with the agreement of the artists). The rest is a variety of other music and sounds, including recordings from 78-rpm records, presidential speeches, lectures, Creative Commons materials, radio programs, and conference proceedings. The advanced search page can be used to search by title, creator, description, collection, date, and other more specific criteria.

Audio Resources: Radio Stations (Real and Virtual)

With thousands of radio stations now providing audio archives of their programs and/or streaming audio of their current broadcasts, great possibilities are open to Internet users. Besides the recreational possibilities, these radio resources not only provide another channel for news (see Chapter 9), but they can supply answers for "Who said what and when?", "Did so-and-so really say what she was quoted as having said?", and "What have people been saying about a particular topic?". Although recent interviews may not be available in transcribed form, the audio may be there, whether on a well-known source such as BBC or on a local radio station. These radio stations can also be valuable to those who are learning a foreign language. The Radio-Locator site will be useful in locating a specific station.

In addition to these "real" radio stations, the Internet also provides "virtual" radio stations so you can tune in on your computer and listen to your own choice of musical genres. Some of this on-demand music is free and some requires a subscription. If you subscribe to satellite radio for your car, check with your provider for the added capability of accessing their services on your computer as part of your subscription.

Radio-Locator (formerly the MIT List of Radio Stations on the Internet)
www.radio-locator.com

Radio-Locator provides links to more than 10,000 radio station sites worldwide and includes 2,500 with live, streaming audio (for continuous listening). From this site you can search for radio stations by country, U.S. state or ZIP code, Canadian province, call letters, and station format (classical, rock, etc.). The advanced search page provides searching by multiple criteria, but it limits your results to only the U.S. or Canada.

Yahoo! LAUNCHcast Radio

music.yahoo.com/launchcast

With Yahoo!'s LAUNCHcast radio, you can listen to your own choice of genres and customize your stations with "My Station Profile." The Radio Station Guide offers a choice of music arranged by themes (more than two dozen of them) and more than 80 genres. LAUNCHcast Plus is a premium service that provides more customization, premium sound quality, and other features. The stations with the earphone symbols offer free access; those with plus signs require the LAUNCHcast subscription.

MSN Radio—Windows Media Player

radio.msn.com

To get to MSN Radio you can either go to radio.msn.com or open the Windows Media Player on your computer, and then click the Radio tab— either serves as the gateway to MSN Radio. Clicking on a station may lead you to either actual or virtual radio stations. Some stations are free, while those listed as Exclusive to Radio Plus require a paid subscription. In addition to classical, country, jazz, etc., you will find that the 20+ genres/topics on the main page also include Fan Favorites (all require a subscription), Recently Played, Featured Sounds, and MSN Local Sounds. The latter is a directory to MSN-created channels that mimic the mixes found on 1,400 local stations. The International category leads to 47 stations from 23 countries. If you have signed up for Radio Plus, use the plus sign in the circle to the right of a station listing to add that station to your own list.

Podcasts

Podcasts are downloadable audio recordings (broadcasts), analogous to Weblog postings, that are quickly becoming a source for valuable information and commentary for Internet users. Podcasts are "published" using feeds (e.g., RSS) that can be downloaded via the Web and transferred to an MP3 player (or to your computer) so you can listen to it at your convenience.

There are a number of programs that will periodically check for new downloads and download them automatically, including, among others, iTunes, iPodder, Doppler, and BlogMatrix Sparks.

For locating podcasts of interest, there are several podcast directories and search engines, including the four following podcast search engines discussed. Other sites, such as Yahoo! Audio Search and Blinkx, cover podcasts as well as other audio formats.

For users of the podcast search and directory sites, the important difference between them may be the particular categories under which the podcasts are organized, and whether those categories match your needs.

Yahoo!'s Podcast Search

podcasts.yahoo.com

Yahoo!'s podcast search easily identifies podcasts of interest, identifying individual podcast episodes on specific topics, while also providing a way to listen to episodes and subscribe to podcasts. (The "Publish a Podcast" link on the site provides a good introduction to podcasts, including how to use them and even a tutorial on how to create your own.) It provides access to video podcasts as well as audio.

When searching, the terms you enter in the search box are automatically ANDed; you can use a minus for NOT and quotation marks for phrases. To find podcast series that cover a particular subject, choose the Series option from the pull-down window. Limiting to a series will retrieve those podcasts that have your term(s) in the title or description of the podcast series or in the tags that the owner and readers have applied. If you want to find every episode (individual podcast broadcast session) that mentions a topic, use the Episodes pull-down option. An episode search will retrieve all individual episodes (programs) with your term(s) in the episode's title, description, or tags.

If you searched for both series and episodes, on the search results pages you will see series listed first, followed by individual episodes mentioning your term(s). For the series listings, you will see the name of the podcast, a brief description, and usually a thumbnail image. Click on either the name or the image, and you will be directed to a Series Information page created by Yahoo! that provides more information about the series including the URL of the podcast home page, the URL for its RSS feed, ratings and reviews by Yahoo! readers, and a list of recent episodes. You can also add your own tags so others can find the podcast more easily. On results pages and on Series Information pages, you will find links to Listen and Subscribe for each series. Click on the Listen link to hear the most recent episode; click on the Subscribe link and Yahoo! will easily get you subscribed, including choosing your own "jukebox" (iTunes, Yahoo! Music, etc.). The Download button that comes with each episode record will download the program to your computer and create a player so you can listen.

Podcastdirectory.com

www.podcastdirectory.com

While Yahoo!'s podcast search emphasizes "search," Podcastdirectory.com emphasizes browsing by category. With it, you can browse for podcasts by country, region, city, state, genre, language, popularity, "buzz" (what people are searching for on the directory today), and Google Map. The latter is a Google mashup with the location of the podcasters on a map. Each of the browsing options provides extensive subcategories. A keyword search is also available on the main page. The terms you enter there are automatically ANDed, and you can use ORs, a minus in front of terms for a NOT, and quotation marks for phrases. Podcastdirectory.com also covers video podcasts with a separate search box for finding them.

Browsing results usually show the podcast's logo, its name, and a brief description. Click on the name to get to a fuller description and a list of episodes, each with its own description. Search results show similar information and also provide, at the top of results pages, links to search episodes, search Internet radio, and video podcasts.

PodSpider

www.podspider.com

PodSpider is both a podcast search engine and a directory, with listings for more than 30,000 podcasts, arranged in six main themes. Each main theme is subdivided into two more category levels. On category pages, the search box helps you search all podcasts or just those in that category.

When searching, you can use multiple words, but if you do, they are automatically treated as a phrase. Because of this limited search functionality, you may want to browse a category first, then search within that category. Searches yield a list of matching podcasts with the title, logo, description, and when it was last updated. Click on Details or the name for a list of episodes, and then click on the title of an episode to hear it. You can limit your searches to All, German, English, or French.

PodSpider also provides, for a price, a powerful, easy-to-use program with which you can locate, subscribe, download, listen to podcasts, and synchronize them with your mobile device. A free demo is available.

Podscope

www.podscope.com

Podscope bridges three of the main topics discussed in this chapter—audio search, podcasts, and video search. It also exemplifies one of the important technological directions for audio and video: the ability to search for the spoken word, not just by the indexing of transcripts, but by the use of voice recognition technology. The aim of the Podscope creator (TVEyes) is to ultimately cover a broad range of multimedia content, but to begin with podcasts.

On the main page you can search for audio, video, or both, or you can search by clicking on one of the more popular tags that you see on the main page. As this site gets underway, search capabilities are quite limited (to a single word) and results can be pretty far off (largely because every word spoken in a podcast episode can be indexed). Search results show the episode title, the date, and the source (the podcast). Click on the title or the plus sign to see a description, and a link to hear a snippet of conversation and links to the podcast Website, to play the episode, and to get the URL for the RSS feed for the podcast. Results are sorted by ranking score, but there is also a link that sorts them by date. Though the initial search functions that the searcher can use are limited, the voice recognition and indexing technology is very promising and Podscope is a good place to explore some of the possibilities.

A Sampling of Other Audio Resources

The History Channel: Speeches & Video

www.historychannel.com/broadband

A search in the search box on this section of The History Channel site will deliver links to a variety of audio and video resources on the site. On the main page, you can browse by show, for great speeches, and by topic. Even if you are not a history buff or scholar, you will be at great risk of being captivated by what this site provides.

The Movie Sounds Page

www.moviesounds.com

This is a source for sound clips from more than 90 major movies. The Sound Tools page has a very good collection of links to audio editing tools.

Music Search and Sales

Some of the sites already mentioned provide a way to search for music and serve as "music stores." More and more companies are getting into the online music sales competition. The following two sites are among the current leaders in legal music downloads; their descriptions will provide a glimpse of the possibilities.

Apple: iPod & iTunes

www.apple.com/itunes

On the iPod and iTunes Web site, you can download iTunes, a combination of digital jukebox, music download store, music manager, CD burner, general player for other audio files, and more. Early on, and especially because of the iPod connection, iTunes took the leadership among online music stores, allowing you to not just purchase songs legally, but to create your own library of music and video by both purchasing music online and importing music and videos from your own digital music library. From there, you can organize your library, "synch" to your iPod, listen on your computer, create your own CDs, and do several other tasks. On the "store" side, you can use the iTunes software to go online and download any of more than 3 million songs, 3,000 music videos, and some TV shows, plus audiobooks and podcasts (the latter usually free).

When you select the Music Store option under the list of sources from iTunes, you can use the search box near the top of the window to search by keyword (artists, song, etc.). On search results pages, you will see a Power Search option that will allow you to search specifically by Artist, Composer, Song, Album, or Genre. The Radio option in iTunes Source section will provide access to more than 900 radio stations arranged by genre (both Internet and "real"). For some stations, you will not be able to go online unless you have a (paid) Preferred Member status.

iTunes also provides a podcast directory (Figure 8.4). Click on Podcasts from the iTunes Source list, and you will see a Podcast Directory link toward the bottom of the resulting screen that will take you to the Podcasts section

Figure 8.4

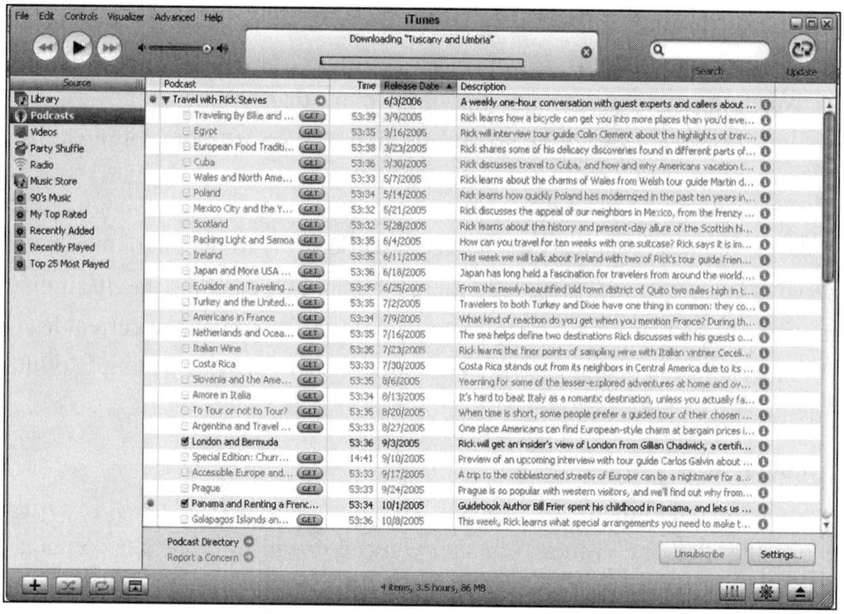

List of podcasts on iTunes

of the Music Store. From there, you can either search or browse for podcasts of interest to download.

Yahoo! Music

music.yahoo.com

Just as iTunes is required software for purchasing from Apple's music store, Yahoo!'s music store, Yahoo! Music, requires that you download (free) software, in this case, the Yahoo! Music Engine. The latter also lets you play music, search for music, create playlists, share music over a home network, rip and burn CDs, and transfer music to portable devices. Yahoo! Music Unlimited (Y! Unlimited) has fewer songs than does iTunes, with a little more than 1 million. You can either purchase songs on a per-song basis or buy them at a discounted rate for a small subscription. Yahoo! uses DRM (Digital Rights Management) that embeds a code in each piece of music so you can use it as long as your subscription is active. With an active subscription, you can download music, share it with others (on Yahoo! IM), transfer it to your portable player, etc.

You can download music through the Music Engine, but the Yahoo! Music Web site also provides features directly (most of which you can also get to from the Music Engine). These include a music search, customizable radio stations, music news, music videos, and information about musicians, groups, and recordings.

- Search Music – Search by artists, albums, songs, videos, or all of those.
- LAUNCHcast Radio – Listen to your own choice of genres and customize your station. You can customize (Edit) your station and use the Radio Station Guide to choose songs from 19 main genres/ themes and more than 230 subcategories. About half of those are free and the rest (those identified with a plus sign) require a LAUNCHcast Plus subscription. On the free side, you are limited to listening to 600 songs per month. After that, you need a LAUNCHcast subscription for full access to songs and your cus- tomized station.
- Music Videos – Yahoo! claims "The most Videos on the Web!". You can choose videos from Pop, Rock, Country, Rap, and R&B categories or by artist, and can create and edit a Video Station similar to the radio stations.
- Artists – Use the search box to find an Artist's Page, which includes a discography, reviews, news and interviews, message boards, a list of fans, perhaps a biography and photos, and an opportunity to rate the artist.

The Yahoo! Music Engine also provides access to the Yahoo! Podcast Search, discussed earlier.

Video

In terms of usefulness and applications, most of what can be said about audio resources on the Internet is also true for video resources. In most cases, the same players that can be used for audio are used for video. You may find that your computer is not equipped with Apple's QuickTime Movie Player (available also for PCs), which is worthwhile to download if you run across a file that requires it.

To look for video, try the following places:

- For news, try news services such as BBC, CNN, and MSNBC, plus local radio and TV station Web sites

- Use the video search capabilities of Yahoo! or Google
- Look around in subject-specific sites such as The History Channel and American Memory (discussed previously under "Audio")
- Use the BUBL LINK video resource guide that follows

Directory of Video Resources on the Internet

BUBL LINK: Catalogue of Internet Resources—Video
bubl.ac.uk/link/v/video.htm

The BUBL LINK page is actually a directory of directories, providing annotated descriptions and links to more than a dozen sites, each of which, in turn, provides collections of links to video resources for a variety of subject areas.

Video Search Engines

Until 2005, if you wanted to do a wide-reaching search of video on the Web, you went to AltaVista or AlltheWeb. This has now changed with the video search offerings from Yahoo!, Google, and others. The video indexing and search technologies these engines are beginning to incorporate are a first step toward a wealth of other video search possibilities. As referred to in the earlier discussion of audio files, one of the most powerful of these technologies is the use of enhanced RSS to provide additional metadata that can be attached to a video or audio file. The provision of better metadata is only the starting point for what RSS can do for video search engines, particularly by using "enclosures" to attach full-text transcripts that have been created by closed captioning and voice recognition technologies. As well as its application by Yahoo!, this is a natural for TV programming and there are at least two places on the Web where you can already get a sense of what is coming for TV: Google's video search and Blinkx.

Yahoo!'s Video Search
video.yahoo.com

In terms of quantity of video, Yahoo!'s video search is ahead of all others, with millions of videos that Yahoo! has identified by crawling Web pages. In addition, Yahoo!'s collection also contains video gathered directly from video publishers by means of RSS delivery. This aspect means that Yahoo! can get to videos that "crawling" can't identify and, because of RSS "enclosures," a lot of metadata can be gathered to enhance the indexing of those videos.

To get to Yahoo!'s video search, go to video.yahoo.com or use the tab above Yahoo!'s main search box. On the main page of Yahoo! Video Search, you will find tabs to browse by Features, Popular, Categories, or Tags. The My Studio link will take you to a page where you can upload your own videos.

When using the search box, all terms you enter are automatically ANDed and you can use quotation marks for a specific phrase. Results pages show 10 thumbnails per page and, along with each thumbnail, the video's file name, URL of the video itself, duration, file type, and the URL of the page on which the video is found. If you see a Channels section, this will take you to other videos from the sources (e.g., producers, Yahoo! News) found among the results. Click on one of the thumbnails to go to a page from which you can play the video. From that page, you also can see a rating of the video (by Yahoo! users), a link to rate it yourself, how many times it was viewed, links to e-mail or IM it, and perhaps a description of the content. The More Videos box lets you easily go to other videos that appeared in your search results. There is also a link to save it on your My Favorites page, a Yahoo! page containing a collection of videos you have saved.

Yahoo! Video also provides an advanced video search page, letting you narrow your search by format, size (resolution), duration, and site/domain.

Google's Video Search

video.google.com

Google's Video Search emphasizes the "hosting" by Google of commercial (as well as amateur) video, providing a showcase and marketplace for TV shows, movies, documentaries, music videos, etc. (Figure 8.5). Uploading videos for sale is not limited to big production companies—anyone can place video they have created online by using Google's Video Upload Program. For commercial videos that have been uploaded, you can purchase them online, in some cases a downloadable version that you can keep and in some cases a "day pass" for viewing it as many times as you wish within a 24-hour period.

In searching for videos, links beneath the search box can be used to narrow your search results to the Top 100, Comedy, Music Videos, Movies, Sports, Animation, or TV Shows. On results pages, you have the options, at the top of the results page, to view the results as a list rather than in "grid"

Figure 8.5

Example of video found through Google's Video Search

format, to further narrow your results by seeing just the free ones or just those for sale, and to narrow results by length (All, Long, Medium, or Short).

In the main search box, you can also narrow your results by searching by a prefix, such as "title:" and "owner:" (for example, *title:star trek*). In most cases, it will be simpler to do a straightforward search using keywords describing what you are looking for, and then narrowing your search by the links on the search page or the narrowing links on the results pages.

Google Video has great potential. If you want to get a sense of some of the great video you can get for free, check out the film available from the U.S. National Archives and Records Administration (search for *owner:nara*).

YouTube
youtube.com

YouTube, once thought of as a Web site used mostly by teens, has an increasing amount of high quality useful video, including news, how-to videos, interviews, and a variety of other interesting content.

Search Engines for Video—TV-Specific

If you are looking for video of TV news and other shows and want to search for it easily and effectively, take advantage of the following sites. The

first one, Blinkx, is free (and includes more than just TV), while the other two
that follow require a fee.

Blinkx

www.blinkx.tv

At Blinkx, you can get more than 1 million hours of video, audio, podcasts, and vlogs (video weblogs), including, of course, lots of TV footage.
For a number of major news suppliers, you will be taking advantage of the
full-text searching of every word spoken on the video, made possible through
advanced voice recognition and speech-to-text technology that lets Blinkx
automatically create transcripts of the audio and video content and index it.
The searching, though, also extends to metadata beyond just the content of
those transcripts. On top of that, it's free.

The main page features an impressive list of participants, including almost
all major TV networks, newspapers such as *The Times* and the *Washington
Post*, plus other sources such as *Forbes*, Public Radio, the Discovery
Channel, the Biography Channel, and the Comedy Channel. When searching,
terms you enter are automatically ANDed, and you can use both ORs and
NOTs. Using the list of suppliers, you can also limit your choice to one or
more suppliers (or categories: Entertainment, News, Information,
Commercials, Self-Cast, Radio). On the results pages, you will find a slider
that lets you put more or less emphasis on either relevance or date, and there
is also a Safe Search filter option.

ShadowTV

www.shadowtv.com

ShadowTV is a fee-based service that monitors (and serves as a clipping
service with automatic notification) for more than 120 stations, including
major networks, cable stations, and local affiliates. At present it just covers
U.S stations. It makes video available within a few minutes of when it was
broadcast and also includes an archive dating back four years (though the
material that is more than six months old is not available online). Closed
captioning of programs is both searchable and readable. You can search by
keywords and date/time, making use of an extensive collection of operators
and features (AND, OR, NOT, NEAR, soundex, stemming, fuzzy, and
wildcards).

TVEyes

www.tveyes.com

TVEyes is a fee-based search of radio and TV content from stations in the U.K., Canada, Australia, and the U.S. It indexes the audio feeds from these by means of voice-recognition technology and provides alerts and a searchable archive. Though it is fee-based, look at either the sampling you can get online for free, or sign up for a full demo.

Television News Archive

tvnews.vanderbilt.edu

This archive at Vanderbilt University (Tennessee) has more than 30,000 network evening news broadcasts from major U.S. national broadcast networks (ABC, CBS, NBC, CNN, and PBS) and more than "9,000 hours of special news-related programming including ABC's *Nightline* since 1989." From the site, you can search headlines and abstracts and use Boolean, and limit by date, broadcast type (regular evening news or special broadcasts), and reporter. Content is not delivered online but is ordered as videotapes.

CHAPTER 9

NEWS RESOURCES

Once more, the word "amazing" has to be used. To be able to read the headline stories from a newspaper 10,000 miles away, sometimes before the paper appears on local residents' doorsteps, is indeed amazing. This chapter covers the range of news resources available (news services and newswires, newspapers, news aggregation services, etc.) and how to most effectively find and use them. Very importantly, the chapter emphasizes the limitations with which the researcher is faced, particularly in regard to archival and exhaustivity (comprehensiveness) issues.

TYPES OF NEWS SITES ON THE INTERNET

Understanding news resources on the Internet is challenging not just because there is such a broad and rich expanse of news available, but because almost every news site is designed differently from the next, with differing functions and missions. In "ancient" times, it was relatively easy to group news resources into categories such as newspapers, magazines and journals, radio, and TV. Today, it is harder to definitively categorize the types of places to go on the Internet for news. Although many typologies of news sources are possible, using the following categories can prove to be helpful in sorting things out (while recognizing there is considerable overlap and that many sites fit in more than one category):

- Major news networks and newswire sites – Sites that are original sources for news stories but may also gather and provide stories from other sources
- Aggregation sites – Sites that serve primarily to gather news stories from multiple sources
- Newspaper and magazine sites – Sites that serve as the online version for a printed newspaper or magazine

- Radio and TV sites
- Multi-source news search engines – Sites that provide extensive search capabilities for a broad range of news sources
- Specialized news services – Sites that focus on news in a particular subject area
- Alerting services – Sites that provide a personalized selection of current news stories on a regular basis

FINDING NEWS—A GENERAL STRATEGY

A good starting point for finding news on the Internet is to ask the question, "What kind of news are you looking for?":

1. Are you interested in breaking news (today's headlines)?
2. Do you need older news stories?
3. Do you want to be kept up-to-date automatically on a topic?

For breaking news, you might start with virtually any of the categories listed earlier, depending upon the breadth of your interests, both with regard to subject and with regard to the local, national, or international perspective needed. If you want to browse headlines, consider bookmarking and personalizing a general portal (such as My Yahoo!) and perhaps using it as the start page for your browser. Headlines in categories of your choice will show up every time you open your browser (or click Home). Alternatively, you might choose a news network site (BBC, MSNBC, etc.) or your favorite newspaper as your start page.

For older news stories, the choice is much more limited. If you are interested in the last few weeks, one of the search engines may serve best. For international or high-profile news going back a few years, BBC may be a good choice, because it provides searching of all stories covered on its site back to 1997. If your interest is more local, check to see if the local paper has searchable archives.

If you need to keep up-to-date on a particular topic, take advantage of one of the alerting services and have headlines relating to your interests delivered to you by e-mail.

Characteristics to Look for When Accessing News Resources

For a research project or question, particularly when it is important that you know what you have and have not covered in your research, it is imperative that you be aware of exactly the kinds of items and time frames particular news sites include. You certainly do not need to know this for every search, but the following factors are among the major content variables encountered among news sources on the Internet:

- Time frame covered – Some sites cover only today, others go back weeks, months, or years.
- Portion of original actually included – Particularly for newspapers and magazines, there is great variation as to how much of the print version is available online.
- Sources covered – Some sources may draw only from a single newswire service, others may include thousands of sources.
- Currency – Although "old news" can be tremendously valuable, "news" often implies "new." Depending on the site, the stories may be only minutes old, whereas for other sites the delay in including stories may be considerably more.
- Searchability – Some sites only allow you to get to stories by browsing though a list or by category. Other sites allow searching by keyword, date, and other criteria. Look around on any news site for a search box.
- Availability of alerting services – Although it may not be emphasized, on many sites, if you dig around a bit, you may find that a free e-mail alerting service is available. Some sites specifically exist as alerting services.
- Availability of RSS feeds – RSS as a concept is discussed near the end of the chapter. However, until you get there, RSS stands for Really Simple Syndication and, briefly, is a mechanism whereby a Web site, such as a news source, can code its pages so that stories are automatically distributed ("syndicated") to any Web site (or Web user) that chooses to automatically receive those stories.
- Personalization capabilities – Some sites may allow you to personalize the site, so that when you go to it, categories of headlines of your choice and your local news, weather, and sports are displayed.

NEWS RESOURCE GUIDES

With thousands of news sites out there, this chapter can only include a few selected sites. To find out about other sites, take advantage of one of the several good news resource guides. The ones listed here are among the more highly regarded. Each provides somewhat different options in terms of coverage and searchability or browsability. One of the most important uses of the first five sites listed here is the easy identification of newspapers and other news resources for virtually any country and large city in the world. If you need to know the Web site for the local newspaper in Kathmandu, these resource guides will lead you there. You will find it worthwhile to go to one of these guides, choose a country, and spend a few minutes browsing through the sites for that country. The other guides mentioned here focus on finding specific news features—political cartoons and "news in pictures" sites.

Kidon Media-Link

www.kidon.com/media-link

Kidon Media-Link is arranged to let you browse more than 18,000 media sites by continent and country, but it also has a search page so you can search by a combination of media type (newspaper, radio station, etc.) and either by city or by words in the title of the site. It will also display sites by language (English, Spanish, French, German, Italian, Portuguese, Arabic, Russian, Chinese, and Dutch). Symbols indicate the presence of streaming audio and video for each site.

ABYZ News Links

www.abyznewslinks.com

ABYZ News Links contains mostly newspapers, but it also includes many broadcast stations, Internet services, magazines, and press agencies (Figure 9.1). For some countries and localities, ABYZ offers more links than Kidon Media-Link (and for some, fewer links). The search link on the page does a Google "site-search." You can browse by continent and country.

Metagrid

www.metagrid.com

Metagrid covers not just newspapers but magazines, for which it provides a nice browsable directory by subject. It covers, altogether, 8,000 sites.

Figure 9.1

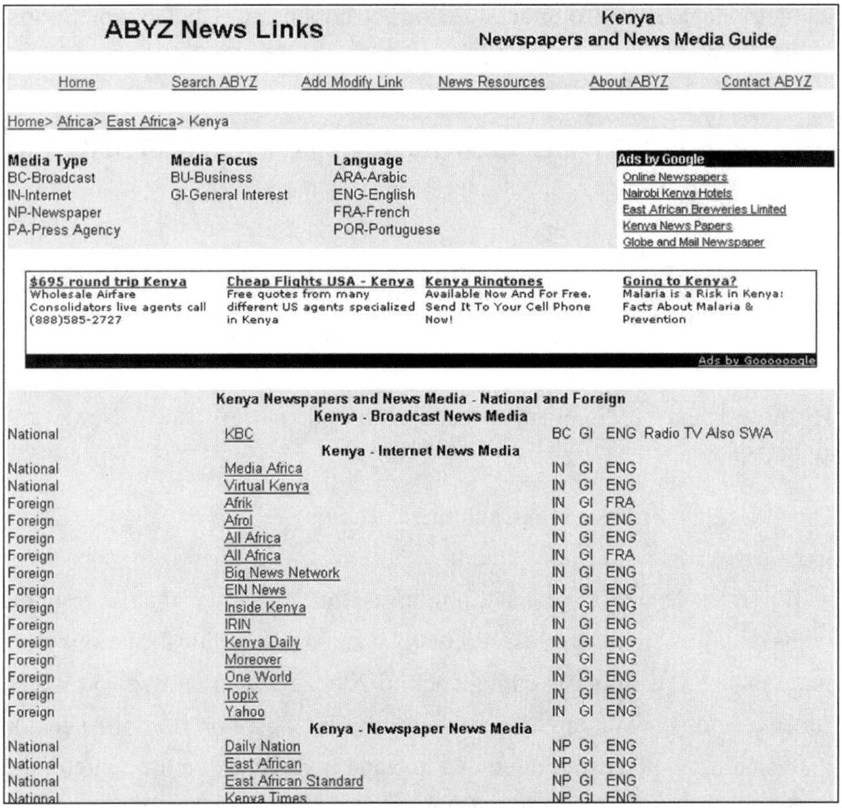

List of media links at ABYZ News Links

NewsLink

newslink.org

In addition to browsing newspapers worldwide by country, NewsLink allows you to browse U.S. newspapers by the following categories: National Papers, Most-linked-to (state or type), Major Metros, Dailies, Non-dailies, Business, Alternative, Specialty, or Campus papers by state. You can also search by city and state, and specify All, Newspaper, TV, or Radio. It covers considerably fewer sites than Kidon Media-Link and dead links are frequently a problem.

NewsWealth

www.newswealth.com

NewsWealth has a few links to newspapers around the world, but its strength is in the other kinds of browsable news resource categories it provides. These include Magazines, Columnists, Blogs, Cartoons, Celeb Gossip, Sports, Business, Weather, Live Cams, Scanners Live, and Lotto Results.

News Resource Guides—Specialty Content

News in Pictures
www.newsinpictures.com

News in Pictures is a collection of links to more than 100 sites with sections such as Photos of the Day and News in Pictures. Links are arranged according to the following categories: News, Sports, Disaster, Entertainment, History, Science, Miscellaneous, News in Video, USA Local News, and World News.

Daryl Cagle's Professional Cartoonists Index
www.cagle.com

Daryl Cagle's Professional Cartoonists Index is more than a resource guide with links to other sites; it actually contains the political cartoons from more than 100 cartoonists dating back to 2001. You can browse and search for free, and you can purchase rights to re-print a cartoon from the site. On the home page, you can browse by topic and if you click on the Search for a Cartoon link, you can search by keyword, date, color, and artist.

MAJOR NEWS NETWORKS AND NEWSWIRES

Major news networks and newswires have sites that provide news items that they themselves have produced, although they may use and incorporate other sources as well. Sites such as BBC, CNN, and MSNBC are the choice of many Internet users for breaking news, because the headlines are updated continually. They also typically provide a number of other items of information beyond news headlines, such as weather. These are sites for which the "click everywhere" principle emphatically applies. By spending some time clicking around on the page, clicking through the index links at the bottom of the main page, and browsing through the site index, you can get an idea of the true richness of these sites.

Newswire services such as Reuters, UPI, AP, and Agence France Presse are primarily in the business of providing stories to other news outlets.

Their sites contain current headlines, but may also be more a brochure for the service.

BBC

news.bbc.co.uk

A large portion of searchers throughout the world consider BBC (Figure 9.2) the best news site on the Internet. It is particularly noted for its international coverage (BBC "World Edition"). In the international section of some U.S. services, "international" seems to be defined as "news from abroad that is of particular interest to the U.S." BBC's international coverage, though, is much more truly "international." Among its other strengths are its easy browsabilty, its extensive search capability, and the availability of free searchable archives going back to November 1997. The BBC news site is only one small portion of what the overall BBC site offers. If you go to the U.K. version, you will find a link to the "A–Z Index." Browse through that

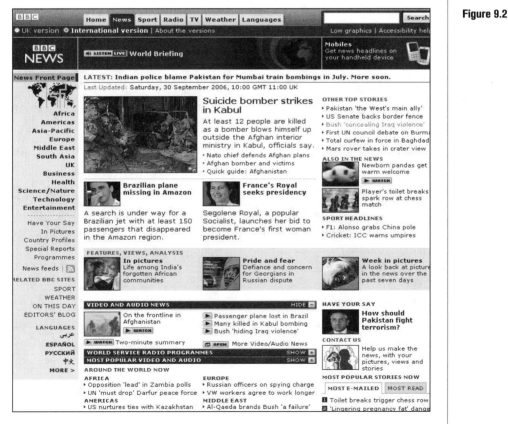

Figure 9.2

BBC News home page (international version)

to find things from the Arabic Language News to Zoos. On the news home page, look for the languages options, the Country Profiles, and the free e-mail service.

All content comes from BBC writers, though they may utilize other sources such as Reuters in writing their stories.

The search box allows searching by multiple keywords, and all the terms you enter are automatically ANDed. You can also make use of quotation marks for phrase searching. On the results pages, you can use tabs near the top of the page to narrow your results to BBC News & Sport or BBC Audio & Video. On the right side of the results pages, the first few audio and video records are displayed along with links to play them.

CNN

www.cnn.com

CNN.com, a Time Warner company, has been displaying an increasingly international perspective, partly in connection with CNN's strong presence on European TV. It has U.S. and international versions, as well as interfaces in several languages (Arabic, English, Japanese, Korean, and Turkish). The site, which is particularly rich in video, features a Watch Video section of the home page that makes it easy to select and watch video. Once the player opens, you can easily move to other videos and search for video (though you will encounter some video ads). Archived video (more than seven days old) is only available with a CNN Pipeline subscription. The Preferences link at the bottom of the page lets you set the edition, personalize your weather, and receive e-mail alerts. CNN has a variety of other services including audio news you can download to your MP3 player, daily and weekly e-mail news alerts, RSS feeds, a desktop ticker, and mobile access. The subscription-based CNN Pipeline service offers access to more than 2,000 hours of video from an interface that can display up to four live streams.

MSNBC

www.msnbc.com

The MSNBC site has an excellent "fly-out" menu for browsing through headlines by category and subcategory. The front page also provides lead stories, a stock market overview, video, and a search box. In addition to MSNBC's own stories, you will find stories from local NBC stations, Associated Press, *Newsweek*, and other sources. Most stories are available online for a few weeks, some for many months. U.S. users can personalize this site by entering their ZIP code; they will then see local news, weather, and sports headlines at the bottom of the main page. There is a free e-mail option and a number of RSS and podcast feed options, including an RSS feed for any specific search you have done.

Reuters

reuters.com

Reuters.com provides content from more than 2,000 Reuters journalists around the world. The site, which was significantly expanded in 2002, lets you browse through general, financial, and investment news for the last day or so, and the search box allows retrieval of stories going back two to three weeks. The site, which is searchable by keyword, company name, or stock symbol, lets you limit your search to news or photos, and you can browse using eight main news categories. A search in the Quote search box takes you to the Company Search page, which provides stock quotes for the company and excellent company profiles, news, and other enterprise information. Reuters also provides a free e-mail alert.

Aljazeera.net

english.aljazeera.net

There is definitely some truth to Aljazeera's motto that "now when Aljazeera speaks, the world listens and 'reads'." The content on this site is aimed primarily at the Arab world and from an Arab perspective. Sections include News, Economy, Culture, Sci-Tech, Special Reports, and Polls. The Arabic version is available at www.aljazeera.net, and it is particularly interesting to note that the content there is not identical to the English version.

NEWSPAPERS

Thousands of sites for individual newspapers are available on the Internet. There are still a few newspaper sites that contain an insignificant number of actual stories, but most contain at least the major stories for the current day, and most contain an archive covering a few days, a few months, or even several years. Most online versions of newspapers do not contain sections such as the classified ads (or display ads) that appear in the print version. Some online versions contain things that are not in the print version, such as profiles of local companies.

Although most people are not likely to completely desert the print version of their favorite newspaper for a while to come, the online versions do provide some obvious advantages, such as searchability and archives. Some also provide greater currency, with updates during the day. Perhaps the most obvious advantage is simply availability—the fact that newspapers from around the world are available at your fingertips almost instantly. Take advantage of the availability of distant papers particularly when doing research on issues, industries, companies, and people. For industries, take advantage of specialization of newspapers dependent upon their location. For example, the *San Jose Mercury* is strong on technology because of its location in Silicon Valley, the *Washington Post* is strong on coverage of U.S. government, and Detroit papers are strong on the auto industry. For companies and for people, the local paper is likely to give more coverage than larger papers.

More and more newspaper archives are available online. In some cases, you can get recent stories for free, but have to pay for earlier stories. The price is usually quite reasonable, especially considering the cost to obtain them through alternative document-delivery channels.

Use the news resource guides mentioned earlier to find the names and sites for papers throughout the world. For availability of newspaper archives, check the site for the particular paper. Keep in mind that commercial services such as NewsLibrary, Factiva, LexisNexis, and Dialog may have archives for newspapers that predate what is available on the newspaper's Web site. If you are not in an organization that has a library that provides access to some of these, your local public library may.

Newspapers—Front Pages

The following two sites provide a look at the actual pages of newspapers.

Today's Front Pages
www.newseum.org/todaysfrontpages

Brought to you by the Newseum, this site offers a look at the actual front pages of 573 newspapers from 54 countries. On the front page, the thumbnails of the pages are listed alphabetically (by U.S. state and city, and then by other countries and city). Tabs at the top of the page let you choose by map or regional list. Click on a thumbnail to see a larger view, and from there you can click on a link that gives you a PDF version that can be enlarged further.

PressDisplay.com

www.pressdisplay.com

The main page of the PressDisplay.com site at first looks like many other news sites, with news headlines and images. When you click on one of the images of a newspaper front page though, you will go to images of the full front page and from there you can go to images of all of the news pages of the paper. The front page is free, but for more you will need a subscription (a seven-day trial is available). Using the Select Newspaper link or the search box at the top of the PressDisplay.com main page, you can go to the pages of 500 newspapers from 70 countries. The window by the search box permits you to search by time frame, but on results pages you will find an advanced search section enabling you to search (within the papers) by newspaper, date, language, author, and limit to headline.

RADIO AND TV

Sites for radio and TV stations are excellent sources for breaking news and may also contain audio (and sometimes video) archives of older programs. The next two sites make it easy to locate radio stations from around the world. The third site, NPR, is particularly valuable for its archives of National Public Radio shows.

Radio-Locator (formerly the MIT List of Radio Stations on the Internet)

www.radio-locator.com

Radio-Locator's site offers links to more than 10,000 radio station sites (and 2,500 audio streams) worldwide and allows you to search for radio stations by country, U.S. state or ZIP code, Canadian province, call letters, and station format (classical, rock, etc.).

TVRadioWorld

radiostationworld.com

TVRadioWorld is a directory of thousands of radio stations worldwide organized first by continent, then country, and then type of station within the country.

NPR

www.npr.org

This site provides easy access to National Public Radio stations through-out the U.S., and also provides a searchable audio archive of NPR stories and a facility for ordering transcripts. Using the pull-down menu at the top of the page, you can find a list of programs or schedules, or the list of stories and schedules for individual programs ("All Things Considered," "Car Talk," etc.).

AGGREGATION SITES

There are a number of sites whose main function is to gather news stories from a variety of newswires, newspapers, and other news outlets. Also, two of the largest general search engines (Google and Yahoo!) provide extensive news searches of thousands of news sources. (Ask.com's news search is at present rather limited in terms of searchability and the uniqueness and amount of content. Among the following sites are the two search engine sites and five that are among the most prominent sites focusing specifically on news aggregation. (See Table 9.1 for a comparison of the numbers of sources, types of sources, language coverage, and retrospectiveness of these sites. Be aware that the numbers will tend to change.) These are all good places to go to make sure you are covering a wide range of sources, and each does it in a somewhat different way, with differing content and differing browsing and searching capabilities. The final site covered (not included in the chart) is World News Network, an international network of news sites.

Google News

news.google.com

Google's main news search covers about 4,500 English language sources, with sites crawled continually. This means that you may be able to find some things on Google only minutes after they appear in the original source. Items are retained in Google's news database for 30 days, and Google provides a powerful free alert service, along with a news search for many of its country-specific versions. You can access these by means of the pull-down menu on the main news search page.

On Google's news page, you will find a browsable newspaper-type layout, with titles and brief excerpts for Top Stories (Figure 9.3) and three records for each of the following sections: World, U.S., Business, Sci/Tech, Sports, Entertainment, and Health. Each news record has the title, an indication of how long ago the story was indexed, a 30- to 40-word excerpt, and links to related stories from other sources. If the story has a photo, a thumbnail appears beside the story summary. The small In the News section provides links to 10 hot topics.

News Search Engine Comparison Chart   **Table 9.1**

News Search Engine	No. of Sources	Main Types of Sources	Languages	Retrospective
Google	4,500	Newspapers, newswires, TV, radio Web-only news sites	Main site in English 20 other sites in 7 other languages	30 days
Yahoo!	7,000	Newspapers, newswires, TV, radio Web-only news sites	35 Languages	30 days
Findory	a few thousand"	RSS, Blogs, newspapers, newswires,	English	4 weeks
Topix.net	10,000	Newspapers, newswires, TV, radio Web-only news sites	English only	More than 1 year
NewsNow	22,000	Newspapers, newswires, TV, radio, RSS, Blogs Web-only news sites	15+ languages	1 week free
RocketNews	16,000	Newspapers, newswires, TV, radio, RSS, Blogs Web-only news sites	English, some French, Spanish, others	4 days
Feedster	30 million	RSS, including Blogs, newspapers, newswires, TV, radio Web-only news sites	Many	1 month

On the left side of the page, links for each of the news categories will take you to a full page of 20 top stories for that category. Below that are links for setting up news alerts, RSS feeds, and Google's mobile news service. The Personalize link lets you (if signed in) add news sections to the main page (including sections from other country versions), show headlines only, and rearrange the sections.

Figure 9.3

Google News home page

In the search box, you can use prefixes such as "intitle:" and "inurl:". (However, for "inurl:" only use the main part of the URL; for example, *inurl:reuters* works well, but *inurl:reuters.com* misses most of the Reuters stories.) Google has an advanced news search that allows you to use simple Boolean, search by source, location, and date, and narrow by limiting to occurrence of your terms in the headline, the body, or the URL of the record. Search results look very similar to Web search results, but you will also find a Sort by Date link that conveniently arranges results by latest first.

Although news records are retained on Google for 30 days, for some sources the article may not be there when you click, especially for newspapers that have dynamic pages that change frequently, or that keep older articles in a separate archive database (mainly for fee-based access). Unlike regular Google, there is no cached copy of news pages.

Yahoo! News

news.yahoo.com

For years, Yahoo! News has been a favorite place on the Web for newsseekers. It covers more than 7,000 news sources in 35 languages, all searchable

Figure 9.4

Yahoo! News home page

at once from Yahoo!'s main page. The content comes from Yahoo!'s news "partners" (AP, Reuters, Agence France Presse, *Washington Post*, *USA Today*, *LA Times*, *Chicago Tribune*, NPR, and *US News and World Report*), plus from crawling thousands of other news sites on the Web. Most stories are retained for 30 days.

The main page displays a featured article (usually with links to video and a photo slideshow) and five headlines from each of 15 news categories (U.S., Business, World, Entertainment, etc.). Links to a full news page for each section are located across the top of the main page (Figure 9.4). The Site Index link there leads to a clickable display of each of the news sources (AP, NPR, Wonkette, etc.) covered in each category. On the Site Index page, you will also find menus for Local News, Comics, and Editorial Cartoons.

The main page also contains links to video news, This Week in Photos, photo slideshows, links to "Full Coverage" on major current news topics, local weather, and links to get RSS feeds, news alerts, and weather alerts.

With the search box on the main page, you can search All News, Yahoo! News Only (the news from partner sources), News Photos, or Video/Audio. In the search box, you can use the same techniques (Boolean, prefixes, etc.) you use in a Yahoo! Web search. If you use the Advanced link next to the search box, you can use simple Boolean, sort results by relevance or date, narrow your search by date, source, location, categories, and language, and specify the number of results to be shown on each results page.

News search results look much the same as Web search results, with the story title, source, date, and first line of the story, but without a cache link. For crawled, non-partner sources, click on a story to take you to the page on which it was found. Click on the link for a story from a Yahoo! news partner for access to many additional features, such as links to video, RSS feeds, links that will place that source automatically on your My Yahoo! page, a link to create an alert on the topic, links to related stories (Full Coverage), links to e-mail, IM, or discuss the story, and more. Within these stories, you will often find particular topics highlighted along with a small purple icon next to them. These are Y!Q links that, when clicked, will result in a pop-up window with a Web and News search of that topic.

Findory

www.findory.com

Findory, which covers several thousand news sources and Weblogs, creates a personalized page for each user, with recommended content based on the statistics it has gathered about the story types you have previously read on the Findory site. The more you use the site the more personalized your own Findory page becomes. The Blogs section of Findory works in the same way.

Topix.net

www.topix.net

Topix.net's strong point is the very detailed categorization it applies to its stories. On the site, you will find news and Weblogs from more than 10,000 sources. The stories from these sources are placed in more than 360,000 categories, by locality, country, industry, company, etc. These include categories for 30,000 U.S. cities and towns and 5,500 companies and industries. To see the categories, click the Directory link near the top of the page. One of the very potent aspects of the site is that you can create e-mail alerts or use RSS feeds for any of these topics, including alerts or feeds for any U.S. ZIP Code. The site contains one year of archives and has an advanced search where you can limit to source, URL, ZIP code or city, category, country, and time frame.

NewsNow

newsnow.co.uk

NewsNow is in the business of providing newsfeeds to other organizations and sites, and it was the first major site providing news aggregation dedicated to a U.K. audience. It covers more than 30,000 sources and updates from them every five minutes. From the NewsNow home page you can either search or browse by category. The categories are a major strength of the site and the 12 main categories are broken down into a total of more than 700 subcategories. Using these categories you can quickly and easily focus in on news relevant to your specific areas of interest. To use some features, such as the advanced search, a subscription is required.

RocketNews

www.rocketnews.com

RocketNews covers more than 30,000 sources that provide RSS feeds (news, Weblogs, and podcasts) and includes a substantial number of non-English sources. From the main page, you can search news, Weblogs, audio/podcasts, and video, limit your search by date, and have your results sorted by date or relevance. News is retained on the site for four days. You can browse the news by nine categories, each of which provides an RSS feed. RocketNews is also known for its easy-to-use RSS Reader software, which can be downloaded for free from the RocketNews site.

Feedster

www.feedster.com

As with RocketNews, Feedster covers sites that have RSS feeds, including more than 33 million feeds from Weblogs, news sources, and podcasts. From the main search box, you can limit to any or all of those categories. The terms entered in the search box are automatically ANDed, plus you can use phrases and Boolean (OR, NOT, or parentheses).

World News Network

wn.com

World News Network is an impressive network of more than 1,000 sites for individual countries, industries, regions, and more. The main page provides headlines and a list of categories for Regions, Business, Countries, Current Events, Entertainment, Environment, Science, Society, and Sport, with subcategories for each. The regional categories lead to the individual country news sites; the subject categories lead to news for a tremendous variety of subjects ranging from nuclear waste to cocoa.

The search options on the main page offer a search by a combination of keywords and language, and the advanced search lets you search by keywords, simple Boolean, and language, and sort your results by relevance or date and specify the number of results per page. Consider taking advantage of the free e-mail alert services found within the various sections.

SPECIALIZED NEWS SERVICES

Having a site for specialized news for a particular industry, area of technology, and so on, can be not just useful, but sometimes critical for those who need to make sure they are not missing important developments in that area. Such sites exist for a tremendous variety of subjects. In some cases, they are news-only sites, but in some cases specialized news is just one function of the site. For a good idea of the possibilities, go to the World News Network (just discussed) and click on Site Map. There alone, you will find more than 200 specialized news sites. One very simple yet effective approach to finding a specialized news site is to use a Web search engine and search for the industry or topic and the word "news," for example, *paper industry news*.

WEBLOGS

Fitting, somewhat, into the category of specialty news sites is the Weblog phenomenon. These sites began to appear in very large numbers around 2001. Weblogs (also known as "blogs," with the verb form "blogging") are, according to blog pioneer Dave Winer, "often-updated sites that point to articles elsewhere on the Web, often with comments, and to on-site articles."

These often focus on topics of very specialized interest and are a good way of keeping up-to-date on such specialized topics. They can range from very useful sites that gather news and provide well-informed commentary to inane ramblings. In any case, they have become a significant part of the "news" content available on the Web and being able to locate either Weblog sites or individual Weblog items is now a part of news searching, as indicated by the fact that many of the news sources already discussed in this chapter include Weblog content.

Weblog Search Engines and Directories

The popularity and usefulness of blogs provides professional searchers with the inevitable challenge of finding useful blog sites, and among the billions of postings, those individual postings that discuss a specific topic. Fortunately there are a number of sites that provide some substantial search capabilities, often in addition to other Weblog-related functions such as readers, Weblog publishing services, and directories.

Be aware though that blog searching presents some unique search problems. Many Weblog search sites cover only Weblogs that provide an RSS feed (thereby leaving out a lot of Weblogs) and exactly what gets indexed for a particular posting will vary, depending upon how much of the Weblog posting was included in the RSS feed (title, summary, full-text, etc.). As with news search engines, how many sources these cover and how retrospective they are will vary greatly. You will also notice a lot of variability in what search features are provided.

Among the dozens of Weblog search engines, the following are among the most popular, fully featured (for searching), and/or extensive in terms of retrospective coverage. Because of the problems mentioned, if you really don't want to miss something, use more than one of these engines.

Bloglines

bloglines.com

Bloglines, which is owned by Ask.com and covers both blogs and newsfeeds, has content that goes back to January 2004, and with its advanced search you can use simple Boolean, and limit results to blogs or news, to where the term occurs (title, author, subject, body, or URL), to language (20 options), and to date posted. You can sort results by popularity or date, and, in addition to searching "All Blogs," if you use the Bloglines "reader," you can narrow by or exclude those blogs to which you have subscribed.

Technorati

technorati.com

With content dating back to late 2004, Technorati includes more than 40 million sites and 2.5 billion links. Its Options link lets you search using simple Boolean and phrases, search blog sites that focus on a specific topic, search links to a URL, or search by user-applied "tags."

Blogger—Blog Search

search.blogger.com

Now owned by Google and going back to mid-2005, Blogger's Blog Search offers an advanced search page for searching by specific blog, date, and links. The advanced search additionally provides search by simple Boolean, title, URL, language, or adult filter. Check the About link for several prefixes that can be used and expect this to be integrated into Google's News search.

Bloogz

www.bloogz.com

Covering blogs back to late 2003, Bloogz allows you to search by language (English, Italian, Spanish, German, French) and sort by relevance or date. By default, search terms are ORed and you can use "+" for AND, "-" for NOT, quotation marks for phrases, and "*" for truncation. Click on the Search Guide link to get the syntax for some interesting user-applied relevance ranking.

IceRocket

www.icerocket.com

Also going back to late 2003, IceRocket's advanced search enables searching by simple Boolean, title, tag, author, or date. The following prefixes can also be used in the main search box: "title:", "author:", and "tag:".

RSS

Depending on whom you ask, RSS stands for either Really Simple Syndication or Rich Site Summary, though the former definition seems to be more popular. RSS is a format that lets news providers (and others) easily syndicate (distribute) their content. It makes use of XML language, which is a cousin of HTML (on its mother's side). The "product" is an "RSS feed," which is basically a specially coded Web page that feeds the information to those who request it. Using RSS feeds, sites can gather the headlines from a broad range of sources and create simple links on their own pages that lead to the stories. RSS has been increasingly used by the broad range of news sites, from networks such as BBC and MSNBC on down to individual newspapers. It is also used extensively by Weblogs, though not all Weblogs (nor all *news* sites for that matter) offer an RSS feed.

On the slightly more technical side, there are actually a number of "formats" that provide these kinds of feeds, and are referred to as RSS, RDF, OPML, Atom, etc. For the user, they are all essentially the same, so unless you are producing a feed yourself, don't worry about the differences.

For a user (you) to make use of these feeds you need an RSS reader—software, or a Web site, that goes out and gathers the feeds that you request. To request the feeds, make use of orange RSS or XML buttons, or similar buttons or links, you find on news sites or Weblogs. For someone who has not yet gotten into RSS, that is where the surprise comes. When you click on one of those buttons what you usually see is a page of code that makes little sense to the average Web user. The secret: Ignore the code, look at the address bar, and copy the URL of the page. It is the URL of that page that you need in order to sign up for an RSS feed. Take that URL to your RSS reader.

If you see a My Yahoo! link, click it and, if you are signed up for My Yahoo!, another click or two and that feed will show up on your My Yahoo! page.

RSS Readers

The following tools, most of which have already been mentioned, can be used for locating RSS feeds of interest and reading them. These are just a few of many RSS readers available. Most allow you to not just add and read feeds, but to organize them into folders or groups, and perform other functions.

Bloglines

bloglines.com

If you click the My Feeds link in Bloglines, you will see links to RSS feeds you have already signed up for and a link to add new feeds (Figure 9.5). For the former, just click on the name of the feed to see the new items.

Figure 9.5

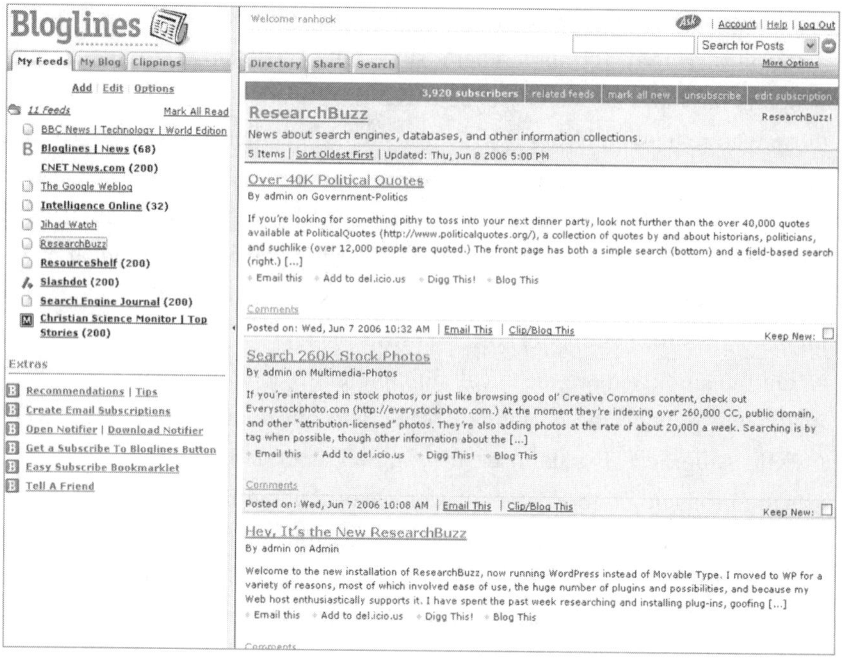

Bloglines RSS reader

Rocketinfo

reader.rocketinfo.com/desktop

Rocketinfo's RSS reader lets you easily add feeds, read them, and organize them into "channels."

My Yahoo!

my.yahoo.com

Almost all of the readers are easy to use, but with a My Yahoo! account, when you see an Add to My Yahoo! link on a news site, you can have the feed appear on your My Yahoo! page with just a couple of clicks. If you find a news site with an RSS button, but no Add to My Yahoo! button, you can still add it to My Yahoo! by copying the URL. In My Yahoo!, click the Add Content link and then the Add RSS by URL link.

ALERTING SERVICES

Among the most underused news offerings on the Internet are the numerous, valuable, and easy-to-use news alerting services. These are services that automatically provide you with a listing of news stories, usually delivered by e-mail and that are sometimes very personalizable according to your interests. You don't have to go to the news; it comes to you. Although the concept has been around for decades, it has gone through many incarnations, ranging from mailings of 3 x 5 cards in the 1960s to the overhyped "push" services in the mid-1990s to the more typical (free) e-mail mailings that have now stood the test of Internet time. If you are not familiar with this concept, the way it works is that you find a site that provides such a service, you register and, in most cases, pick your topic, and thereafter, you will receive e-mails regularly that list news items on that topic. Many newspapers provide alerting services, some allowing you to receive just selected categories of headlines. Some alerting services cover a number of sources and allow you to be very specific with regard to the topic. The best way to find out about these is simply to keep an eye out as you visit sites. Several sites already mentioned in this chapter provide alerting services. The following are two sites that epitomize the possibilities presented by this kind of service.

Google Alerts

www.google.com/newsalerts

Google offers a free alerting service for its 4,500 news sources. You can enter your search and then specify the delivery frequency (daily or "as it happens"). Multiple alerts can be established.

Yahoo! Alerts

alerts.yahoo.com

From Yahoo! News pages, click the News Alerts link to set up keyword alerts on any topic you wish, using the Yahoo! Keyword Alerts option. The Yahoo! Alerts page also provides other alert options, including delivery of alerts by e-mail, Yahoo! IM, or mobile devices.

CHAPTER 10

FINDING PRODUCTS ONLINE

Whether for one's own purchase, for one's organization's purchase, or for competitive analysis purposes, many searchers frequently find themselves searching for and comparing products online. The Internet is a rich resource of product pages, company catalogs, product directories, evaluations, and comparisons. From the rather mundane purchase of a pair of slippers to finding vendors of programmable "servo motion" controllers, the Internet can make the job quicker and easier. This chapter takes a look at where to look and how to do it efficiently and effectively. As with other chapters, the intent is not to be exhaustive, but rather to provide readers with a bit of orientation and some tips, point them in a useful direction, and provide examples of some leading sites.

CATEGORIES OF SHOPPING SITES ON THE INTERNET

A wide variety of types of "shopping" sites on the Internet serve a wide variety of functions. Most sites could fall into one (or more) of the following categories:

- Company catalogs
- Online shopping malls
- Price comparison sites
- Auction sites
- Product and merchant evaluations sites
- Consumer rights sites

Used in combination, these types of sites enable the user to find the desired product, check on the quality of both the product and the vendor, and feel confident and safe in making a purchase. ShoppingSpot.com, the first site listed here, is a good place to start if you want to explore, in an organized way, the variety of shopping resources available on the Web. Many of the sites covered in this chapter serve multiple functions. They are placed in the category that seems to best fit the site's primary function.

ShoppingSpot.com
shoppingspot.com

ShoppingSpot.com will not only point you in a good direction as to where to shop, but it also has a lot of links related to how to shop, with review sites, price comparison sites, consumer protection sites, coupon sites, and other resources. It has an excellent directory of specialized sites, from Antiques to Travel.

LOOKING FOR PRODUCTS— A GENERAL STRATEGY

The all-purpose rule of "keep it simple" works very well when looking for products online. If you know whom you want to buy from, start out with that site. If you have a specific brand, product, or set of characteristics, jump into a general Web search engine and get a quick (and perhaps a bit random) feel for what information is out there about the product. In the first 20 or so records, there is a good chance that you may get some links to vendors, some pages on specific models, links to some reviews, and often, for popular items (for example, photo printers), links to sites about selecting that kind of product.

Then move on to a more systematic approach. For a business-related purchase, you might next go to ThomasNet to identify vendors and specific products. For consumer products, you might go to one of the online shopping malls such as Yahoo! Shopping or eBay. Once you begin to focus on a likely choice, you can check out some reviews of the product itself at one of the review sites, do a search engine search on the specific model or products (ANDing the word "review" to your search), use one of the merchant rating sites, and look around in newsgroups to see what other buyers have said about it.

COMPANY/PRODUCT CATALOGS

If you know the name of the company you might want to buy from and don't know its Web address, put the name in a search engine and you usually will be at their site in seconds. If you don't know who manufactures or sells the product, go to one of the following company/product directories. Each will lead you to companies that produce a product, with a brief description of the company, how to contact the company, and usually a link to the company's Web page.

ThomasNet

www.thomasnet.com

ThomasNet is the online equivalent of *Thomas Register* and *Thomas Regional*—what library users and librarians in the U.S. recognize as that shelf full of thick green books that for decades has been the starting place in many libraries for identifying industrial products and manufacturers. ThomasRegister contains millions of industrial product listings from 650,000 U.S. and Canadian distributors, manufacturers, and service companies, with products listed under 67,000 headings. You can either browse through the categories or make use of the search box (Figure 10.1). If you prefer to search, the tabs near the top of the page will direct your search toward Products/Services, Company Names, Brand Names, or Industrial Web (information from supplier Web sites, catalogs, etc.). Browsing is probably the best way to get a feel for what the site has to offer and the breadth and detail of the categories. (There are 17 categories just for various types of fuel cells.)

Figure 10.1

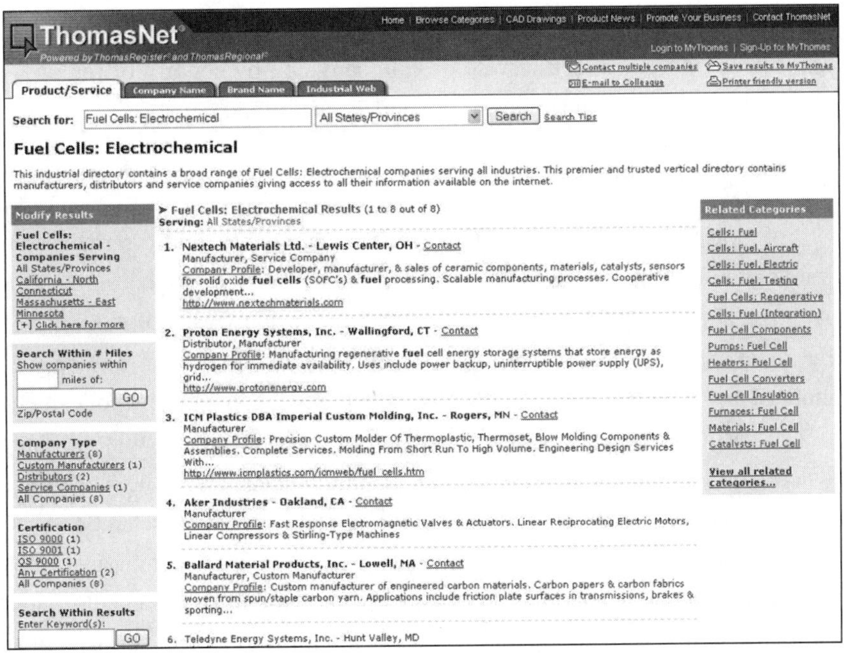

ThomasNet search results

Kompass

www.kompass.com

The Kompass directory includes products from 1.9 million companies in 70 countries. Products are searchable by 54,000 product/service keywords and 750,000 trade names; 3.5 million executive names are also included and searchable. On the Kompass main page, you can search by Products/Services or by Companies and search worldwide, by region, or by country. The More Search Criteria link provides a search by trade names and executives as well. The advanced search requires a subscription, but there is also a pay-as-you-go option. The specificity of the categories and the searchabilty by location make it easy to precisely and thoroughly locate providers (for example, the 141 companies in Western Europe that provide velvet gloves). The site also has sections for Public Tenders and Requests for Quotations. These sections require registration (which is free).

Kellysearch

www.kellysearch.com

From a company that goes back to 1790, Kellysearch covers more than 10 million products from 2 million companies in 13 countries. From the main page, you can browse through 135,000 product headings and you will also find alphabetic indexes to companies and products. Using the search box, you can search either Product/Service or Company and by country or region. A search covers product headings, trade names, and brand names.

SHOPPING MALLS

You don't have to look hard to find sites that enable you to purchase an item online from hundreds or thousands of online stores through a single site. Amazon and Overstock.com are among the most widely used of these malls, but there are many, many more that serve the same function or may be specialized for a particular category of product (see ShoppingSpot.com, mentioned earlier). The sites (online "malls") included in this section are ones where you can purchase items directly from the site, paying the site easily, securely, and confidently, without having to go to other merchant sites to make the purchase. This distinguishes them from the price comparison sites where the site leads you to the Web sites of the individual merchants. Most shopping mall sites use Shopping Cart technology, enabling you to gather multiple items and then check out all items at once.

Both categories (shopping mall and price comparison sites) have some features in common. A third category, auction sites, likewise demonstrates a lot of similarities. Pretty obviously they all give basic information about products (name, brand, model, price, pictures, and a brief description). All of the sites discussed here also provide a search box in which you can search multiple terms (the terms are automatically ANDed). With the exception of Froogle, all of the shopping sites listed here have a directory where you can browse by category and subcategories. Also with the exception of Froogle, all of these sites allow you to perform your search in a specific category as well as across all categories.

The following descriptions will focus on the ways in which these sites differ from one another.

Amazon

www.amazon.com

Initially just an online bookstore, Amazon has expanded to a full shopping mall, where you can buy almost anything, from rare books to sweaters and software. As well as a search box, the main page provides a detailed directory for browsing. (If you hold your cursor over the See All Product Categories tab, you will also get a fly-out box from which to browse categories.) Because of the richness of the site, both in terms of shopping breadth and shopping features, you will find it worthwhile to try the "click everywhere" approach to exploring the Amazon site. On product pages, you will find a section that allows you to narrow your results by category, brand, or price range, and in some cases, additional criteria related to the kind of product. Among the other things you will find are: personalized recommendations based on your previous purchases; sites for Canada, the U.K., Germany, Japan, China, and France; shipment tracking; gift registries; selling options; personal lists where you can store items of interest; and the ability to "Look Inside" a book and view selected actual pages from the book.

Overstock.com

www.overstock.com

Overstock.com, as hinted by its name, is an online "outlet mall" with an emphasis on discounts, and even includes tabs for Liquidation Bins, New Arrivals, and Clearance Bins sections. It also has auctions. On search results pages, you can narrow your search by category, price, and brand, and use the tabs at the top of the results list to narrow your results (depending upon the product) to shopping only, auctions only, etc. For some items, you will find product ratings and reviews.

PRICE COMPARISON SITES

Basically any time you look at the same product from two different suppliers, you are doing a price comparison. In that sense, most of the sites discussed in this chapter are price comparison sites. The following sites discussed, however, put emphasis on the comparison aspect. Those that emphasize consumers' own reviews and opinions are grouped together as a separate subcategory. This division is somewhat arbitrary and reflects more a matter of emphasis of the site than a definitive distinction. The sites that follow are ones that cover the broad range of shopping. Although the interfaces are all different, you will notice a number of commonalties. For most, expect to find the obvious information (name of the product, make, model, a brief description, and price); name of the merchant; product and merchant ratings and reviews; links to compare prices for the same product from multiple merchants; links to do side-by-side comparisons for items that you select from the results page; and links on results pages that allow you to further narrow your selection by brand, store, price range, category, etc. Most have a directory that allows you to browse by category, and most have a search function. There are also sites on the Web that do such comparisons for particular types of products or services, such as computers or travel. (For links to sites that do comparisons for travel, see www.extremesearcher.com/travel.)

Directory of Price Comparison Sites

Open Directory: Consumer Information—Price Comparisons
dmoz.org/Home/Consumer_Information/Price_Comparisons/

This section of Open Directory provides a listing of more than 20 price comparison sites that cover shopping in general.

Yahoo! Shopping
shopping.yahoo.com

Yahoo! Shopping contains millions of products from more than 100,000 stores and provides perhaps the largest range of shopping features of any of the shopping sites. Whether you get to a products page by browsing or searching, you will find there the following options and features:

- Links to save the item to your list of saved items and to see your list.
- Link to more items of that type from that merchant (Yahoo! Shopping only displays one item from each store on the initial product page).
- Merchant rating (ratings of that merchant by buyers).
- Compare Prices button – When the specific brand and model is found in other stores, clicking this button will produce a page showing a grid that compares prices, etc. from the various merchants.
- Compare Side-by-Side button – Use the checkboxes by each item to select those you wish to compare, and then click this button to see a comparison chart of the various brands/models.

On product pages, you will also see a link to view the products in a grid rather than a list and a link to sort the results by product rating (Figure 10.2).

Figure 10.2

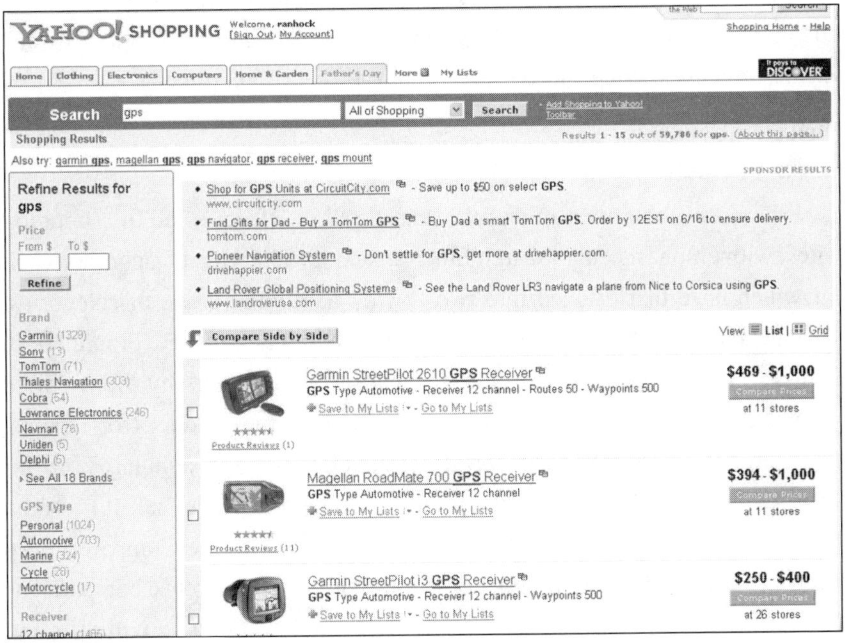

Yahoo! Shopping product page

With the Refine Results section on the left side of the page, you can specify a price range or choose from lists more items from a particular brand, store, or "Special Deals" (25% Off and More, etc.). For some types of items, such as computers, cell phones, and cameras, when you are browsing through the categories, you will find Buying Guides, "Top 5" lists, and more.

mySimon

www.mysimon.com

mySimon, one of the earliest comparison shopping sites, gathers price and other information from thousands of merchants. On the home page, take advantage of the Expert Buying Advice, Shopping Guides, and Consumer Reports sections for advice on a range of popular products. To get to what mySimon can tell you about specific products, use the category tabs or the search box near the top of the page. On the results pages, you can narrow your search by price range, brand, or other criteria specific to the product. The Compare Prices button next to a product will give you a table that provides a price comparison chart for the various stores that sell that item, plus, for each store, shows you the merchant rating, the availability of the item from the store, and a box that enables you to calculate the shipping cost and total cost for the item from each store. Depending upon the product, you may also find product ratings. On the Compare Prices page, you can sort results by best matches, price, store name, store rating, or total price.

PriceGrabber.com

www.pricegrabber.com

PriceGrabber.com has one of the "cleanest" interfaces of all the shopping sites, with emphasis on its search function and its 22 product categories, each of which is further divided into two to four additional levels of categories. Product pages are likewise easy to use, but rich in functionality (Figure 10.3). On the left is a panel where you can narrow your results by brand, price range, etc., with additional criteria depending on the product (for laptops, there are 14 criteria). You can sort the results list by price, popularity, or rating. A Compare button above the product list enables you to select from the list and then see a side-by-side comparison chart. With the Compare Prices button, for an individual product, you can see prices and other comparisons for the stores that sell the product. On PriceGrabber.com, you will also find discussion groups for categories of products.

Figure 10.3

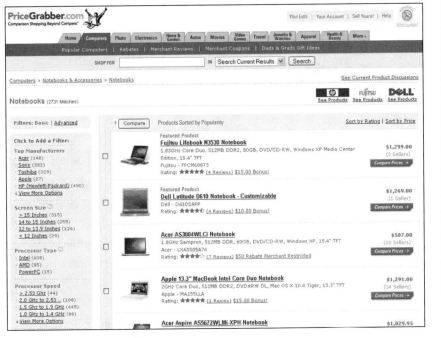

PriceGrabber.com product page

Shopping.com

www.shopping.com

Shopping.com, owned by eBay, has Web sites in the U.S., the U.K., France, and Germany. It has millions of reviews from Epinions as well as millions of products and thousands of merchants. Get to a product listing by either browsing the categories on the home page or by using the search box. Once on a product page, you will find options to further narrow your results by category, price range, brand, keyword, and other product-specific criteria. As with both Yahoo! Shopping and PriceGrabber.com, you will find buttons to get charts comparing selected products from the list, or prices for a particular product from different merchants.

Shopzilla

www.shopzilla.com

Shopzilla provides information on more than 26 million products from more than 76,000 stores. Either Shopzilla's search box or its categories will lead you to a product page where you can narrow a search by price range, brand, and other criteria. Results can be sorted by best match, price (high–low or low–high), or product rating. With the Compare Prices buttons, you can compare prices for the particular product from various stores. Shopzilla is strong on the product ratings and reviews, with an extensive collection of reviews for both products and merchants.

Froogle

froogle.com

Froogle (clever name, eh?) was introduced by Google in 2002, a cousin of Google's under-recognized and marginally promoted Google Catalogs (catalog.google.com), which includes the content of thousands of catalogs. However, Froogle goes beyond just listing the content of catalogs: It includes content that (1) is the result of Google's crawling of the Web to identify product sites, and (2) was submitted by merchants. On Froogle's home page, you will see a search box, a link to the Advanced Froogle Search page, and a sampling of product headings. Froogle does not show a categorized directory of products, so you are limited to searching.

Froogle's advanced search page allows you to search by simple Boolean, price range, and category, and also limit your search to product name or description. On the results pages, you can narrow by subcategory (even though Froogle does not display a list of categories, it does have some categories tucked away), price range, brands, stores, seller rating, and sometimes additional criteria. It also suggests some related searches, and provides links to seller ratings and reviews and a link to add items to your shopping list. On the results page, you can also sort your results by relevance and price (high-to-low or low-to-high), and see a grid view rather than a list of products. You can also search by ZIP code for stores near you, and a Compare button allows you to compare prices from multiples stores.

AUCTIONS

Auction sites on the Web have a lot in common with the shopping malls and price comparison sites, but differ, of course, in the "bidding" approach. The best-known auction site is eBay, though there are a number of others, including a very large auction site that is part of Yahoo! (auctions.yahoo.com).

eBay

ebay.com

Although many people think of eBay as an auction site where almost anything but body parts are auctioned off, it is also a shopping mall where you

Figure 10.4

eBay product page

can buy things outright, avoiding either the fun or effort (however you see it) of having to go through the auction process. When you do a search or browse through the categories, you will see tabs that take you to All Items, Auctions, or Buy It Now. The latter is for items that can be purchased without the auction process. eBay has one of the most sophisticated sets of search features of any of the shopping sites. Look for the Advanced Search links on the main page and other pages. eBay's advanced search allows you to search by simple Boolean ("all the terms" or "any of the terms"), phrase, category, price range, location, seller, etc.

On search results or browsing pages (Figure 10.4), you will find a section that contains links to categories that match your search terms, related buying guides, and a number of narrowing criteria that relate particularly to the "auction" side of eBay, such as location of the seller, payment methods accepted, price range, etc. Also on the results pages, you will find suggested related searches, a button to compare items you select from the results list, and options to sort your results by auction times (newly listed, ending today, etc.). You can sort your results by whether the seller takes PayPal, by price (auction starting bid), and by either the time when the item was listed or time left for the auction. Click on the name of an item to find full details about both the item and the auction status. On the main page, look for the Helpful Links section and click on the Learning Center link. If you are new to auctions, the Learning Center is an excellent place to find out how it all works.

PRODUCT AND MERCHANT EVALUATIONS

Some of the sites just discussed may build both product and merchant reviews into their results. Other sites on the Internet *specialize* in reviews and evaluations, including consumer opinion sites and merchant rating sites. Among these are Epinions, BizRate, Consumer Reports, Consumer Search, and ConsumerREVIEW.com.

In addition to using these sites, Web search engines can also be used effectively to find reviews and evaluations by simply doing a search on the name of the product (e.g., *Nikon F100*) or the type of product (e.g., *digital cameras*), in combination with the terms "evaluations" or "reviews."

Example: *"digital cameras" (reviews OR evaluations)*

Going one step further, especially if you are tracking your own or competitors' products, take advantage of the frequent comments that appear in newsgroups regarding products. Look both at Google Groups (groups.google.com) and Yahoo! Groups (groups.yahoo.com) discussed in Chapter 6.

Epinions
epinions.com

On the surface, Epinions looks much like other shopping sites, with a search box and browsable categories that include more than 2 million products or services. What differs is that the emphasis in Epinions is on the reviews. For each product, you will find links to further details about the product and to reviews written by Epinions users. To provide reliable reviews, even the reviewers can be reviewed by Epinions' "Web of Trust" system. For various products, you will also find advanced search options, buyer's guides, and store ratings.

BizRate
bizrate.com

BizRate is also both a shopping site and a review site, and you can browse by category or you can search. Once you identify a particular product, you will typically have access to details about the product (often detailed specifications in the case of electronic and other technical products), reviews of the product, and the list of stores and their prices. For each store, you will see a rating, based on feedback from BizRate users.

Consumer Reports

consumerreports.org

Consumer Reports, the publisher of the well-known product review journal, has its evaluations available online, but only to paid subscribers.

ConsumerREVIEW.com

consumerreview.com

ConsumerREVIEW.com, one of the specialized product review sites, focuses on reviews of outdoor, sporting goods, and consumer electronics products.

ConsumerSearch

consumersearch.com

ConsumerSearch takes a different approach to providing reviews by having its editors "scour the Internet and print publications for comparative reviews and other information sources relevant to the consumer." The reviews on the site are based on those sources and a set of criteria developed by ConsumerSearch.

BUYING SAFELY

Although many Internet users quickly began to take advantage of the benefits of online purchasing, some users are still quite shy about giving up their credit card numbers to a machine. Having a healthy skepticism is indeed a reasonable approach. Knowing where caution ends and paranoia begins is the problem. In general, following a few basic rules should keep the online purchaser fairly safe. There are few guarantees, but there are also few guarantees that the waiter to whom you gave your credit card in the restaurant did not do something illegal with it. If the following precautions are kept in mind, online purchasers should feel reasonably secure:

1. Consider who the seller is. If it is a well-known company, there is some security in that. (Yes, we *do* remember Enron.) If you don't

recognize the seller, do you know the site? Sites such as Amazon and Barnes & Noble are respected and want to protect their reputation. If you are buying through an intermediary such as eBay, it likewise has a reputation to protect and builds in some protections, such as providing access to feedback about sellers from other customers. On some merchant sites, you will see symbols displayed that indicate the merchant is registered with organizations that are in the business of assuring that member merchants meet high standards. The best known of these organizations is BBBOnline (from the Better Business Bureau, www.bbbonline.org). On its site, you can search to see if a company is a member. For various legitimate reasons, even large and reputable sites may not participate in programs such as these, so the lack of a seal of approval alone should certainly not keep you from buying.

2. When you get to the point of putting in payment information, check to see that the site is secure. Look for the closed padlock icon on the status bar at the bottom of your browser, or the https (instead of http) in the address bar of the browser.

3. As with traditional purchases, read the fine print. Look for the payment methods, terms, and return policy. Also look around for seller contact points, such as phone number and address.

4. Print and keep a copy of the purchase confirmation message you receive when you complete the purchase.

5. When possible, pay by credit card to be able to take advantage of the protections this provides regarding unauthorized billings. Some sites, such as eBay, will also provide services. These services charge the seller a fee and may cause a slight delay, but hold the money until the product is received. Payment services such as PayPal also build in some safeguards.

For additional advice, take advantage of the safeshopping.org site created by the American Bar Association. If you encounter problems with a purchase, you may want to consult the Federal Trade Commission's site for E-Commerce (www.ftc.gov/bcp/menu-internet.htm). For cross-border complaints, consult eConsumer.gov (www.econsumer.gov).

CHAPTER 11

BECOMING PART OF THE INTERNET: PUBLISHING

The Internet is, obviously, a two-way street. So far, this book has primarily discussed using the Internet to *find* information. The other direction is *providing* information to be found. Creating and participating in groups (discussion groups, etc.), which were discussed in Chapter 6, is one way of contributing to the content on the Internet, but the more systematic way of providing information to others is to have your own "place" on the Web—a Weblog, a podcast, a Web site, or a variation of those.

A "PLACE" ON THE WEB

The general nature and purpose of the Web is "communication," and the Web provides not just the ability to receive information, but to transmit ("publish") information, to go beyond the now-mundane ability to communicate with a set group of people via e-mail, to go out to the Web "worldwide," to get a message across—to share yourself, your knowledge, your work, and your opinions, with a virtually unlimited audience.

There are numerous ways to make a "place" for yourself on the Web, ways that provide varying levels of simplicity, exposure, and impact. As just mentioned, the ways include the use groups and forums, covered in Chapter 6. Particularly by using something like Yahoo! Groups, you can have a place to put text, photos, and files, interact with visitors to the site, and more. Weblogs likewise can be a "place" on the Web for you, with even greater simplicity. They have a different nature than groups, and have a reputation for being a good place to express opinions and share news and ideas. There are also specialized publishing opportunities for things such as publishing your own photos, with descriptions, comments, and viewer interaction, on sites such as Flickr. If you just want to be "social," you can get a page on a site such as MySpace. If your spoken word conveys your message better than the written word, you can become a podcaster. Beyond that, for the full experience and the greatest level of exposure, versatility, variety, and communications power, you can set up an actual Web page or Web site of your own, with, as you wish, your own design, photos, links, images, audio, video, and much more. Achieving a presence on the Web can be as simple as a Weblog or as intensive an endeavor as a full-fledged Web site with many pages and a broad range of features.

As for why you may wish to do any of this, there are many reasons for considering publishing: providing a "personal" space for yourself, a space for an organization to which you belong, a committee of which you are a member, a course you teach, a "cause," your own business …

Whatever your reasons, as you move into publishing, keep two words in mind: *content* and *style*. It is a truism that on the Web "Content is King." You must have useful content to make visitors to your place feel it was worth the trip and to make them come back. Have something to say! What you say may be as simple as family news, family photos, your resume, or a syllabus for a course. As for style, the term in this context has two aspects: personal style and presentation style. For the first, don't put yourself on the Web unless you can do so with "style." You don't need to come across as suave, sophisticated, sexy, or debonair, but what you put on the Web of yourself should reflect the best you have to offer.

The other aspect of style is your writing style and the style of your page. You want the look of your place to convey neatness, thoughtfulness, and organization. If you are going the Weblog route or are creating a Web site using a template, the style of the page itself will pretty much take care of itself. As for what you write, do it correctly. Poor grammar and other writing problems definitely communicate something, but not what you want. (Think about your own reaction when you encounter a page with multiple spelling errors.) Though it is written primarily for people building Web pages, the following site can be useful for most people who want to have any form of effective Web presence.

Web Style Guide

www.webstyleguide.com

Written for people who are creating Web sites, the well-known Web Style Guide presents, in an easy-to-read, non-technical way, the basic principles of design that should be considered for any Web site. Even for those who are using templates or just "involved" in some way in the management of a Web site, the time-tested Web Style Guide is worthwhile and interesting reading. (Though the Web Style Guide Web site is great, the inexpensive, beautifully presented book version is slicker and perhaps more convenient to read. Sometimes "books are better.")

On "Personal" Web Places

We are all our own "company" even if we work for someone else. As Tom Peters said, "To be in business today, our most important job is to be head marketer for the brand called You" (www.fastcompany.com/online/10/brandyou.html). This is true not just for executives and aspiring executives, but very true for academics, artists, writers, entrepreneurs, and others. Having a place of your own on the Web, where you can send people or where people can find you, is both easy and (for many but not all people) important. If you choose to have a personal Web site, do it with style. Make sure it conveys the degree of professionalism you want it to convey. Then advertise it. Submit it to search engines. Put the URL in your automatic e-mail signatures. Put in on your business cards.

WEBLOGS

If you have something you wish to say and/or information that you feel should be shared, there is really no easier way to get yourself a place on the Web than to get yourself a Weblog. The Weblog ("blog") alternative has found much favor and publicity in the last few years and requires little effort. Discussed earlier in Chapter 9 from the news content perspective, blogs provide an easy means to gather and distribute news, commentary, advice, and so forth (Figure 11.1). The main intent of blogs is to provide a place for short and frequently updated postings. Although they may lack the graphics and other capabilities of a Web site, their ease of use has been a major factor in their popularity.

Software and Sites for Creating Blogs

There are a number of sites and software programs (blogging tools) that allow you to create blogs, some that you can use through your browser and some that you download and install on your server. Those that allow you to

Figure 11.1

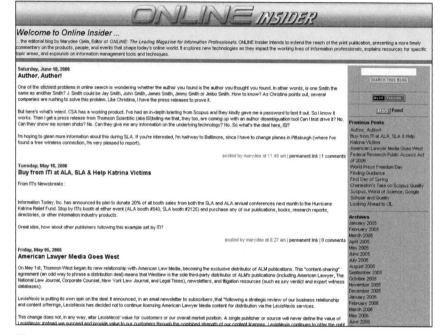

Example of a blog

do your blogging online through your browser typically will also host your blog on their site. The following are some of the more well-known examples of places where you can go to create a blog.

Blogger

blogger.com

Blogger is a free blogging tool and hosting service. It is one of the best known and is both simple to use and powerful. On the Blogger site, you can create your blog and Blogger will also host the site for you on Blogger's hosting site, blogspot.com. Indeed, in the five minutes or less that Blogger advertises, you really can get your blog created and up on the Web. You can choose from several templates for your page or, with some HTML skills, you can modify one as you wish. Posts can be made from the Blogger site using a WYSIWYG interface, by e-mail, or from your mobile device. You cannot categorize your posts on Blogger, but among the other features that Blogger provides, you can moderate and otherwise control visitor comments, block spam robots, post photos from your computer or your camera phone, post audio blogs, and easily create a news feed.

WordPress.com

wordpress.com

WordPress.com provides a free, quite full-featured, easy-to-use Web-based interface for creating and hosting your blogs and you can get a blog set up in barely more than five minutes. With the features WordPress.com offers, you can categorize posts; RSS feeds for both your posts and for comments received are automatically set up; you can create a site index and have multiple pages; you can import posts you have posted on another Weblog service; statistics are automatically provided (volume, referrers, and top posts, for both the blog and feeds); you can control spam with your own list of spam words and your own blacklist; you can create bookmarklets for each post. At present you cannot post by e-mail or mobile devices. WordPress.com in general gives you quite good control both over how posts are displayed and over comments. Posting images is a bit complicated, but on the other hand (after a few setup steps), you can easily post pictures directly from Flickr to your WordPress.com Weblog.

Blogs created on WordPress.com can be hosted elsewhere, as well as on the WordPress.com site, and if you wish, you can download the program to your own server. The basic WordPress.com service is free but for advanced services such as extra storage and domain hosting there is a fee. WordPress.com can get a beginner going quickly, easily, and free, yet it allows users to take advantage of features that should keep even experienced bloggers happy.

Moveable Type

www.sixapart.com/movabletype

Moveable Type, a pioneer in blogging software, is client software that you download (rather than making use of a Web site such as Blogger). It is very full-featured and because of that, even though it is less easy to use than Blogger and some other programs, it is the favorite of many professional bloggers, and it is designed to be able to manage many blogs from many people. There is a free downloadable version, but for a supported version, you must pay. Moveable Type does not itself provide hosting of your Weblogs. The installation of the program is best handled by someone with some technical expertise.

LiveJournal

www.livejournal.com

LiveJournal is a community-focused blogging tool and hosting site from Six Apart, the people who created Moveable Type. When you are signed up with LiveJournal, you can join its Communities, which are interest-specific or region-specific. LiveJournal has two levels of free service (the "sponsored" service that comes with ads, the other comes without ads) and a paid version. By allowing ads, you get access to more features. The ad-free subscription is limited to very basic blogging features (plus a few additional features such as tagging of entries), the sponsored membership gives you substantially more, and the paid version gives you access to all features, which includes such things as posting by phone and e-mail and creating a poll; use of Scrapbook, which is LiveJournal's image and video hosting service; an advanced search feature; customized themes (templates); text messaging to members; and more. A "Memories" feature allows you to organize entries into a keyword archive system. These can include not just your own posts but those from communities and other members. As well as being able to use LiveJournal through your browser, there is downloadable client software available that you can use.

Weblogging Hybrids

The following two sites are examples of "hybrid" blogging tools that go beyond blogging into the realm of "social networking."

MySpace

myspace.com

One of the blogging tools previously discussed, LiveJournal, provides standard blogging features, but with a significant focus on online "communities," a concept also referred to as "social networking." MySpace is foremost a "social networking" site, a site that makes use of blogs as one feature of what it provides. MySpace is primarily populated with teens, twenty-somethings, bands, and celebrities (or, more likely, their publicists). It is about socializing, it is about the "personal." In one sense it is about what blogs were initially about—personal journals—but in the MySpace context, the topics are typically about "me" and about fun, leisure, and enjoyment, rather than the types of commentary and content provided by the more traditional blog sites. MySpace is, though, a phenomenon about which even the "more-than-thirty-somethings" should know, because of its current role in the Internet "culture."

Yahoo! 360°

360.yahoo.com

Yahoo! 360° is a personal Web page that you can easily create and that has at its core a blog. In addition, you can post pictures and do some "social networking" by providing links to "friends" you have invited to have a link on your page, and you can share your Yahoo! LAUNCHcast radio station selections, your own reviews of restaurants and businesses, the list of Yahoo! Groups to which you belong, and your favorite links.

PODCASTS

Podcasts, which were discussed in Chapter 9 from the perspective of finding them, are also a way for anyone to publish on the Internet. For messages that are best conveyed aurally, for genres such as storytelling, or as an avenue for reaching a sight-impaired audience, podcasts present a very viable publishing option.

To create a podcast of your own, you need the following, some of which should be pretty obvious: (1) something to say; (2) a microphone; (3) a computer with an Internet connection; (4) sound recording software; (5) an MP3 encoder to convert what you record into an MP3 format; (6) a place on the Web to host your podcast. For the latter, a Weblog or Web site can work fine. For more detail, visit the following site.

Yahoo! Podcasts—Publish a Podcast

podcasts.yahoo.com/publish

This section of the Yahoo! Podcasts site provides a good introduction to what is involved in publishing a podcast, including links to where you can download the necessary software.

WEB SITES

Of all of the ways to publish on the Web, the classic and ultimate way is having your own Web site. From there, you have the greatest flexibility and unlimited content and the possibilities are virtually (there is a pun there) unlimited.

In addition to the reasons previously mentioned, having a site of your own is also useful for another reason. For those who are involved in contributing input to their organization's site or to someone else's site, having done your own Web site can provide a healthy perspective. It can, on one hand, take away a lot of the mystique (you won't be unnecessarily awed by some of the cute little things you see), and on the other hand, you will have a better appreciation for the more sophisticated things you see. Also, if your time and inclinations permit such, building your own site can be a lot of fun.

What follows is not intended to teach you how to build a Web site, but intends to provide an overview of what is involved in order to help answer the questions: Can I do it (build my own Web site)? What is involved in doing so? What will it cost?

If you go with the Web site option for publishing, you have a range of options and levels of sophistication. You can have, or not have, your own domain name, you can use templates or a Web page editor, or if you are, or want to be, in the *techie* category, you can build pages from scratch by writing HTML.

What's Needed

The main tools needed for building a Web site of your own are a purpose, time, software, skills, and a place to publish. Depending on what you want to produce, each of these can either be minimal or extensive.

Purpose

The introductory paragraphs to this chapter mentioned some of the reasons for creating your own place on the Web. Before you start with a Web site, though, it is advisable to give a fair amount of consideration to why you are doing it and what you want to accomplish. Though those things may seem very obvious, a focus on those two considerations is important for all Web site designers, from beginner to the most experienced. Your aims may change continually, but the more direction you have established to begin with, the less you may have to go back and change later. Write down your purpose. The main purpose of almost any page is "communication." What do you want to communicate and why?

Tied in closely to your statement of purpose will be an analysis of your intended audience. Who are you addressing? What background are they likely to have in connection with your topic? What age level are you addressing? How skilled are they likely to be in using and navigating through Web pages? What is their level of interest? For the latter point, if your page is the syllabus for a course you are teaching, users have a high level of interest in that they may be required to use the page. If you are selling something, you need to design a page that will do a good job of attracting and keeping the readers' attention.

Time

If you are using a free Web site service such as Tripod or GeoCities (discussed later in this chapter) and you take advantage of their templates and already know what information you want to put on the site, you can have a Web site created and available for use in an hour or so. The time required to build and maintain a site goes up from there, depending upon how fancy you want to get, how much content you want to include, and how much maintenance the site will require (updating, etc.).

Software

If you are building a site using a free Web site service such as GeoCities or Tripod, you will not need any software other than your browser. These sites provide what you need to make a basic but at the same time very attractive site, with room for lots of content and many pages. Beyond that, unless you decide to learn how to write HTML (HyperText Markup Language) code, you will need a Web page editing program such as Dreamweaver, FrontPage, HomeSite, Claris HomePage, or Netscape Composer (there are many, many more). These are basically word-processor-like programs that convert what you enter, and the features you choose, into HTML code.

The cost of these can range from free (e.g., Mozilla Composer or Netscape Composer) to several hundred dollars. If you are using the editor for educational purposes, you may find an educator's rate for some programs that will be substantially less than the full price.

Composer (either Mozilla or Netscape) provides the basics of what you need to build a Web page. Parts of the program can be a bit clunky and it does not provide the more sophisticated features such as forms and cascading style sheets. It does, however, provide what most beginners need, and the fact that it is free is significant.

If you think you are going to want to get more sophisticated, have many pages on your site, and make it interactive, you may want to start with a sophisticated, but still relatively easy-to-use program such as Dreamweaver (Figure 11.2).

Figure 11.2

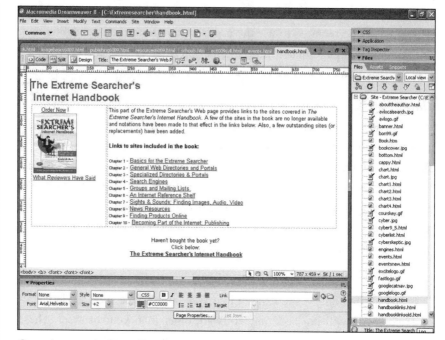

Sample page built on Dreamweaver

Uploading your finished pages to a Web server will require file transfer software. HTML editors usually build in this feature.

Graphics Software

It is likely that you will want some images on your site and unlikely that you will want to put them on your page without making some modifications to the images, such as cropping and some other easy changes that will improve the image. Chances are that you already have graphics software that will do what you need. If you have purchased a scanner or a digital camera, it probably came with a program for editing photos. These programs are surprisingly robust and adequate for most operations that need to be performed on images to make them ready to be placed on a Web page. If you want to move up a step, consider Adobe PhotoShop Elements, a program that does the vast majority of things that the well-known and much more expensive PhotoShop does.

Skills

To build a Web site with the minimalist approach (using templates on a free Web site service) requires only the ability to follow step-by-step instructions.

Beyond that, the ability to use (or learn how to use) an HTML editor will be needed and the ability to work with graphics will be useful. Be aware that the use of graphics software can be addictive—as well as using it for your Web site, you may find yourself up at 3 A.M. fixing the cracks and tears in that photo of your great-grandfather and adding feathered edges, drop-shadows, and other special effects to your pictures.

If you are new to using Web editors and graphics software, there are a number of ways to learn. Your choice will probably depend upon your own learning styles. Most programs you purchase will have a built-in tutorial, and if you commit an hour or so, you can be on your way. If you are willing to commit several hours, you will probably find yourself in quite good control of the program. There are also tutorials available on the Web for most popular programs, and they sometimes provide a more simplified, yet effective, approach to Web page editing and graphics software. Do a Web search for the name of your program and the word "tutorial" and you will probably find several. There are also numerous books and classes available for the more popular programs.

The alternative to using an HTML editor is to learn to write HTML code. Most people would probably consider this the hard way, but it can actually be fun. (Then again, some people also consider jumping into an icy river on New Year's Day "fun.") For most, starting with a Web page editing program makes the most sense, but as you get more heavily into Web page building, you eventually will want to learn the basics of HTML because of the added control it can give you. (In the interest of full disclosure, the author admits to having had fun writing HTML code.) Knowing some HTML code can make the use of an editor such as Dreamweaver easier, quicker, and more flexible.

Domain Names

If you make use of one of the free Web site hosts, your site will have an address that looks something like *geocities.com/yourname*. If you go with a paid hosting service, you will need to get a domain name of your own. For someone who has a company and/or needs to make the most professional impression, having one's own domain name is the way to go. The cost of purchasing (registering) a domain name has come down tremendously and when you sign up for a Web-hosting service, the service will usually bundle the process and cost of getting the name of your choice registered into the hosting.

Related to that last point is the issue of whether you would prefer to sign up through a domain registration service and then, separately, choose a host, or whether you want to just have your chosen hosting service do the registration process for you. The latter is easier, but if you decide later to switch hosts, some extra steps will be involved.

Even if you aren't ready to build a site, you may want to get a domain name for your own name (*yourname.com*) or "reserve" a name for the company you dream of having. (This is called "domain parking" and is a way of protecting some of your "intellectual property.") Some domain name registration services will not only register and "park" your name for you, but will throw in an e-mail service so that you can use your domain name for your e-mail even if you do not yet have a Web site. These services can be very inexpensive (less than $15 per year). Regarding the e-mail service, as long as you keep your name registered, your address will always be there. If you change jobs, you will still have your personal e-mail address, and it also provides that backup e-mail address you can use when you don't want to, or shouldn't be, using your employer's e-mail system. (For that purpose, you can of course just use a free e-mail service such as Yahoo! Mail or Gmail, but the e-mail addresses you have with them do not convey the same "importance" as an address from your own domain name.) The following is one example of a registration service that specializes in providing these added services.

000Domains.com
www.000domains.com

000Domains.com provides registration services for more than 30 top-level domains including the usual general domains (.com, .net, etc.), plus several country domains such as .us, .uk, and .de. In addition to the domain registration, 000Domains.com includes, among other services, the following at no additional charge: domain parking; e-mail forwarding; domain forwarding (from multiple addresses to an existing site); and unlimited ownership changes (you can assign your domains to someone else).

Where to Publish

Among the main options for places where an individual Web-site builder may place a Web page are the following: on a Web-hosting service with your own domain name, on your organization's server, or on one of the "free Web site" sites.

Web-Hosting Services

Once you have decided that you want to have a Web site of your own with your own domain name, you will need to choose a Web-hosting company (service) where your Web pages will reside. These companies can easily be located through their ads in computer magazines, a yellow pages directory, or a Web search. There are numerous directories specifically of Web-hosting services. To locate these directories, you can use the following Open Directory category (at dmoz.org):

> Computers > Internet > Web Design and Development >
> Hosting > Directories

Web-host services will host your site for as little as $5 or even less for basic service and will also guide you through the process of getting your own domain name. One of the big advantages of these services is that they handle most of the paperwork of the domain name registration. Compare the ads, call their toll-free numbers, and talk to two or three of them, partly to get a feel for their degree of customer service orientation.

As you explore these, you will get a feel for the various levels of service provided and be able to decide which you need. (If, for example, you aren't selling a product, it is unlikely that you will need a Shopping Cart service as part of your hosting contract.) Be sure to check the reviews of Web-hosting services. The following site will help.

Upperhost

www.upperhost.com

Upperhost is an independent Web-host reviewing service. It provides up-to-date benchmarking and reviews, done by Webmasters, on a very wide range of Web-hosting companies. You will also find user comments and a useful collection of articles on Web hosting.

Putting Your Site on Your Organization's Server

If you are in an academic institution, there is a good chance that your institution may provide free Web space for you. For other organizations, there may be similar possibilities depending on your purpose and the nature of the organization. Do not be surprised if you are presented with a list of criteria that must be met, with regard to both content and format. If you are a faculty member at a university, you may easily be assigned Web space with minimal restrictions and the permission to upload your pages when and as you like. At the K–12 level, there is a very good chance that there will be cooperation and enthusiasm for teachers or others to create school and classroom pages. In other situations, it may not be as easy, and there are situations where you will encounter institutional Webmasters with requirements that make little sense. Fortunately, a larger proportion of those in charge of organizational sites are realistic and helpful.

Free Web Page Sites

For many people who want to get started, using a free Web site service is an excellent starting place. Even if you are planning to eventually place your site on your organization's server or have your own domain name on a hosting service, these free Web site services provide a good initiation. Free Web sites are available from a variety of sources. The ISP (Internet Service Provider) you use at home may provide a free site for subscribers. There are also commercial sites that specialize in providing free space. You pay for these by putting up with the ads that will come along when your page is displayed, but it is often a good bargain. They usually also offer upgrades (that avoid the ads) for a relatively small monthly fee. The leading free Web-site services are GeoCities (a part of Yahoo! at geocities.com; see Figure 11.3), Tripod (tripod.com), and Angelfire (angelfire.com).

Each of these services provides 15 to 20 megabytes of storage, which is enough for a very substantial Web site. They also provide templates that can be used, Web editors, and uploading capabilities, as well as allowing you to upload pages you have created elsewhere, such as in another Web editor. These sites also make it easy to place features such as the following on the pages you create: photos, a counter, news headlines, weather for places you choose, online messages, and guest books. In most cases, you will have at least a little control over the kinds of ads that appear by your choice of the interests or communities that you select as part of the sign-up procedure.

In addition to the three services listed above, Google of course has gotten into the game with Google Page Creator (pages.google.com).

Sites to Help You Build Your Web Sites

There are thousands of Web sites that provide help in building Web pages, ranging from the tutorials already mentioned to sites that provide specific

Figure 11.3

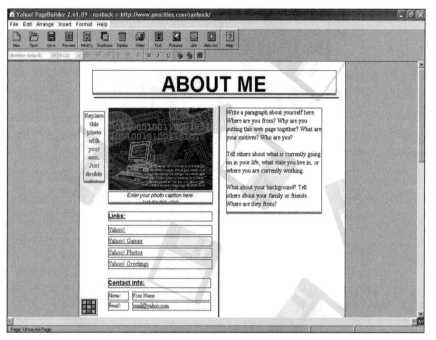

Example of a GeoCities template

features you can place on your pages (such as graphics and JavaScript scripts) to sites that bring together a large collection of a variety of tools. The following three representative sites are those that the beginner may want to explore, particularly to get a feel for the kind of help that is out there.

Webmonkey

www.webmonkey.com

Webmonkey is especially strong on tutorials for a variety of things you might want to place on your page (Figure 11.4). Look particularly at the Beginners page. The content of the site is presented and arranged in a way that you can, at your own speed, build up your Webmaster skills one step at a time.

Reallybig.com: The Complete Resource for All Web Builders

reallybig.com

Reallybig.com contains more than 5,000 links of use to both the beginner and the advanced builder, including resources for "free scripts, CGI, counters, fonts, HTML, Java, clipart, animation, backgrounds, icons, HTML editors, buttons, photographs, site promotion, easy-to-follow Tips and Tricks, and much more."

Figure 11.4

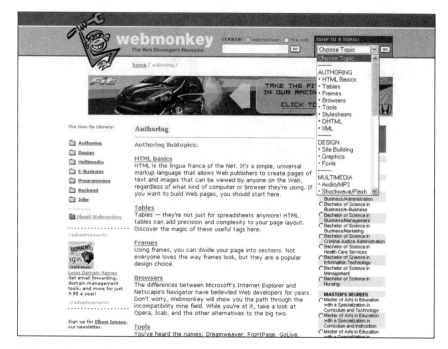

Webmonkey authoring page

About.com—Web Design

webdesign.about.com

This section of the About.com site contains articles, tips, tutorials, and an excellent collection of links to resources such as clip art collections, JavaScript collections, Web hosting services, and so on.

Though it wasn't emphasized in the discussion of reasons for creating Weblogs and Web sites, if you are the kind of person who is inclined to try out the publishing side of the Web, an added benefit that will almost undoubtedly accrue is that you will have some fun, probably a lot of fun, doing it.

Conclusion

It is hoped that the preceding chapters have provided some new and useful ideas, information, and sites, even for the very experienced Internet user. My final bit of advice is: "Explore!" As you use the sites I've mentioned, or any site, take a few extra seconds to look around. Poke into the corners of a site, and if it looks very promising, "click everywhere."

—*Ran Hock*

GLOSSARY

The following words are defined in the context of the Internet and are not necessarily intended to be applied generally.

Ajax. Asynchronous JavaScript and XML. A technique for creating interactive Web applications. It increases the interactivity of a page by making it unnecessary to reload the entire page when only a portion of the page needs to be changed.

algorithm. A step-by-step procedure for solving a problem or achieving a task. In the context of search engines, this is the part of the service's program that performs a task, such as identifying which pages should be retrieved or ranking retrieved pages.

ALT tag. Text associated with an image, in the HTML code of a page, that can be used to identify the content of the image or for other purposes. Standing for "alternate text," it initially provided a description while waiting for the image to load, but it is now used more for other purposes, such as providing a description of the image that can be read by screen readers for sight-impaired users. In some browsers, you will see this text pop up when you hold your cursor over an image.

AND. The Boolean operator (or connector) that specifies the "intersection" of sets. When used between words in a search engine query, it specifies that only those records are to be retrieved that contain *both* words (the words preceding and following the "AND"). For example, *stomach AND growling* would only retrieve records containing both of those words. For major search engines, you do not actually type AND since it is implied (automatically applied). (See **Boolean**.)

API. Application Program Interface. An interface that one program provides to allow requests for services or interchange of data from another program.

applet. A small Java program used on a Web page to perform certain display, computational, or other functions. The origin of the term refers to "small applications programs."

blogs. See **Weblogs**.

bookmark. A feature in Web browsers, analogous to bookmarks in a book, that remembers the location of a particular Web page and adds it to a list so a user can return to the page easily. Firefox, Netscape, and others refer to these as "bookmarks," while Internet Explorer uses the term "favorites."

Boolean. Mathematical system of notation created by 19th-century mathematician George Boole that symbolically represents relationships between sets (entities). For information retrieval, it uses AND, OR, and NOT (or their equivalents) to identify those records that meet the criteria of having both of two terms within the same record (AND), having either of two terms within the records (OR), or eliminating records that contain a particular term (NOT).

broadband. High-speed data transmission capability. In the home or office context, it usually refers to DSL (Digital Subscriber Line), cable, high-speed fiber-optic access, or T1 (or higher) Internet access.

browser. Software that enables display of Web pages by interpreting HTML code, translating it, and performing related tasks. The first widely-used browser was Mosaic, which evolved into Netscape. Internet Explorer is the browser developed by Microsoft. Among the several others are Firefox, Opera, and Safari.

browsing. Examining the contents of a database or Web site, etc., by scanning lists or categories and subcategories. When a site provides this capability, it is referred to as having browsability.

case-sensitivity. The ability to recognize the difference between upper and lower case. In information retrieval, it means the difference between being able to recognize *White* as a name versus *white* as a color, or *AIDS* as the disease versus *aids* as something that provides assistance.

classification. Arrangement of items (such as Web sites) by subject area, often using a hierarchical scheme with several levels of categories and subcategories. In some cases, alphanumeric codes are used instead of words (for example, Library of Congress or Dewey Decimal classifications).

concept-based retrieval. Retrieval based on finding records that contain words related to the concept searched for, not necessarily the specific word(s).

co-occurrence. Occurrence of specific different terms within the same records. Analyzing the frequency of co-occurrence is one technique used to find records that are similar to a selected record.

cookies. Small files of information generated by a Web server and stored on the user's computer, used for personalization of sites, etc.

crawler. See **spider**.

diacritical marks. Marks such as accents that are applied to a letter to indicate a different phonetic value.

directory (Web). Collection of Web page records classified by subject to allow easy browsing of the collection.

domain name. The part of a URL (Web address) that usually specifies the organization (computer) and type of organization where the Web page is located (e.g., in www.microsoft.com, "microsoft.com" is the domain name). Domain names always have at least two parts: The first part usually identifies the organization or specific machine; the second part (e.g., ".com") identifies the kind of organization. In some cases, there will be a two-letter code indicating the country of origin. All domain names have a corresponding numeric address, such as 207.158.227.228.

domain name server. A computer that converts the URL you enter into the numeric address of a domain and identifies the location of the requested computer.

field. A specific portion of a record, or Web page, such as title, metatags, URL, etc.

file extension. In a file name, such as letter.doc or house.gif, the part of the file name that follows the period, usually indicating the type of file.

folksonomy. A process whereby users of a site, such as one that contains photos, can "tag" items with their own choice of descriptive terms. Theoretically, this is an aid to help other users locate items of interest.

FTP. File Transfer Protocol. Computer protocol (set of instructions) for uploading and downloading files.

gopher. A menu-based directory that allows access to files from a remote computer. Gophers were supplanted in the mid-1990s by Web tools such as directories and search engines.

home page. The main page of a Web site. It is also the page designated by a user as the page that should be automatically brought up when the user's browser is loaded.

HTML. HyperText Markup Language. The coding language used to create Web pages. It tells a browser how to display a record, including specifications for fonts, colors, location of images, identification of hypertext links, etc.

Internet. Worldwide network of networks based on the TCP/IP protocol.

Invisible Web. Those pages that are not indexed by Web search engines and therefore cannot be retrieved by means of a search on those engines.

Java. A programming language designed for use on networks, particularly the Internet, which allows programs to be downloaded and run on a variety of platforms. Java is incorporated into Web pages with small applications programs called "applets" that provide features such as animation, calculators, games, etc.

JavaScript. A computer language used to write "scripts" for use in browsers to allow creation of features such as scrolling marquees, navigation buttons that change appearance when you hold your mouse over them, etc.

metasearch engines. Search services that search several individual search engines and then combine the results.

metasites. See **resource guides**.

metatags. The portion (field) of the HTML coding for a Web page that allows the person creating the page to enter text describing the content of the page. The content of metatags is not shown on the page itself when the page is viewed in a browser window.

NEAR. A "proximity" connector that is used between two words to specify that a page should be retrieved only when those words are near each other in the page. (See **proximity**.)

nesting. The use of parentheses to specify the way terms in a Boolean expression should be grouped (i.e., the order of the operations). For example, *landmines (detection OR disarming)*.

newsgroup. An online discussion group. A group of people and the messages they communicate on a specific topic of interest. The term also refers more narrowly to such a discussion group on Usenet.

NOT. The Boolean operator (connector) that when used with a term eliminates the records containing that term. (See **Boolean**.)

OR. The Boolean operator (connector) that is used between two terms to retrieve all records that contain either term. (See **Boolean**.)

podcasts. Downloadable audio recordings (broadcasts), analogous to Weblog postings. Podcasts are usually published using feeds (e.g., RSS) that can be downloaded via the Web and transferred to an MP3 player (or to a CD) so the user can listen to it at his or her convenience.

portal. A site that serves as a gateway or starting point for a collection of Web resources. Portals typically have a variety of tools (such as a search engine, directory, news, etc.) on a single page that is usually designed so a user can use the page as their start page for their browser. Portals are often personalizable for content, layout, etc.

precision. In information retrieval, the degree to which a group of retrieved records actually match the searcher's needs. More technically, precision is the ratio of the number of retrieved relevant items to the total number of retrieved items (multiplied by 100 percent to express the ratio as a percentage). For example, if a query produced 10 records and six of them were judged relevant, the precision would be 60 percent. This is sometimes referred to as relevance.

proximity. The nearness of two terms. Some search engines provide proximity operators, such as NEAR, which allow a user to specify how close two terms must be for a record containing those terms to be retrieved.

ranking. The process by which it is determined in what order records retrieved by a search engine should be displayed. Search engines use algorithms that evaluate records to assign a "score" that is meant to indicate the relative "relevance" of each record. The retrieved records can then be ranked and listed on the basis of those scores.

recall. In information retrieval, the degree to which a search has actually managed to find all the relevant records in the database. More technically, it is the ratio of the number of relevant records that were retrieved to the total number of relevant records in the database (multiplied by 100 percent to express the ratio as a percentage). For example, if a query retrieved four relevant records, but there were 10 relevant records in the database, the recall for that search would be 40 percent. Recall is usually difficult to measure since the number of relevant records in a database is often subjective and difficult to determine.

record. The unit of information in a database that contains items of related data. In an address book database, for example, each single record might be the collection of information about an individual person, such as name, address, ZIP code, phone number, etc. In the databases of Web search engines, each record is the collection of information that describes a single Web page.

relevance. The degree to which a record matches the user's query (or the user's needs as expressed in a query). Search engines may assign relevance "scores" to each retrieved record with the scores representing an estimate of the relevance of that record.

resource guides (metasites). Small, specialized Web directories that provide a collection of related links on a specific topic. Also known as cyberguides, resource guides, special directories, Webliographies, etc.

RSS. Acronym for Really Simple Syndication or Rich Site Summary. This is an HTML format by which news providers (and others sources such as Weblogs) can easily syndicate (distribute) their content over the Internet.

search engines. Programs that accept a user's query, search a database, and return to the user those records matching the query. The term is often used more broadly to refer not just to the information retrieval program itself, but also to the interface and associated features, programs, and services.

spider. Programs that search the World Wide Web to identify new (or changed) pages for the purpose of adding those pages to a search service's (search engine's) database. Also known as "crawlers."

start page. The page that loads automatically when you open your browser, sometimes called your "home page." You select what you want your start page to be by using the "Edit > Preferences" or "Tools > Internet Options" choices on your browser's menu.

stopwords. Small or frequently occurring words that an information retrieval program does not bother to index (ostensibly because the words are "insignificant," but more likely because the indexing of those words would take up too much storage space or require too much processing).

submitted URLs. URLs (Internet addresses) that a person directly submits to a search engine service to have that address and its associated Web page added to the service's database.

syntax. The specific order of elements, notations, etc., by which instructions must be submitted to a computer system.

tagging. The process of attaching descriptive terms by users to pictures and other items found on the Web. In its most typical application, it refers to the capability of any user of a site to add their own terms to help other users search for items on a particular topic.

TCP/IP. Transfer Control Protocol/Internet Protocol. The collection of computer data transfer protocols (set of instructions) used on the Internet.

telnet. A program that lets a user log onto and access a remote computer using a text-based interface.

thesaurus. Listing of terms usually displaying the relationship between terms, such as whether one term is narrower or broader than another. Thesauri are used in information retrieval to identify related terms to be searched.

thread. Within a group (newsgroup, discussion group, etc.), a series of messages on a specific topic, consisting of the original message, replies to that message, replies to those replies, etc.

timeout. The amount of time a system will work on a task or wait for results before either stopping the task or the waiting.

truncation. Feature in information retrieval systems that lets a user search with the stem or root of a word and automatically retrieve records with all terms that begin with that string of characters. Truncation is usually specified using a symbol such as an asterisk. For example, in some search engines, *town** would retrieve town, towns, township, etc.

URL. Uniform Resource Locator. The address by which a Web page can be located on the World Wide Web. URLs consist of several parts separated by periods and sometimes slashes. URLs may have various parts such as the domain name, subdomains, paths (directories), and file names.

Usenet. The world's largest system of Internet discussion groups (newsgroups).

videotext. Systems, developed beginning in the 1970s, allowing interactive delivery of text and images on television or computer screens. One of the first applications was the delivery of newspaper content.

Web (World Wide Web, WWW). That portion of the Internet that uses the Hypertext Transfer Protocol (http) and its variations to transmit files. The files involved are typically written in some version of HTML (HyperText Markup Language), thereby viewable using browser software, allowing a GUI (Graphical User Interface), incorporation of hypertext point-and-click navigation of text, and extensive incorporation of images and other types of media and formats.

Web 2.0. A term for a "second generation" of the Web that provides a much greater focus on, and use of, desktop applications on the Web, and collaboration and sharing by users. Forerunners of this include wikis, Weblogs, RSS, and podcasts. Though there is no precise definition, some people also define Web 2.0 in terms of the programs used, including APIs (Application Programming Interfaces), social software, and Ajax (Asynchronous JavaScript and XML).

Weblogs. Web sites or pages, most typically created by individuals, that are updated frequently and usually provide commentary, news, links to news items elsewhere on the Web, etc., usually on a specific topic. Weblogs are now more frequently referred to simply as "blogs."

WikiWiki site (or wiki). A site created and maintained as a collaborative project of Internet users that allows fast and easy input and online editing by users.

WYSIWYG. <u>W</u>hat <u>Y</u>ou <u>S</u>ee <u>I</u>s <u>W</u>hat <u>Y</u>ou <u>G</u>et. Refers to interfaces, such as in word processors, where the way something looks as you are typing is basically what it will look like when it is displayed in its final form (e.g., on a printer, Web site, or blog).

URL List

Links to all of the sites covered in this book can be found at www.extreme searcher.com.

Chapter 1

A Brief History of the Internet, version 3.1
www.isoc.org/internet/history/brief.shtml

Internet History and Growth
www.isoc.org/internet/history/2002_0918_Internet_History_and_Growth.ppt

Hobbes' Internet Timeline
www.zakon.org/robert/internet/timeline

The Virtual Chase: Evaluating the Quality of Information on the Internet
www.virtualchase.com/quality

Evaluating the Quality of World Wide Web Resources
www.valpo.edu/library/user/evaluation.html

Wayback Machine—Internet Archive
www.archive.org

CompletePlanet
completeplanet.com

U.S. Copyright Office
lcweb.loc.gov/copyright

The U.K. Patent Office—Copyright
www.patent.gov.uk/copy

Copyright Web Site
www.benedict.com

Copyright and Fair Use in the Classroom, on the Internet, and the World Wide Web
www.umuc.edu/library/copy.html

Journalism Resources—Guide to Citation Style Guides
bailiwick.lib.uiowa.edu/journalism/cite.html

Style Sheets for Citing Resources (Print & Electronic)
www.lib.berkeley.edu/TeachingLib/Guides/Internet/Style.html

ResourceShelf
www.resourceshelf.com

FreePint
www.freepint.com

ResearchBuzz
www.researchbuzz.com

Internet Resources Newsletter
www.hw.ac.uk/libwww/irn

The Internet Scout Project
scout.wisc.edu

CHAPTER 2

Yahoo! Directory
dir.yahoo.com

Yahooligans
yahooligans.yahoo.com

Open Directory Project
dmoz.org

Librarians' Internet Index
lii.org

Internet Public Library
www.ipl.org

Yahoo!
yahoo.com

My Yahoo!
my.yahoo.com

Excite
excite.com

Lycos
lycos.com

AOL
aol.com

MSN
msn.com

Netscape
netscape.com

Traffick: Frequently Asked Questions about Portals
www.traffick.com/article.asp?aID=9#what

CHAPTER 3

The WWW Virtual Library
www.vlib.org

Search Engine Guide
www.searchengineguide.com

Refdesk
refdesk.com

Internet Public Library Ready Reference
www.ipl.org/div/subject/browse/ref00.00.00

INFOMINE
infomine.ucr.edu

BUBL LINK
bubl.ac.uk/link

Intute
www.intute.ac.uk

Project Gutenberg
www.gutenberg.org

Library of Congress Z39.50 Gateway to Library Catalogs
lcweb.loc.gov/z3950/gateway.html

Tennessee Tech History Web Site
www2.tntech.edu/history

Best of History Web Sites
www.besthistorysites.net

Virtual Religion Index
religion.rutgers.edu/vri

ChemDex
www.chemdex.org

healthfinder
www.healthfinder.gov

MedlinePlus
www.nlm.nih.gov/medlineplus

New York Times > Business > A Web Guide: Business Navigator
www.nytimes.com/ref/business/business-navigator.html

CEOExpress
ceoexpress.com

Virtual International Business and Economic Sources (VIBES)
library.uncc.edu/vibes

Resources for Economists on the Internet
rfe.org

I3—Internet Intelligence Index
www.fuld.com/Tindex

Governments on the WWW
www.gksoft.com/govt

Foreign Government Resources on the Web
www.lib.umich.edu/govdocs/foreign.html

FirstGov.gov
firstgov.gov

Directgov (U.K. Online)
www.open.gov.uk

Political Resources on the Net
www.politicalresources.net

FindLaw
www.findlaw.com

Kathy Schrock's Guide for Educators
school.discovery.com/schrockguide

Education World
www.education-world.com

Education Index
www.educationindex.com

Education Atlas
www.educationatlas.com

Kidon Media-Link
www.kidon.com/media-link

Cyndi's List of Genealogy Sites on the Internet
www.cyndislist.com

CHAPTER 4

Search Engine Shortcuts
www.extremesearcher.com/shortcuts

Google Maps Mania
googlemapsmania.blogspot.com

Yahoo! Maps Application Gallery
developer.yahoo.com/maps/applications.html

Search Engine Watch
searchenginewatch.com

CHAPTER 5

Google
google.com

Yahoo!
yahoo.com

Windows Live
live.com

Ask.com
ask.com

Exalead
exalead.com

HotBot
hotbot.com

Lycos
lycos.com

WiseNut
wisenut.com

AltaVista
altavista.com

AlltheWeb
alltheweb.com

KartOO
kartoo.com

.

Grokker
grokker.com

TouchGraph
touchgraph.com

CHAPTER 6

Google Groups
groups.google.com

Yahoo! Groups
groups.yahoo.com

Delphi Forums
www.delphiforums.com

ezboard
www.ezboard.com

Big Boards
www.big-boards.com

Topica
lists.topica.com

L-Soft CataList, the Official Catalog of LISTSERV Lists
www.lsoft.com/lists/listref.html

CHAPTER 7

HighBeam Encyclopedia
encyclopedia.com

Encarta
encarta.msn.com

Encyclopedia Britannica online
britannica.com

Wikipedia
wikipedia.org

HowStuffWorks
www.howstuffworks.com

yourDictionary.com
www.yourdictionary.com

Merriam-Webster Online
www.m-w.com

Diccionarios.com
www.diccionarios.com

LEO (Link Everything Online)
dict.leo.org

Answers.com
answers.com

InfoPlease
www.infoplease.com

A9.com
a9.com

Infobel
www.infobel.com

Wayp International White and Yellow Pages
www.wayp.com

Yahoo! People Search
people.yahoo.com

AnyWho
www.anywho.com

Superpages.com
superpages.com

The Quotations Page
www.quotationspage.com

Bartleby.com
www.bartleby.com

Yahoo! Finance—Currency Converter
finance.yahoo.com/currency

Weather Underground
wunderground.com

Perry-Castañeda Library Map Collection
www.lib.utexas.edu/maps

David Rumsey Historical Map Collection
www.davidrumsey.com

Global Gazetteer
www.fallingrain.com/world/

World Gazetteer
www.world-gazetteer.com

U.S. Postal Service ZIP Code Lookup
www.usps.com/zip4

CNNMoney
money.cnn.com

Statistical Resources on the Web—Comprehensive Subjects
www.lib.umich.edu/govdocs/stcomp.html

SOSIG—Statistics and Data
www.sosig.ac.uk/statistics

USA Statistics in Brief
www.census.gov/statab/www/brief.html

FedStats
www.fedstats.gov

Amazon
www.amazon.com

Barnes & Noble
www.barnesandnoble.com

Library of Congress Online Catalog
catalog.loc.gov

The British Library Integrated Catalogue
blpc.bl.uk

Google Book Search
books.google.com

Library of Congress Z39.50 Gateway to Library Catalogs
lcweb.loc.gov/z3950/gateway.html

The Online Books Page
digital.library.upenn.edu/books

Project Gutenberg
www.gutenberg.org

EuroDocs: Primary Historical Documents From Western Europe
eudocs.lib.byu.edu

A Chronology of U.S. Historical Documents
www.law.ou.edu/hist

University of Virginia Hypertext Collection
xroads.virginia.edu/~HYPER/hypertex.html

Governments on the WWW
www.gksoft.com/govt

Foreign Government Resources on the Web
www.lib.umich.edu/govdocs/foreign.html

CIA World Factbook
www.odci.gov/cia/publications/factbook

U.K. Foreign & Commonwealth Office—Country Profiles
www.fco.gov.uk

FirstGov.gov
firstgov.gov

GPO Access
www.gpoaccess.gov

THOMAS: Legislative Information on the Internet
thomas.loc.gov

Open CRS
www.opencrs.com

Library of Congress—State and Local Government Information
www.loc.gov/rr/news/stategov/stategov.html

Directgov—Web Site of the U.K. Government
www.direct.gov.uk

CorporateInformation
www.corporateinformation.com

Hoover's
www.hoovers.com

ThomasNet
www.thomasnet.com

Kompass
www.kompass.com

Kellysearch
www.kellysearch.com

American Society of Association Executives Gateway to Associations
www.asaecenter.org/Directories/AssociationSearch.cfm

AMA DoctorFinder
webapps.ama-assn.org/doctorfinder

Lawyers.com
lawyers.com

Free Bibliographies and Bibliographic Databases on the Web
www.leidenuniv.nl/ub/biv/freebase.htm

IngentaConnect
www.ingentaconnect.com

FindArticles
www.findarticles.com

Google Scholar
scholar.google.com

Yahoo! Subscriptions Search
search.yahoo.com/search/options

Peterson's
petersons.com

College Board
www.collegeboard.com

Fodor's
www.fodors.com

Lonely Planet
www.lonelyplanet.com

Travelocity
travelocity.com

Expedia
expedia.com

Orbitz
orbitz.com

Internet Movie Database (IMDb)
www.imdb.com

CHAPTER 8

Finding Images Online—Directory of Web Image Sites
www.berinsteinresearch.com/fiolinks.htm

Digital Librarian: A Librarian's Choice of the Best of the Web—Images
www.digital-librarian.com/images.html

BUBL LINK—Image Collections
bubl.ac.uk/link/types/images.htm

Yahoo!'s Image Search
search.yahoo.com/images

Google's Image Search
images.google.com

Picsearch
www.picsearch.com

Corbis
corbis.com

Fotosearch
www.fotosearch.com

Creative Commons
creativecommons.org

Stock.XCHNG
www.sxc.hu

American Memory Project
memory.loc.gov

WebMuseum (Paris)
www.ibiblio.org/wm (or more specifically, www.ibiblio.org/wm/paint)

Flickr
flickr.com

Free Graphics
www.freegraphics.com

Barry's Clipart
barrysclipart.com

Yahoo! Directory > Graphics > Clip Art
dir.yahoo.com/Computers_and_Internet/Graphics/Clip_Art

World Wide Web Virtual Library—Audio
archive.museophile.sbu.ac.uk/audio

Digital Librarian: A Librarian's Choice of the Best of the Web—Audio
www.digital-librarian.com/audio.html

AltaVista—Audio Search
www.altavista.com/audio

AlltheWeb—Audio Search
multimedia.alltheweb.com

Yahoo!'s Audio Search
audio.search.yahoo.com

Singingfish
singingfish.com

FindSounds
www.findsounds.com

Internet Archive—Audio Archive
www.archive.org

Radio-Locator (formerly the MIT List of Radio Stations on the Internet)
www.radio-locator.com

Yahoo! LAUNCHcast Radio
music.yahoo.com/launchcast

MSN Radio—Windows Media Player
radio.msn.com

Yahoo!'s Podcast Search
podcasts.yahoo.com

Podcastdirectory.com
www.podcastdirectory.com

PodSpider
www.podspider.com

Podscope
www.podscope.com

The History Channel: Speeches & Video
www.historychannel.com/broadband

The Movie Sounds Page
www.moviesounds.com

Apple: iPod & iTunes
www.apple.com/itunes

Yahoo! Music
music.yahoo.com

BUBL LINK: Catalogue of Internet Resources—Video
bubl.ac.uk/link/v/video.htm

Yahoo!'s Video Search
video.yahoo.com

Google's Video Search
video.google.com

Blinkx
www.blinkx.tv

ShadowTV
www.shadowtv.com

TVEyes
www.tveyes.com

Television News Archive
tvnews.vanderbilt.edu

CHAPTER 9

Kidon Media-Link
www.kidon.com/media-link

ABYZ News Links
www.abyznewslinks.com

Metagrid
www.metagrid.com

NewsLink
newslink.org

NewsWealth
www.newswealth.com

News in Pictures
www.newsinpictures.com

Daryl Cagle's Professional Cartoonists Index
www.cagle.com

BBC
news.bbc.co.uk

CNN
www.cnn.com

MSNBC
www.msnbc.com

Reuters
reuters.com

Aljazeera.net
english.aljazeera.net

Today's Front Pages
www.newseum.org/todaysfrontpages

PressDisplay.com
www.pressdisplay.com

Radio-Locator (formerly the MIT List of Radio Stations on the Internet)
www.radio-locator.com

TVRadioWorld
radiostationworld.com

NPR
www.npr.org

Google News
news.google.com

Yahoo! News
news.yahoo.com

Findory
www.findory.com

Topix.net
www.topix.net

NewsNow
newsnow.co.uk

RocketNews
www.rocketnews.com

Feedster
www.feedster.com

World News Network
wn.com

Bloglines
bloglines.com

Technorati
technorati.com

Blogger—Blog Search
search.blogger.com

Bloogz
www.bloogz.com

IceRocket
www.icerocket.com

Bloglines
bloglines.com

Rocketinfo
reader.rocketinfo.com/desktop

My Yahoo!
my.yahoo.com

Google Alerts
www.google.com/newsalerts

Yahoo! Alerts
alerts.yahoo.com

CHAPTER 10

ShoppingSpot.com
shoppingspot.com

ThomasNet
www.thomasnet.com

Kompass
www.kompass.com

Kellysearch
www.kellysearch.com

Amazon
www.amazon.com

Overstock.com
www.overstock.com

Open Directory: Consumer Information—Price Comparisons
dmoz.org/Home/Consumer_Information/Price_Comparisons

Yahoo! Shopping
shopping.yahoo.com

mySimon
www.mysimon.com

PriceGrabber.com
www.pricegrabber.com

Shopping.com
www.shopping.com

Shopzilla
www.shopzilla.com

Froogle
froogle.com

eBay
ebay.com

Epinions
epinions.com

BizRate
bizrate.com

Consumer Reports
consumerreports.org

ConsumerREVIEW.com
consumerreview.com

ConsumerSearch
consumersearch.com

safeshopping.org
www.safeshopping.org

Federal Trade Commission's site for E-Commerce
www.ftc.gov/bcp/menu-internet.htm

eConsumer.gov
www.econsumer.gov

CHAPTER 11

Web Style Guide
www.webstyleguide.com

Blogger
blogger.com

WordPress.com
wordpress.com

Moveable Type
www.sixapart.com/movabletype

LiveJournal
www.livejournal.com

MySpace
myspace.com

Yahoo! 360°
360.yahoo.com

Yahoo! Podcasts—Publish a Podcast
podcasts.yahoo.com/publish

000Domains.com
www.000domains.com

Open Directory > Computers > Internet > Web Design and Development > Hosting > Directories
dmoz.org

Upperhost
www.upperhost.com

GeoCities
geocities.com

Tripod
tripod.com

Angelfire
angelfire.com

Google Page Creator
pages.google.com

Webmonkey
www.webmonkey.com

Reallybig.com: The Complete Resource for All Web Builders
reallybig.com

About.com—Web Design
webdesign.about.com

ABOUT THE AUTHOR

Randolph Hock, PhD

Ran Hock divides his work time between writing and teaching. On the teaching side, he specializes in customized courses designed to help people learn how to use the Internet effectively (through his one-person company, Online Strategies). His courses have been offered in the U.S. and a dozen other countries to companies, government agencies, nongovernmental organizations, schools, universities, and associations. On the writing side, he has written *The Extreme Searcher's Guide to Web Search Engines* (CyberAge Books, Medford, NJ, 1999, 2001), *Yahoo! to the Max* (CyberAge Books, Medford, NJ, 2005), and *The Traveler's Web* (CyberAge Books, Medford, NJ, 2007). He has also been a chemistry teacher and a librarian at two universities, as well as held training and management positions with DIALOG Information Services and Knight-Ridder Information for many years. He lives in Vienna, Virginia, with his wife, Pamela, and their two younger children, Stephen and Elizabeth. (His older son, Matthew, is out in the world, working as the vocalist with the band, The Explosion.) One of Ran's passions is travel, and he hopes to someday have time to return to his hobby of genealogy.

More Great Books
from Information Today, Inc.

Yahoo! to the Max
An Extreme Searcher Guide

By Randolph Hock
Foreword by Mary Ellen Bates

With its many and diverse features, it's not easy for any individual to keep up with all that Yahoo! has to offer. Fortunately, Randolph (Ran) Hock—"The Extreme Searcher"—has created a reader-friendly guide to his favorite Yahoo! tools for online research, communication, investment, e-commerce, and a range of other useful activities. In *Yahoo! to the Max*, Ran provides background, content knowledge, techniques, and tips designed to help Web users take advantage of many of Yahoo!'s most valuable offerings—from its portal features, to Yahoo! Groups, to unique tools some users have yet to discover. The author's Web page helps readers stay current on the new and improved Yahoo! features he recommends.

256 pp/softbound/ISBN 0-910965-69-2 $24.95

The Traveler's Web
An Extreme Searcher Guide to Travel Resources on the Internet

By Randolph Hock
Foreword by David Grossman

Ran Hock has done it again! This time, "The Extreme Searcher" turns to the world of travel—a topic the globetrotting author might say he knows all too well. *The Traveler's Web* presents an amazing range of travel resources, but this is no mere directory of great sites: Savvy search tips and techniques will help improve your planning process and the journeys to follow. You'll learn to make the most of the Web for leisure and business travel, from planning and reservations to the countless ways the Internet can enhance your experience of destinations and cultures the world over. As with all Extreme Searcher books, *The Traveler's Web* is supported by a Web page.

400 pp/softbound/ISBN 0-910965-75-7 $19.95

The Librarian's Internet Survival Guide, 2nd Edition
Strategies for the High-Tech Reference Desk

By Irene E. McDermott • Edited by Barbara Quint

In this updated and expanded second edition of her popular guidebook, *Searcher* columnist Irene McDermott once again exhorts her fellow reference librarians to don their pith helmets and follow her fearlessly into the Web jungle. She presents new and improved troubleshooting tips and advice, Web resources for answering reference questions, and strategies for managing information and keeping current. In addition to helping librarians make the most of Web tools and resources, the book offers practical advice on privacy and child safety, assisting patrons with special needs, Internet training, building library Web pages, and more.

328 pp/softbound/ISBN 1-57387-235-0 $29.50

Teaching Web Search Skills
Techniques and Strategies of Top Trainers

By Greg R. Notess

Educators and information professionals who teach Web searching will welcome this instructor's guide from trainer and search guru Greg Notess. Greg shares his own training techniques along with tips and strategies from savvy search trainers Joe Barker, Paul Barron, Phil Bradley, John Ferguson, Alice Fulbright, Ran Hock, Jeff Humphrey, Diane Kovacs, Gary Price, Danny Sullivan, Rita Vine, and Sheila Webber. In addition to presenting expert training strategies, *Teaching Web Search Skills* demonstrates a variety of approaches to instructional design and methodology, recommends a range of essential resources, and features dozens of helpful figures, search screens, worksheets, handouts, and sample training materials.

368 pp/softbound/ISBN 1-57387-267-9 $29.50

Net Crimes & Misdemeanors, 2nd Edition

Outmaneuvering Web Spammers, Stalkers, and Con Artists

By J. A. Hitchcock
Foreword by Vint Cerf

In this revised and expanded edition of her popular book, cybercrime expert J. A. Hitchcock offers practical and easy-to-follow methods for dealing with spam, viruses, hack attacks, identity theft, and other online dangers. The book covers a broad range of abusive practices and features dozens of firsthand anecdotes and success stories. A one-time victim of cyberstalking who fought back and won, Hitchcock went on to become a leading victim's advocate. Her readable and reassuring book is loaded with tips, strategies, and techniques as well as pointers to the laws, organizations, and Web resources that can aid victims and help them fight back. Supported by a Web page.

496 pp/softbound/ISBN 0-910965-72-2 $24.95

The Visible Employee

Using Workplace Monitoring and Surveillance to Protect Information Assets—Without Compromising Employee Privace Trust

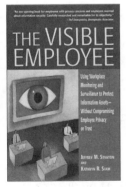

By Jeffrey M. Stanton and Kathryn R. Stam

The misuse of information systems by employees can result in leaked and corrupted data, crippled networks, lost productivity, legal problems, public embarassment, and more. Organizations are increasingly monitoring employee usage of network resources including the Web—but how well are they doing? Based on an extensive four-year research project, *The Visible Employee* reports on a range of security solutions and the attitudes of employees toward workplace surveillance. A must-read for managers, IT staff, and employees with privacy concerns.

376 pp/softbound/ISBN 0-910965-74-9 $24.95

The Web Library
Building a World Class Personal Library with Free Web Resources

By Nicholas G. Tomaiuolo • Edited by Barbara Quint

With this remarkable, eye-opening book and its companion Web site, Nicholas G. (Nick) Tomaiuolo shows how anyone can create a comprehensive personal library using no-cost Web resources. And when Nick say "library," he's not talking about a dictionary and thesaurus on your desktop: He means a vast, rich collection of data, documents, and images that—if you follow his instructions to the letter—can rival the holdings of many traditional libraries. This is an easy-to-use guide, with chapters organized into sections corresponding to departments in a physical library. *The Web Library* provides a wealth of URLs and examples of free material you can start using right away, but best of all it offers techniques for finding and collecting new content as the Web evolves. Start building your personal Web library today!

440 pp/softbound/ISBN 0-910965-67-6 $29.95

Cashing In with Content
How Innovative Marketers Use Digital Information to
Turn Browsers into Buyers

By David Meerman Scott

In failing to provide visitors with great information content, most of today's Web sites are missing a golden opportunity to create loyal customers—and leaving a fortune in new and repeat business on the table. According to Web marketing expert David Meerman Scott, too many marketers focus on style over substance. While a site may win awards for graphic design, Scott demonstrates that the key to Web marketing success is compelling content, delivered in new and surprising ways. In *Cashing In with Content*, he interviews 20 of today's most innovative Web marketers, sharing their secrets for using content to turn browsers into buyers, to encourage repeat business, and to unleash the amazing power of viral marketing. The book features a diverse range of content-savvy organizations from the worlds of e-commerce, business-to-business, and government/non-profit, including the Wall Street Journal Online, CARE USA, Kenyon College, Alcoa, Tourism Toronto, Weyerhaeuser, Booz Allen Hamilton, and United Parcel Service.

280 pp/softbound/ISBN 0-910965-71-4 $24.95

Teach Beyond Your Reach

An Instructor's Guide to Developing and Running Successful Distance
Learning Classes, Workshops, Training Sessions and More

By Robin Neidorf

Distance learning is enabling individuals to earn college and
graduate degrees, professional certificates, and a wide range of skills
and credentials. In addition to the rapidly expanding role of
distance learning in higher education, all types of organizations
now offer Web-based training courses to employees, clients, and
other associates. In *Teach Beyond Your Reach*, teacher and author
Robin Neidorf takes a practical, curriculum-focused approach
designed to help new and experienced distance educators develop
and deliver quality courses and training sessions. She shares best
practices and examples, surveys the tools of the trade, and covers
key issues, including instructional design, course craft, adult learning styles, student-teacher
interaction, strategies for building a community of learners, and much more.

248 pp/softbound/ISBN 0-910965-73-0 $29.95

Super Searchers Go to School

Sharing Online Strategies with K–12 Students, Teachers, and Librarians

By Joyce Kasman Valenza
Edited by Reva Basch

Twelve prominent K–12 educators and educator-librarians share
their techniques and tips for helping students become effective,
life-long information users. Through a series of skillful interviews,
Joyce Kasman Valenza—techlife@school columnist for the
Philadelphia Inquirer and herself a tech-savvy high school
librarian—gets the experts to reveal their field-tested strategies for
working with student learners and educator peers. You'll discover
techniques for teaching search tool selection, evaluating result lists
and Web sites, deciding when to use a professional database or the
Invisible Web, and much more.

272 pp/softbound/ISBN 0-910965-70-6 $24.95

Building & Running a Successful Research Business
A Guide for the Independent Information Professional

By Mary Ellen Bates • Edited by Reva Basch

This is the handbook every aspiring independent information professional needs to launch, manage, and build a research business. Organized into four sections, "Getting Started," "Running the Business," "Marketing," and "Researching," the book walks you through every step of the process. Author and long-time independent researcher Mary Ellen Bates covers everything from "is this right for you?" to closing the sale, managing clients, promoting your business, and tapping into powerful information sources.

488 pp/softbound/ISBN 0-910965-62-5 $29.95

The Skeptical Business Searcher
The Information Advisor's Guide to Evaluating Web Data, Sites, and Sources

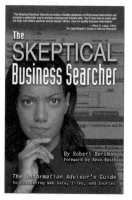

By Robert Berkman • Foreword by Reva Basch

This is the experts' guide to finding high-quality company and industry data on the free Web. Information guru Robert Berkman offers business Internet users effective strategies for identifying and evaluating no-cost online information sources, emphasizing easy-to-use techniques for recognizing bias and misinformation. You'll learn where to go for company backgrounders, sales and earnings data, SEC filings and stockholder reports, public records, market research, competitive intelligence, staff directories, executive biographies, survey/poll data, news stories, and hard-to-find information about small businesses and niche markets. The author's unique table of "Internet Information Credibility Indicators" allows readers to systematically evaluate Web site reliability. Supported by a Web page.

312 pp/softbound/ISBN 0-910965-66-8 $29.95

Ask for these books at your local bookstore or order online at www.infotoday.com

For a complete catalog, contact:

Information Today, Inc.
143 Old Marlton Pike
Medford, NJ 08055
609/654-6266 • e-mail: custserv@infotoday.com